SICILY

SICILY

Pierre Sébilleau

translated by Oliver Coburn

With 168 illustrations
and 4 coloured plates
1 map

NEW YORK
OXFORD UNIVERSITY PRESS
1968

First published in France by
B. ARTHAUD (PARIS AND GRENOBLE)

DG
862.5
S413
1968b

Copyright © 1966 B. Arthaud
English Text Copyright © 1968 Kaye and Ward Ltd.

Plates printed in France
Text printed in Great Britain
by Adlard and Son Limited,
Dorking, Surrey

Also available in this Series
ALGERIA
AUSTRIA
CHÂTEAUX OF THE LOIRE
CÔTE D'AZUR
EGYPT
GARDENS OF ROME
GREECE
ITALIAN LAKES
LONDON
MONT BLANC AND THE SEVEN VALLEYS
PROVENCE
ROME
SIENNA
SPAIN
VENICE
VERSAILLES

LIST OF ILLUSTRATIONS

		Page
IDYLLIC ISLAND		
1.	Palermo. The Harbour	11
2.	Segesta. Temple Interior	12 and 13
3.	Common transport near Nicosia	14
4.	Agrigento. Temple of Juno Lacinia	27
5.	Monreale. Capitals in cloister	28
6.	Syracuse. Ancient Quarries	29
7.	Farm labour between Gela and Piazza Armerina	30 and 31
8–10.	The animal kingdom	32 and 33
11.	Sicilian cart	34

PALERMO

12–20.	NATIONAL MUSEUM	
12.	Lion head from temple at Himera	43
13.	The Syracuse Ram	44
14.	The gallery's small cloister	45
15.	Metopes from C Temple at Selinunte. From left to right: Apollo's; *quadriga* Perseus and the Gorgon; Heracles and the Cercopes	46
16.	Metope from Y Temple at Selinunte: Europa on the bull	46
17.	Metope from E Temple at Selinunte: Heracles and the Amazon	47
18.	Priestess of Isis	48
19.	Terracotta vase in the Casuccini collection, with the myth of Perseus and Medusa (6th century B.C.)	49
20.	Detail from an Etruscan sarcophagus	49
21.	San Giovanni degli Eremiti	50
22.	La Martorana (left) and San Cataldo (right)	51
23.	The Cathedral	51

24–26.	THE NORMANS' PALACE	
24.	Palatine Chapel. Interior seen from the choir	52
25.	Palatine Chapel. Ambo and pascal candelabrum	53
26.	Palatine Chapel. Mosaics on the south side	54
27.	Mosaics in King Roger's Room	55
28.	King Roger crowned by Christ, mosaic in La Martorana	56
29.	National Gallery. The Triumph of Death	56 and 57
30.	National Gallery. Bust of Eleonora of Aragon	58

MONREALE

31.	Chevet of Cathedral	67
32.	The cloister	68 and 69
33–36.	Cloister capitals	69 and 70
37.	Cathedral and cloister	71
38.	William II offers the Cathedral to the Madonna	72
39.	Interior of Cathedral. Mosaics in choir	73
40.	The fountain	74

SEGESTA

41.	Segesta. The Temple	79
42.	Segesta. The Greek Theatre	80 and 81

THE WEST COAST

43.	Mondello. The Harbour	82
44.	Alcamo Marine	91
45.	At Trapani	92
46.	Balestrate. Weighing of grapes	92
47.	Balestrate. Sicilian cart	93
48.	Erice. The Castle	94 and 95
49.	Between Trapani and Marsala. Lifting couch-grass	96
50.	Salt-marshes near Trapani	97
51.	Castelvetrano. The *Ephebe* of Selinunte	98

SELINUNTE

52.	E Temple and, in foreground, stones of F Temple	107
53, 54.	Ruins of G Temple	108 and 109
55.	E Temple	110 and 111

---

1. *Palermo. The Harbour.*
2. *Segesta. Temple Interior.*
3. *Common transport near Nicosia.*

LIST OF ILLUSTRATIONS

56.	Metope of C Temple: the Apollo's *Quadriga* (National Museum at Palermo)	112
57.	C Temple	113
58.	Selinunte. The beach	114

SCIACCA

59.	Irrigation by canals between Selinunte and Menfi	123
60.	Menfi. The Castle	124
61.	Sciacca. The Cathedral	125
62.	Sciacca. The Harbour	126

AGRIGENTO

63.	Temple of Hercules	131
64.	Temple of Castor and Pollux, and view over the town	132 and 133
65.	One of the telamons supporting entablature of the Temple of Olympian Jupiter	134
66.	General View. In background, from left to right: Temple of Concord, columns of Temple of Hercules, and a stretch of the panoramic road	135
67, 68, 70.	Temple of Concord	136, 137 and 139
69.	Detail from sarcophagus of Phaedra in Cathedral	138
71, 73.	Temple of Lacinian Juno	140 and 142
72.	Trunk of olive tree used as seat	141

FROM AGRIGENTO TO SYRACUSE

74.	Porto Empedocle	151
75, 76.	Palma di Montechiaro, village used as model by Tomasi di Lampedusa for his novel *The Leopard*	152 and 153
77.	Gela. Oil wells	154
78.	Near Ragusa	155
79.	Gela. Morning street scene	155
80.	Coping of funerary *stele* from Gela (Syracuse Museum)	156
81.	Ragusa. Church of St George	157
82.	Ragusa. General view	158 and 159
83.	Noto. Church of St Dominic	160
84.	Noto. The Cathedral	161
85.	Noto. Baroque balcony	162

SYRACUSE

86.	Columns of Olympieion	171
87.	Columns of Temple of Apollo	172

88.	Entrance to Tomb of Archimedes	173
89.	The Roman Amphitheatre	174
90.	Euryeles Castle	175
91.	Latomia of Paradise. The Rope-makers' Cave	176
92.	Latomia of Paradise. The Ear of Dionysius	177
93.	The Greek Theatre	178 and 179
94.	Latomia of the Capuchins	180
95.	The Fountain of Arethusa	181
96.	Beneventano Palace	182
97.	The Cathedral	183
98.	The Syracuse Aphrodite (National Archaeological Museum)	184
99.	Columns of Temple of Athene in Cathedral	185
100–104.	NATIONAL ARCHAEOLOGICAL MUSEUM	
100.	Roman sarcophagus (detail)	186
101.	The Mother with Two Children, funerary statue discovered at Megara (560 B.C.) Detail (total height: 2 feet 8 inches)	186
102.	Small Apollo (height 1 foot 6 inches)	187
103.	Lekytos (5th century B.C.)	187
104.	Seated goddess from Grammichele (5th century B.C., height 3 feet 4 inches)	187
105–107.	By the sea	188 and 189
106, 107.	Fishermen repairing hooks on lines, the lines attached to a long thin cord visible on ground	188 and 189
108.	Syracuse. The Harbour	190

IN SICILY'S INTERIOR

109, 111, 112.	Piazza Armerina. Mosaics in the Villa Casale	199, 202 and 203
110.	Near Piazza Armerina	200 and 201
113.	Work in the fields	204
114.	Lake of Pergusa	205
115.	Enna	206 and 207
116.	Between Gangi and Nicosia	206
117.	Near Nicosia	207
118–120.	Nicosia (119 The Cathedral)	208, 209 and 210

CATANIA AND ETNA. TAORMINA

121.	Arrival at Catania	219

	LIST OF ILLUSTRATIONS	
122.	Catania. Former Benedictine Monastery, now a school	220
123.	Catania. Biscari Palace	221
124.	Taormina. Public Gardens	222
125, 126.	Taormina. Greek Theatre	223, 224 and 225
127.	Taormina. Marionette and painted panels from an antiquary's front	226

MESSINA

128.	Outside the 'mussel park'	235
129, 130.	Messina at night (129 The Harbour; 130 Outside the station)	236 and 237
131.	Cathedral façade. Left, detail from central door	238
132.	The Fountain of Orion, outside the Cathedral	239
133.	The astronomical clock and the Cathedral	240
134.	Chevet of the Annunziata dei Catalani	241
135–140.	MESSINA NATIONAL MUSEUM	
135, 136.	Altar-piece of the *Annunciation* by Antonello da Messina.	242 and 243
137.	Christ on the cross (15th century)	244
138.	Marble statue (Hellenistic type) representing Igea (3rd century B.C.; height 5 feet 8 inches)	244
139.	Madonna and Child. Marble statue carved by Baboccio da Piperno (1st half of 5th century; height 6 feet)	244
140.	Scylla by Montorsoli	245
141.	Ceiling of Cathedral	246

FROM MESSINA TO PALERMO

142.	Tyndaris. The Theatre	255
143.	Tyndaris and the Aeolian Islands	256 and 257
144.	Cefalù. Cloister capital	258
145.	Cefalù. Cathedral façade	258
146.	Cefalù Cathedral. Mosaics on apse	259
147.	Cefalù. General view	260 and 261
148.	Solunto. Roman House	262

RETURN TO PALERMO AND CONCLUSION

149.	Quattro Canti Square	267
150.	Panorama from the Normans' Palace	268
151.	Melons for sale	269
152.	The Pretoria Fountain at night	270 and 271
153.	Evening street scene	272 and 273
154.	The art of living	274

155.	Baroque ornament in the Oratory of San Lorenzo.	279
156, 157.	Politeama Garibaldi.	280 and 281
158.	Olive trees at Zucco.	282
159.	Villa Igea.	283
160–164.	Bagheria. Villa Palagonia.	284, 285 and 286

COLOUR PLATES

Frontispiece: Pretoria Fountain (detail).
facing page 38. Selinunte. E Temple.
facing page 118. At Piana degli Albanesi.
facing page 167. The Fire of Etna.

AUTHOR'S NOTE

The earthquake which devastated part of western Sicily in December 1967 occurred while the English edition of this book was being prepared. I would naturally wish to express the deep sadness which I felt, which we all felt, on learning the enormity of the disaster, the number of victims, the misery of the survivors.

I have driven several times along the superb winding road which goes from Alcamo to Castelvetrano, and have a vivid picture of Gibellina, perched high on the hill, and Santa Ninfa. It is hard for me to realise that these same towns are now fields of ruins; though I can easily realise, remembering how populous they were, the severity of the blow which has struck Sicily, the impoverishment it entails, the reconstruction efforts demanded of the Sicilians and of all Italians.

Yet I know that these efforts will be made and that once again Sicily will succeed in overcoming her adversity. Through the ages there have been many such moments as these, in an island resting (according to the ancient legend) on the body of a giant condemned by the gods: Empedocles, who from time to time, crushed by the oppressive weight, writhes abruptly.

We may remember the catastrophe of Messina on 28 December 1908, which razed a large town to the ground, killing more than a hundred thousand people; yet you can see Messina now, reconstructed, populous, bursting with life. Nor should we forget the earthquake of 11 January 1693 which destroyed so many towns and villages, so many ancient churches. One of its consequences was a blossoming of the natural Sicilian genius, the splendid baroque architecture you will find in rebuilt Modica, Noto and Syracuse.

Life in Sicily, like her countryside, is made up of contrasts between sun and shade, light and dark, joy and misery. Had I been rewriting my book now, I might have accentuated the sombre side a little more. Indeed I had already done so in an earlier draft; but then revisited Sicily in a moment of marvellous late September light, so that on my return I could remember little but the beauties and delights of an idyllic island.

Such is the miracle of Sicily, which, after her catastrophes and in spite of her suffering, starts once again to work, to smile and to please. Because of the miracle she will perhaps appeal to you all the more.

P.S., January 1968

IDYLLIC ISLAND

IF you are planning a holiday in Sicily, you will have high expectations, and no wonder. It has such riches to offer, so many marvels of art and nature. Few countries can have been so enthusiastically praised: you have the testimony of great writers of antiquity, Islam and modern Europe; the lavishly illustrated art books, the alluring posters of travel agencies; and not least, the friends who return enraptured by their visit to this beautiful island. It certainly sounds as near a Paradise on earth as you are likely to find.

High hopes indeed, but I do not think they will be disappointed. For four thousand years, travellers and conquerors have been drawn magnetically to Sicily, with its unique geographical position and its abundance of natural blessings. The centuries of intensive cultivation have not exhausted the resources of the soil. Here are the fields of corn which were once the granary of Rome; the gardens of Palermo and Taormina as luxuriant as any Garden of Eden painted by 'Douanier' Rousseau; the orchards of orange and olive trees growing far up the slopes of Etna.

In the middle of the Mediterranean, and therefore in the centre of Western civilization right from its origins, Sicily has an immensely rich history. It has attracted men from all over the world, differing in nationality, race and religion, each leaving some mark of his own genius. These have merged to form a Sicilian people of a very pronounced character, specially gifted, it would seem, for achievement in art and poetry, with a talent for love and hate, comedy and passion.

Sicily has such various delights for your discovery: the beauty of its Doric colonnades, the brillance of its baroque architecture, the grandeur of a still active volcano, its lovely beaches for blissful bathing and sunbathing—a truly idyllic island.

But unfortunately the picture has its darker sides as well. Besides the orange groves and luxuriant gardens, there are parts of the island scorched and barren from sun or

STROMBOLI I.
AEOLIAN ISLES
Lipari I.
Lipari
Vulcano I.
Milazzo
MESSINA
Cape Tinari
Strait of Messina
Mistretta
Tusa
Taormina
Gangi
Sperlinga
Nicosia
ETNA
Enna
Acireale
Aci Trezza
CATANIA
Lake Pergusa
Simeto
Gornalunga
Piazza
Armerina
Caltagirone
Augusta
Anapo
Gela
Palazzolo
Acreide
SYRACUSE
Gela
Comiso
Vittoria
Ragusa
Noto
Tellaro
Modica
Irminio
IONIAN SEA

lava. Throughout her history, which has seen a long succession of invasions, Sicily has very often been a battlefield and Nature has often added to the island's troubles with calamitous earthquakes—the latest so fresh in our memory. Though many Sicilians are gifted in the things of the spirit, many others are apparently dull-witted and morose. The poor are usually dressed in black, and poverty has been almost endemic.

Some of those who have written about Sicily, starting perhaps with Cicero in his 'Verrine Orations', have treated it as a country of complete wretchedness. Certainly these facets are in harsh contrast with the clear light, the splendour of the climate, the beauty of views and works of art. They may sadden you so much that you exaggerate their importance; for the Ciceronian view is no less distorted than its opposite, which sees only the idyllic one. Like a person, a country has its defects and its qualities; but when you are fond of a person or a country, these qualities on closer acquaintance will somehow outweigh the defects. I at least have found that particularly true of Sicily, and I think you will have the same experience: the better you get to know this wonderful island, the greater your love for it will be.

Geography

Sicily is the largest island in the Mediterranean, 9,926 square miles in area, almost the size of Belgium. Because of its triangular shape it was called Trinacria in ancient times and was represented symbolically by three human legs, bent as if in running, extending from a Gorgon's head adorned with intertwined snakes; this representation gives Sicily its striking coat of arms.

If we look at a map, we find the three legs in the form of three mountain ranges starting from a centre at Etna—the 'navel', said Callimachus—branching out to the east, the west and the south west. The three regions thus produced look as if they had deliberately turned their backs on each other. The first faces the Tyrrhenian Sea, the second faces Africa, the third the Ionian Sea.

The northern region of the island is made up of the first two of these ranges, which run almost parallel to the north coast. They are an extension of the Apennines, Italy's backbone, and are separated from Italy by the narrow Strait of Messina, some two miles wide, between Scylla and Charybdis. Like the Apennines, they start in a very ancient range, the Peloritan Mountains, which have granite rocks similar to those of Aspromonte on the other side of the Strait. Also like Aspromonte, they pass into tertiary flexures, the Nebrodi and Caronie Mountains, and limestone formations, the Madonie, which reach almost 6,500 feet; then into the high hills overlooking Palermo; till eventually they plunge into the Mediterranean at the foot of Mount Eryx. These ranges are in fact a 'completion' of the Apennines, for in the south they close the circle of mountains through continental Italy, Corsica and Sardinia, which ends round the Tyrrhenian Sea. Because of the mountains the few rich coastal plains, like Palermo's Conca d'Oro, and their inhabitants' existence, are dominated by that Sea.

The south-eastern region faces Africa and is separated from it by only sixty miles, the Sicilian Channel. This region is very like the North-African coast, with its low inhospitable shores, its salt-marshes, its red soil in which Marsala vines flourish, its limestone hills encrusted with fossils, and its desert-like plateaux. It resembles Africa still more when the dreaded sirocco is blowing, withering even the cactus hedges, forming real Saharan sand-dunes at some points on the coast, saturating the overheated atmosphere with an impalpable but insinuating dust; while overhead the sun is blazing down, a diabolic yellow ball. This is not the region's only Satanic aspect, for Hell disgorges here its more combustible products, the famous Sicilian sulphur, asphalt, and in recent times petroleum.

The Ereian and Hyblean Mountains separate this region from the eastern region, which faces Greece. On the limestone hills above Syracuse, in the rich plain of Catania, or on the cliffs of Taormina, you could imagine yourself in Greece itself; except that, wherever you may be in Sicily, you will see the mighty cone of Etna rising above you far into the clouds. I know of no mountain more satisfying to the spirit than this giant of 10,755 feet, completely on its own, towering above all the peaks round about; legend claims that at dawn it covers the whole of Sicily with its shadow. Though it is perpetually active and often in eruption, I have always felt a sense of calm merely from contemplating its lines.

Of course tourist guides and geography books usually divide Sicily into two parts: the west, rugged, arid, under-developed; and the east, richer, more attractive, more modern. Economically, this division is undoubtably accurate, and it is also true that the Mafia, so powerful in the west, are almost non-existent in the east. However in my view the geographical, historical and human facts are more exactly covered by dividing Sicily into its three 'legs'.

History

Sicily has been inhabited since the most remote prehistoric times. Extremely ancient traces of human life have been found, especially in the west of the island, notably some rock carvings—on which, however, scholars still disagree. Some have connected them with the primitive art of Périgord, others with that of the Sahara. We do not at present know, therefore, whether these first inhabitants of Sicily came from the north or the south, from Europe or from Africa. So for the moment we may consider those whom the Ancients called Sicanes (Sicanians) as the aboriginals, the real 'Sicilians' After them the indigenous history of Sicily comes to an end. Since then, in fact, it has continuously been 'undergoing other people's history', in Benedetto Croce's phrase: the scene of invasions issuing from each in turn of the triangle's three sides— east, south and north.

But although these invasions have produced on Sicilian soil an exceptional mixture of races, none has managed to become dominant. All these men from east and south and north, lured by the bright prospects in Sicily, were so well satisfied with what they found that they let the island mould and absorb them, integrating them into one people with a character of their own. That people could now and then assert their national spirit, as in the rising of the 'Sicilian Vespers' (Easter 1282) celebrated in Verdi's opera; and in modern times they are still enough of a distinct people for Italy to have granted them regional autonomy after the Second World War.

The history Sicily has 'undergone' can be summarized, then, in a list of invasions, which I shall divide into two periods. In the first the invasions were predominantly from the east, except for the last, the Saracen invasion, which came from the south. The invasions in the second period have all been from the north, if we include the most recent of them, though launched from Africa—the Anglo-American 'invasion' of 1943.

From 2000 B.C. *to* 11*th Century* A.D.

The Sikelians

During the second millenium B.C., invaders from the east landed in Sicily. They left arms there in which bronze soon appeared; pottery revealing an Aegean influence; and tombs which were at first mere holes, skilfully terraced on the sides of cliffs, and then real 'monuments' in *tholos* form, after the Mycenaean model. These invaders may have been Cretans, as is suggested by the legend in which King Minos dies in Sicily; or Trojans who escaped from the firing of their city, as the tradition of a Sicilian people, the Elymians, would have it; or the Aegeans whose leader was Ulysses (Odysseus). Whoever they were, they were not of the same race as the Sicanians, whom they drove back into the poorest parts of the island; the Ancients distinguished them from the Sicanians by calling them Sicules (Sikelians).

The Greeks and the Carthaginians

The Carthaginians were the first to settle in the west of the island, soon after the foundation of their city by the Phoenicians, at the very beginning of the 8th century. But the Greeks, landing in western Sicily in 735, established themselves more widely; there was a colonization 'race' between the people of Chalcis, who founded Naxos at the foot of Taormina, and those of Corinth and Megara, who settled soon afterwards on the two neighbouring sites of Syracuse and Megara Hyblaea.

In the years that followed, although it was Cretans and Rhodians who founded Gela, these colonies swarmed. On the coast, Naxos founded Catania and Messina, Gela fathered Akragas (now Agrigento), and the Greek zone joined up with the Carthaginian when Megara established itself at Selinunte and Naxos at Himera. In the interior, the descendants of the first settlers were soon swamped by a horde of new immigrants and Hellenized Sikelians who accepted dictators; these early 'tyrants', like all their imitators throughout history, hoped to solve their problems by empire-building. Phalaris of Akragas is famous only for his legendary cruelty, but Cleander and Hippocrates of Gela gained power over Syracuse, and their successors—Gelon, Hieron and Thrasybulus—controlled three-quarters of Sicily with Syracuse as capital.

Such expansion produced a conflict with Carthage. Gelon won the first round, at Himera in 480. A little later Syracuse and the other Greek cities won further victories, crushing the last revolt of the Sikelians led by Doukhetios; and these victories gave them fifty years of great prosperity. During this first golden age, they built their renowned temples, and became a centre on which great poets and playwrights of the Hellenic world converged: Epicharmes and Simonides, Pindar and Aeschylus.

Invasions which Failed

Sicily had become so Greek that it was even involved in the Peloponnesian War. Segesta, which was threatening Selinunte, appealed to Athens for help; and Athens hoped to exploit this by crushing Syracuse, which, being of Dorian origin, had taken Sparta's side. But the Attic invasions ended in 413 with the celebrated defeat which brought the Athenian prisoners into the quarries of Syracuse, where seven thousand of them perished of sickness and hunger.

Syracuse had nevertheless suffered a shock which the Carthaginians exploited. Emerging from their narrow domain in the west of the island, increasing their forces to the point where one can talk of a new invasion, they started on a war which was to last for over a century. But Syracuse resisted under Dionysius—the tyrant who had Plato in his entourage. As for Agathocles, counter-attacking in Africa, he reached the very gates of Carthage.

Yet in 298 Carthaginian pressure became so great that Syracuse appealed to King Pyrrhus of Epirus, who was waging war in Italy. Pyrrhus occupied the whole island, but failed to take Lilybaeum, the final Punic bastion. When he withdrew, he is said to have cried: 'What a fine battlefield I am leaving for the Carthaginians and the Romans!'

The Romans

The Mamertines, Italiot mercenaries, were in occupation of Messina. Attacked by Syracuse in 264, they asked for help from their neighbours just opposite, the Roman garrison at Reggio. Syracuse appealed to the Carthaginians, and soon everything Greek, Mamertine or Sikelian disappeared in the great struggle between Rome and Carthage, fought out on Sicilian soil.

---

    4. *Agrigento. Temple of Juno Lacinia.*
    5. *Monreale. Capitals in cloister.*
    6. *Syracuse. Ancient Quarries.*
    7. *Farm labour between Gela and Piazza Armerina.*
8–10. *The animal kingdom.*
  11. *Sicilian cart.*

4

5 6

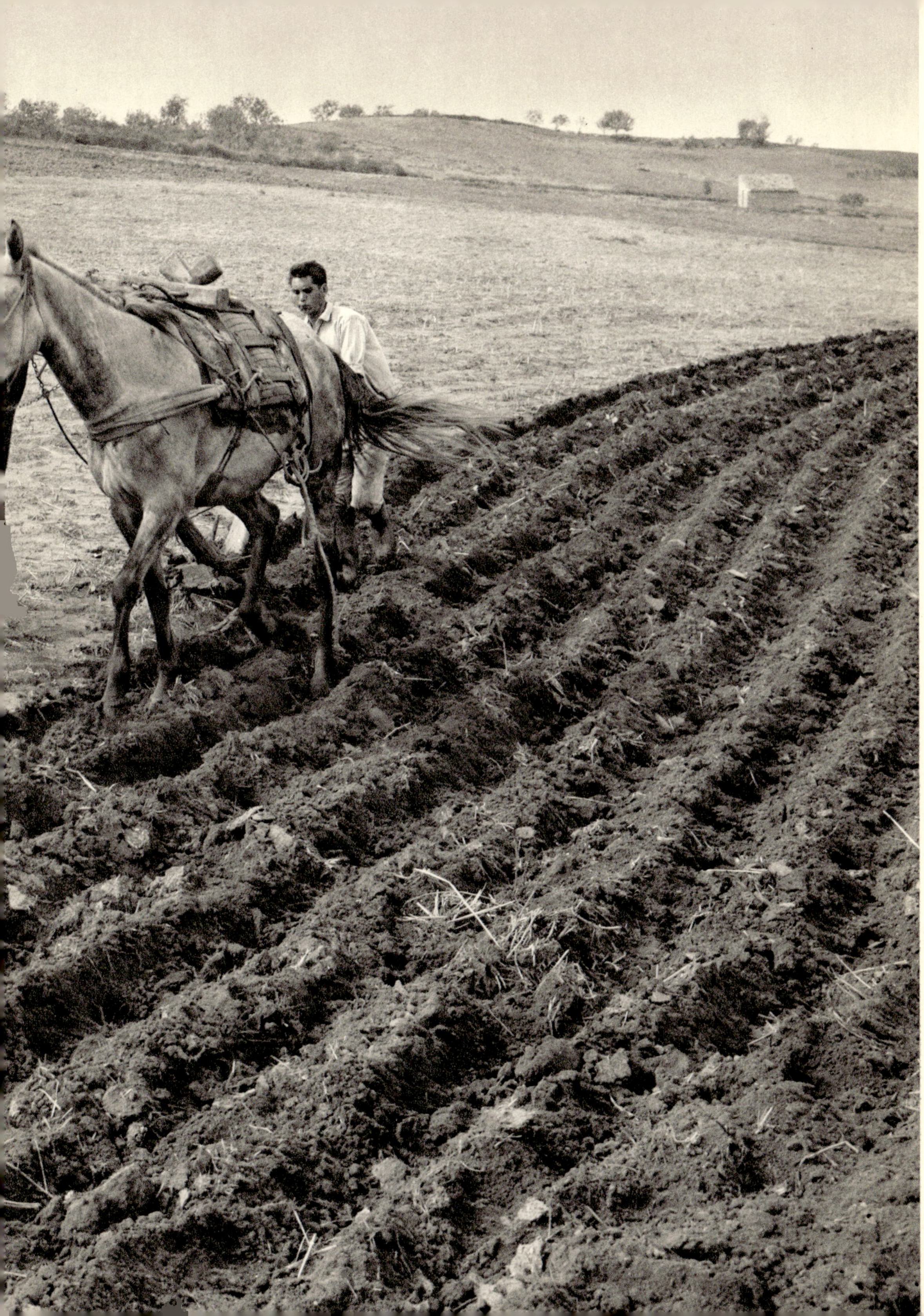

9

8

10

II

The vicissitudes of the struggle are well known. The Roman invasions were blocked by the resistance of places which Carthage supplied from the sea; Rome decided to form a navy, and won naval victories at Mylae, Ecnomus and the Egadi Islands (260, 256 and 241 B.C.); the Carthaginians were finally driven out, and Sicily was turned into a Roman province (227).

It was to remain one for six centuries, during which the *Pax Romana* was disturbed only in the earlier days. In 212, during the Second Punic War, Syracuse, having betrayed Rome for Carthage, was taken by Marcellus despite the inventions of Archimedes; in 139 and 104 Sicily was the scene of two terrible slave wars; and from 44 to 36 it served as base for the revolt of Sextus Pompaeus. Well or badly administered —very badly in the case of the notorious Verres—it was used by Rome as a corn granary and by the Senate as a special preserve for sinecure offices. But this island, which had become the geographical centre of the Roman Empire, played a very unobtrusive role in the Empire's history, literature and art. Silently, Sicily digested the most formidable of its invaders.

During this period, however, it experienced another invasion, also from the east, but quite different in kind: the Christian invasion, which established at Syracuse the first church in the Western world.

The Vandals

The Germanic invasions finally reached this forgotten province, but from the south, curiously enough. This was in the beginning of the 5th century A.D., when the Vandals travelled all round the Mediterranean area, from Spain to North Africa, till they too landed on the shores of Sicily.

Byzantium

At the beginning of the 6th century the Vandals were supplanted by the Goths, who were quite soon driven out during Hellenism's last rally. Sicily was part of the territory reconquered by Belisarius in Justinian's great attempt to re-establish the Augustan empire with Byzantium as capital. This was the most lasting success which the attempt achieved; and it was the final invasion of Sicily from the east.

Saracens

Twenty years after Mahomet's death the Arabs (Saracens, as the Christians of the Middle Ages called them) reached Tunisia; and they too heard talk of Sicily as an earthly Paradise. But they did not succeed in invading it until 827, and Syracuse only fell in 878.

Their occupation, under the dynasty of the Kalbite Emirs, first governors, then more or less independent sovereigns, brought to Sicily a new civilization then at the peak of its creative vitality. Sicily became Muslim, but still absorbed the Arabs. By the 11th century they were in a state of such anarchy that one of their leaders made the mistake of taking into his service a Norman adventurer then fighting in Italy, a certain Roger de Hauteville.

2. *From 11th Century to the Present Day*

The Normans

Roger landed at Messina in 1061, and by 1091 had completed the conquest of Sicily. He was the youngest of an extraordinary brood of Norman 'squires'. Setting out from a manor at Cotentin with only a handful of their fellow-countrymen, they had already conquered Southern Italy, and now Roger added Sicily to the family possessions.

Under the reign of his son Roger II (1105–54) Sicily had its second golden age. After gaining the continental inheritance of his uncle Robert Guiscard, Roger II made his kingdom the most highly developed in Europe. He took Palermo as his capital and, besides the Norman architects, the Arabs, whom the king treated with tolerance and even favour, contributed to the city's embellishment.

But despite the ideas and new blood brought by this invasion, Sicily continued its work of absorption. Soon the Norman warriors began to wear satin, keep harems and write poetry. Under Roger's successors his creation degenerated, and in 1187, when William II died, the kingdom was a prey to anarchy and furthermore in the hands of women.

The Germans

William II had no children, and his rightful heiress was his aunt Constance, Roger II's posthumous daughter. Having earlier become a nun, Constance contracted a late marriage with Henry VI, the Germanic Holy Roman Emperor, son of Frederick Barbarossa. In Frederick's train the Germans eagerly invaded Sicily; this led to a long period of revolts and cruelties. But the strange marriage between Constance, the soured nun, and Henry VI, a one-eyed cripple, produced a figure of exceptional stature: the Emperor Frederick II.

Frederick was brought up at Palermo, where there was a state of anarchy. Before he was thirteen, he put an end to the anarchy by seizing power for himself. Throughout his long reign (1197–1250) he never completely abandoned Sicily and his capital, although he preferred southern Italy. Carrying on with Roger II's administrative and economic work and developing it still further, he turned his Mediterranean kingdom, which he considered far more important than his German empire, into a state far in advance of his time. Impelled by his immense culture and insatiable curiosity, he followed a line which made him to an astonishing degree a precursor of the Renaissance.

The French

The handsome Manfred, Frederick's bastard, usurped the rights of Conrad, the rightful heir. The Holy See, which was hostile to Manfred, claimed the sovereignty over his kingdom which Roger II had once accepted, and assigned it to Charles Duke of

Anjou and by marriage Count of Provence. But Charles was nothing like as good a man as his brother, King Louis IX. He immediately destroyed the modern state created by Roger and Frederick, establishing instead a French-style feudal regime, with land endowments for his friends from Anjou and Provence. He reached southern Italy, but in Sicily encountered a revival of nationalism, which burst out at Easter 1282 outside the Church of Santo Spirito at Palermo, and which History has called 'the Sicilian Vespers'.

The Spaniards

But the national awakening did not last. The Sicilians felt they must seek a protector in the person of Peter III of Aragon. He and his successors defended them against the Anjou rulers, who had remained in possession of Naples, and pretended to respect their independence. But in reality, succeeding where Charles of Anjou had failed, they set to work establishing in Sicily a feudal system in the Spanish style. They were so successful that in 1412 Ferdinand 'the Just' had no trouble in placing the island under the rule of a viceroy, the first of a series which was to last until 1712.

So Sicily relapsed into obscurity, stifled beneath the black cloak of the Spanish viceroys. For three hundred years it had no history apart from some revolts by Palermo, and the revolt of Messina in 1672 which involved the intervention of Louis XIV—Duquesne defeated the Dutch-Spanish fleet, commanded by Ruyter, off Augusta.

The British: Savoy, Habsburgs, the Bourbons of Naples

This Sicilian battle between two Nordic and Protestant admirals resulted in a new invasion carried out by a 'third party', the British. With Spain defeated, and incapable of holding on to Sicily, they wanted to stop the French becoming masters of the Mediterranean instead. In 1712, by the Treaty of Utrecht, Britain had Sicily given to one of her clients of the time, Victor Amedaeus II of Savoy; then in 1718 to the Habsburg Emperor of Austria. In 1734 she suffered a setback when 'the Two Sicilies' went to Charles III of Bourbon, son of Philip V of Spain and great-grandson of Louis XIV. But she managed to reassert her power under the reign of Ferdinand III, nicknamed 'Nasone' (Big-Nose); he was forced to take a British Prime Minister, Sir John Acton, who also became the lover of Queen Maria Carolina, sister of Marie Antoinette. British control, encouraged by Lady Hamilton with Nelson's support, grew so powerful that the French Republic had to drive Ferdinand IV out of Naples. He took refuge in Sicily, where the British protected him throughout Napoleon's reign; and Napoleon's armies were never able to cross the Straits of Messina.

The Italians

Meantime a new factor was emerging in Sicily. The population responded to the ideas of the time and began to realise that they belonged to the united Italy then in course of gestation. Palermo was the first European city to rise in 1848 in the name of freedom, and on 11 May 1860, when Garibaldi landed at Marsala with his thousand Red-Shirts, Sicily accepted him with enthusiasm.

The island became an integral part of the kingdom of Italy; but although it provided several prime ministers, such as Crispi and Orlando, it figured as rather a poor relation—a victim, like the whole of southern Italy, of the insoluble 'problems of the South'. During the Fascist era some Sicilians imagined that their island was at last going to fulfil its mission as the centre of an Italian Mediterranean, the *Mare Nostrum* Mussolini dreamed of. These illusions were finally shattered after 10 July 1943, when Anglo-American forces landed between Cape Passero and Gela.

Under their occupation Sicily experienced a brief blaze of separatism. A movement for independence was created; but with the Mafia involved, this soon degenerated into a banditry business, in which the handsome Salvatore Guiliano achieved his renown. The Sicilians then decided to stay within the Italian Republic, on condition that they were granted provincial autonomy. This was conceded on 15 May 1946, giving extensive powers in economy and finance to the president, government and assembly of the Sicilian Region.

The People

If you are one of those who believe you can best get to know a people by studying their folk-lore, you will be in your element in Sicily. On the roads you will meet the famous painted carts, bright yellow, red and blue, drawn by feather-tufted mules; the carts are adorned with panels of crude paintings, generally showing bearded knights cutting moustachioed Moors into vermillion slices! In the few surviving marionette theatres you will find the same knights, with tin armour, hanging by strings, 'performing' dramas based on the Song of Roland or the Round Table narratives. On public holidays you can admire superb costumes of Balkan origin—at Piana degli Albanesi, for instance; and see processions following statues of holy figures dressed in Spanish style, surrounded by hooded penitents intoning Arab-style chants. Finally, in the Park of the Favorita at Palermo, you can visit the excellent Pitré Museum to study this folk-lore which is a legacy from all Sicily's invaders. Scholars like A. t'Serstevens have found it invaluable for their observations of the Sicilian character.

But folk-lore, however intriguing, often contains an element 'for tourist consumption', and may not reflect the actual lives of the people: of these men in dark clothes, whom you will see at dusk strolling elbow to elbow in the main street of every village; sitting at café tables in the public gardens of towns—without any sign of a drink; or standing right in the sun, gazing downwards, leaning against the rail of a bridge which spans a dried-up river.

Statistics indeed may act as a useful counterweight to folk-lore; they show that this Paradise on earth, although an integral part of the European Common Market, is still in certain respects an under-developed country.

First and foremost, Sicily is over-populated. Despite a recent reduction in the rate of increase, the Island's population is rising today towards the five million mark,

Selinunte. E Temple.

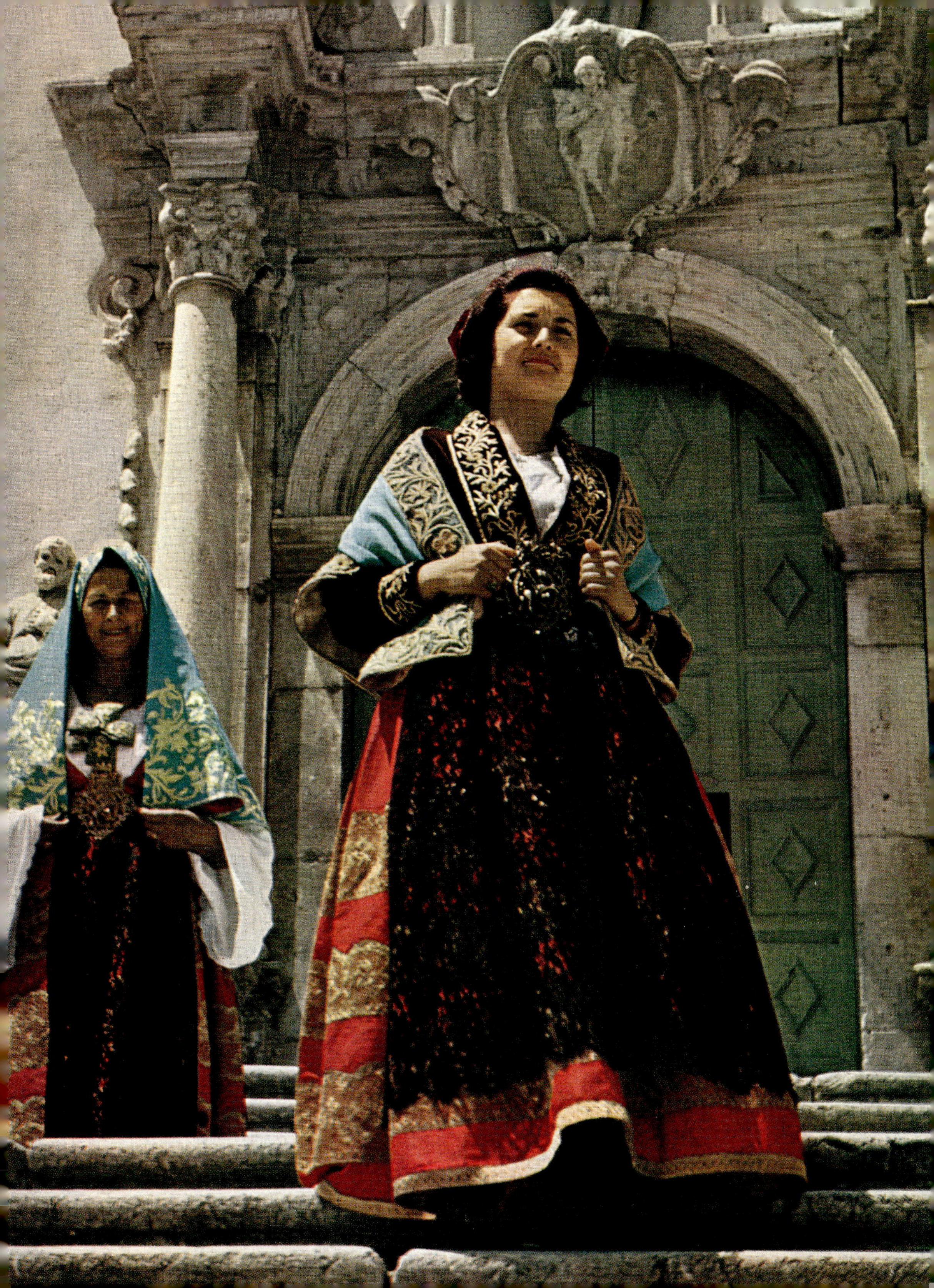

and shade, wealth and poverty. Here a splendid palace or a beautiful ancient ruin; there, right opposite, a mass of hovels or a mean, ugly village. Such stark contrasts, so often repeated, may possibly induce people to doubt their own eyes, then distrust themselves and others, finally keep aloof and silent.

You come across this apathy, suspicion and scepticism in the works of the Sicilian writers. These, indeed, will provide you with another valuable way of learning about the Sicilian character: particularly the works of Pirandello; *The Leopard* by Giuseppe Tomasi, Prince of Lampedusa; Vitaliano Brancati's *Don Juan in Sicily* and *The Handsome Antonio*.

Pirandello likes pitting the traditional Sicilians—attractive and home-loving though sometimes near to madness in their cultivated scepticism and unconcern—against the new men, eager to get-rich-quick and be successful in the framework of the unified Italy. Tomasi's *Leopard* would like to embrace the cause of that Italy, which offers him so much vaster a field of action than Sicily; but he refuses from haughty indifference and a desperate loyalty to an order of things he knows is finished. As for Don Juan, he ends by wearying of the successes he wins at Milan in business and with the ladies, and returns to Catania to enjoy his big bed with wrought-iron volutes, where he at once falls asleep like a true indolent Sicilian.

You may think this mere literary stuff, and very old-fashioned at that, when you are on your tour and see Sicilians in field or factory working with great industry and intelligence; or at Palermo, Catania, Messina, when you meet some of the men of action who are building the new Sicily or the men of letters who are imagining and designing it. But although these may prove quite loquacious on questions of politics or economics, philosophy or art, I cannot guarantee that even they will prove very communicative if you touch on certain taboo subjects or ask them to talk about themselves.

There are of course a great many Sicilians who have emigrated to France and other European countries, and they are much less reserved. But that is quite a different aspect of Sicily, though it plays a big part in the country's life. 146,000 people emigrated in the record year of 1913, and all over the world they form thriving colonies; the money they send home keeps alive a great many of the families who have stayed in Sicily. Mainland Italy is calling for them, and will do so more and more, in an era when for the first time in history the Italian economy is short of labour. Of course by no means all these emigrants make their fortunes; but some exploit the exceptional gifts of their race, to achieve brilliant success in Italian business, politics and the civil service—the Sicilians and the Piedmontese traditionally form the backbone of the Italian service.

What is more, the further the Sicilian is from his native island, although he retains a strong sentimental attachment to it, the more he can break free from complexes and inhibitions, and begin to talk frankly and openly. I owe so much of what I know about Sicily to my friends who have emigrated from it; and I would ask them here to accept my thanks.

Itinerary

For a successful holiday it is essential, I think, to organize your tour so that you can get to know Sicily as thoroughly as possible, while also savouring its idyllic side. There are so many sights to see and places to visit, and these must be balanced against the equally justified desire for relaxed enjoyment.

The itinerary will depend, of course, on what you are most interested in seeing. If it is Greek temples and theatres, many of the ones at Segesta, Selinunte, Agrigento and Syracuse are better preserved than those of Greece itself. For traces of the Roman occupation, go especially to Piazza Armerina. In the churches of Palermo, Monreale and Cefalù you will find unique and truly Sicilian architecture and art, that strange fusion of Romanesque, Byzantine and Arab traditions. You may be attracted to the fortresses left by Frederick II and the Aragonese and Spanish sovereigns. You will certainly want to see the Renaissance masterpieces of sculpture carved for so many churches by Antonello Gagini and Francesco Laurana; the paintings by Antonello da Messina, one of the greatest painters of all time, preserved in the galleries of Palermo, Syracuse, Messina and Cefalù; the profusion of baroque palaces and churches at Palermo, Syracuse, Catania and Noto. You will want to take in something of modern Sicily, its dams and buildings and oil refineries; and everywhere, of course, there are wonderful views and scenery, perhaps especially at Erice, Taormina, Enna and Tyndaris.

Among all these facets of interest or beauty it would be presumptuous to try to dictate your choice; so I shall only suggest an itinerary which seems to me fairly complete, and also offer one piece of advice. Begin and end your holiday at Palermo, where you can fly from Rome. The ferry-boat from Naples will land your car there, unless you prefer to hire one on the spot, which is easy, practical and relatively cheap.

Palermo, you will see at first glance, is above all a capital. Like any capital worthy the name, it provides an epitome of the country's artistic history. This will be enlightening for the whole of your tour, so it may be a good idea to see something of it on your arrival, but without trying to take in too much.

Thus prepared, you can start on your tour of Sicily by going westwards, to Segesta, Erice, Trapani. Then visit the south, Selinunte, Agrigento, Gela, Noto and Syracuse. From Syracuse go inland to Piazza Armerina, Enna, Nicosia. Then back to the sea at Catania, get to know Etna at closer quarters, enjoy the delights of Taormina. Then, by way of Messina, Cefalù and the north coast, return to Palermo.

After seeing the rest of Sicily, you will be better able to appreciate the capital, which is a complex city not easily absorbed. You will have found the places and things which you liked when you were here before, so you can now see them again more thoroughly. You will also discover new wonders as you stroll down the alleys in the old districts and along the roads on the outskirts. And to enjoy the idyllic island once more before you depart, I would recommend you simply to sit at a café table watching people pass. It may be the same table to which Giuseppe Tomasi, Prince of

Lampedusa, would come every day, so that he could sit there and write in peace, after pulling from an old shopping basket the manuscript of *The Leopard*.

12–20. NATIONAL MUSEUM.
12. *Lion head from temple at Himera.*
13. *The Syracuse Ram.*
14. *The gallery's small cloister.*
15. *Metopes from C Temple at Selinunte. From left to right: Apollo's quadriga; Perseus and the Gorgon; Heracles and the Cercopes.*
16. *Metope from Y Temple at Selinunte: Europa on the bull.*
17. *Metope from E Temple at Selinunte: Heracles and the Amazon.*
18. *Priestess of Isis.*
19. *Terracotta vase in the Casuccini collection, with the myth of Perseus and Medusa (6th century* B.C.*).*
20. *Detail from an Etruscan sarcophagus.*
21. *San Giovanni degli Eremiti.*
22. *La Martorana (left) and San Cataldo (right).*
23. *The Cathedral.*

24–26. THE NORMANS' PALACE
24. *Palatine Chapel. Interior seen from the choir.*
25. *Palatine Chapel. Ambo and pascal candelabrum.*
26. *Palatine Chapel. Mosaics on the south side.*
27. *Mosaics in King Roger's Room.*
28. *King Roger crowned by Christ, mosaic in La Martorana.*
29. *National Gallery. The Triumph of Death.*
30. *National Gallery. Bust of Eleonora of Aragon.*

12

13

14

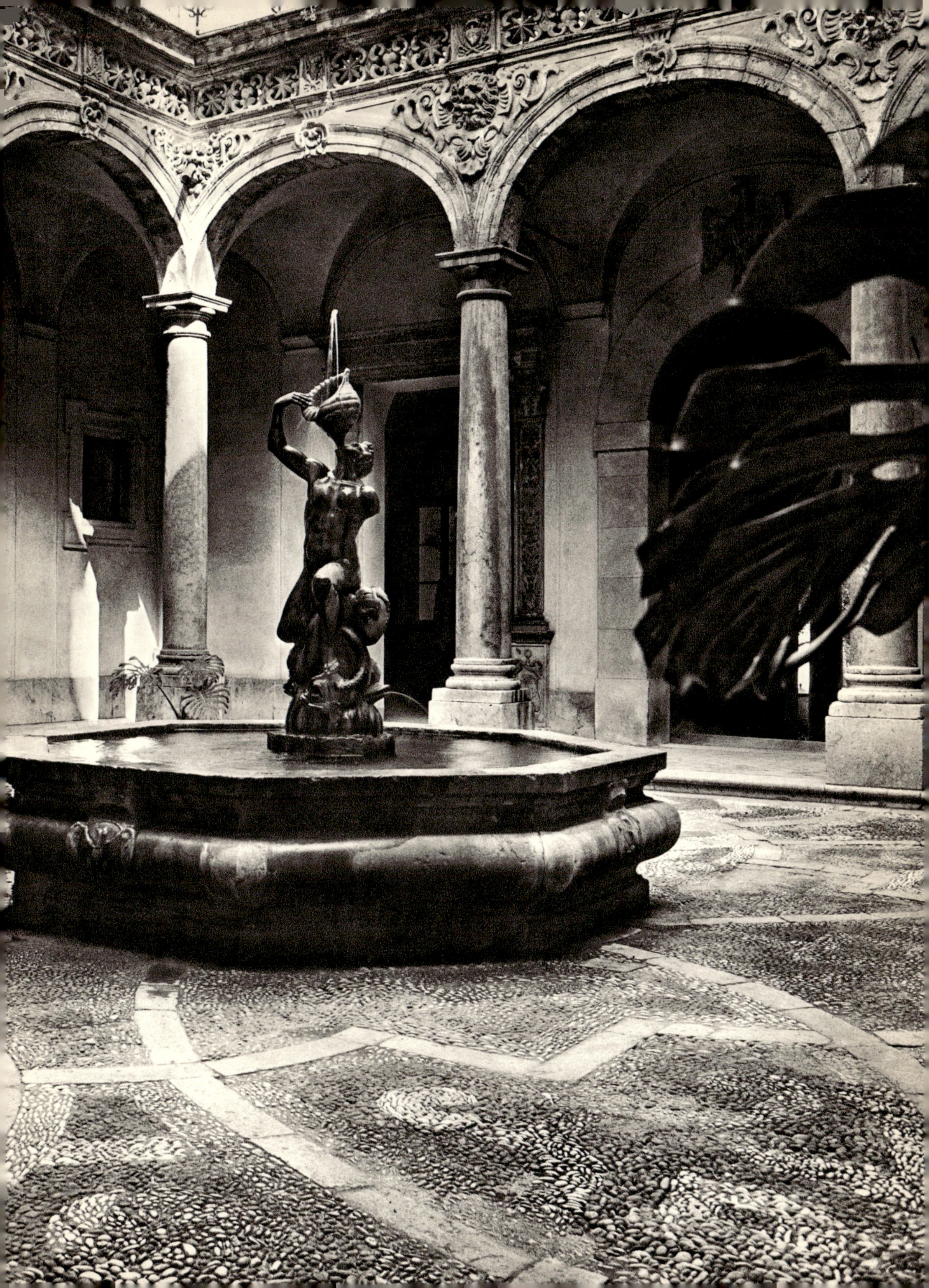

15

16

17

18

19

20

21

22

23

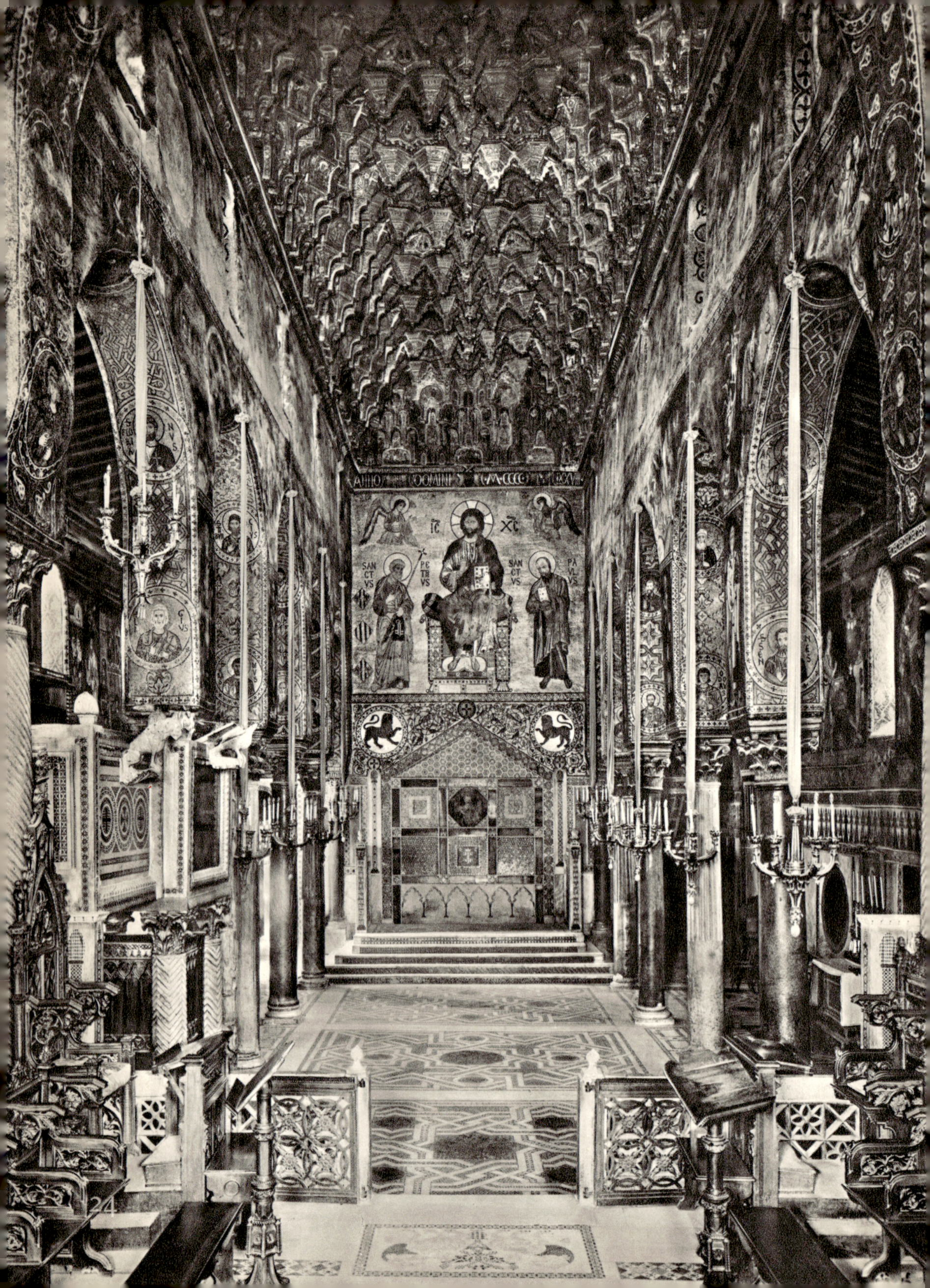
IC XC
SANCTVS
PETRVS
SANCTVS
PAVLVS

25

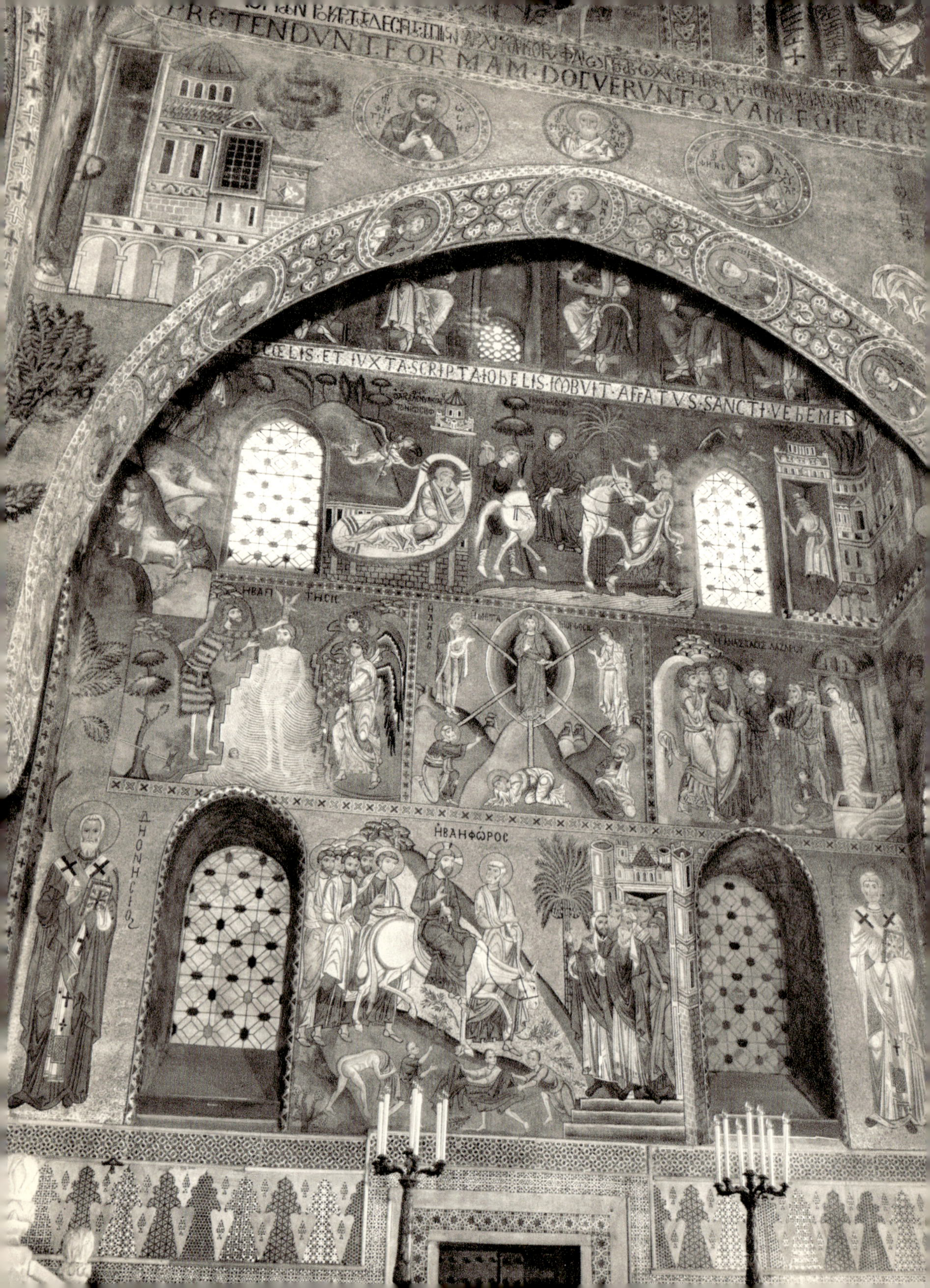

26 27

28

29

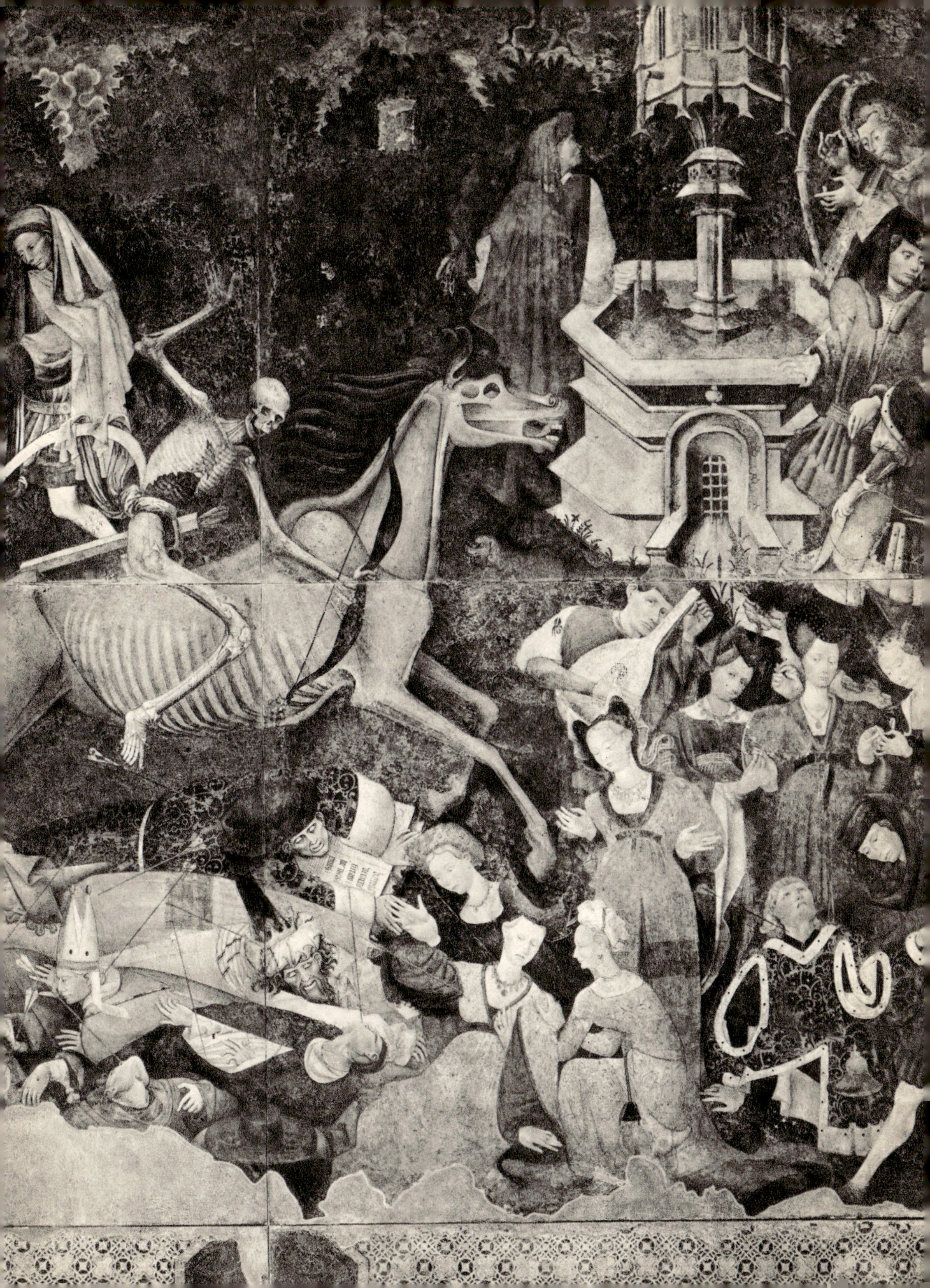

30

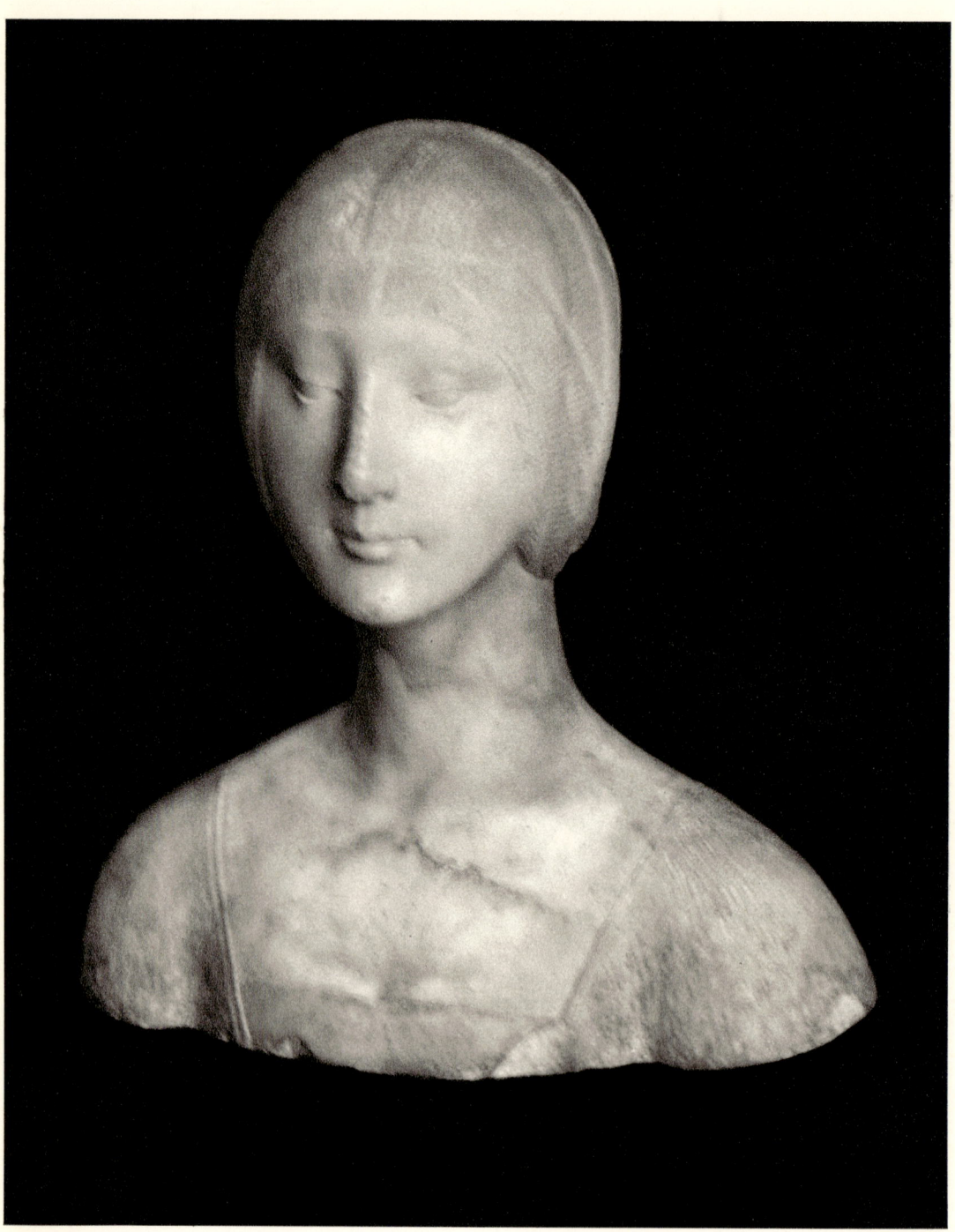

PALERMO

P ALERMO, as I have said, is above all a capital. It has half a million inhabitants, but even with far fewer, it would still be Sicily's queen of cities.

I began to gain this impression of it the day I arrived there for the first time, travelling overland, and discovered it from the hill of Monreale. But the impression was even more inescapable two years later, when I landed there by sea.

In the early morning, coming up on deck, I found the outlines already there on the horizon. On the right lay Monte Pellegrino, which Goethe called 'the finest headland in the world'; as long as you are at Palermo you will go on admiring its tremendous mass. On the left was Monte Catalfano, less spectacular; at the back the circle of mountains surrounding the Conca d'Oro (the shell of gold).

But I could not yet distinguish the city, submerged in the glittering light of morning and the remains of a mist lingering over the sea. Gradually, starting from bottom and top, main features appeared: the Royal Palace, the pines of the Villa d'Aumale, the campaniles of the Cathedral, the roof of the Grand Theatre. Then on the right I saw the buildings of the new districts, the crowded houses of the old city; on the left the terraces of the Foro Italico and the gardens of the Villa Giulia. As we came nearer, all this knit together and spread out, forming a big city.

I was so happy to see it again in the clear morning light, that without wasting a moment I made my way towards Castelnuovo Square, centre of modern Palermo, swarming with people and cars. From there, admiring the smart shops and well-dressed women, I joined the long street parallel to the sea which is the city's main artery, and which is called in turn Via della Libertà, Via Ruggero Settimo and Via Maqueda. The Via Maqueda took me to the centre of the old city, Quattro Canti Square, where I greeted two old friends in passing: the fountain of Piazza Pretoria and the church of La Martorana. But I did not stop; it made it all the better to think that I could return to them as often as I liked.

I turned left into the Corso Vittorio Emmanuele, the second main artery, at right angles to the sea. I reached the sea at La Cala, the old harbour, which is a little reminiscent of Marseilles, cluttered with fishing boats, gleaming with oil, extending in the distance into the powerful installations of the modern harbour. Palermo here is very far from the image of a capital; it is content to be the typical maritime city on the Mediterranean, with tall, closely packed houses, sometimes peeling and damaged by the air-raids of the last war, enlivened by noisy urchins and the shouts of sailors, gossiping women, and merchants gesticulating behind their stalls crammed with colourful vegetables and fruit. I walked for a while on the big street along the sea, among the alleys of the old district, before returning to the atmosphere of a capital in the Via Roma, parallel to the Via Maqueda.

If you had the time, you could carry on strolling indefinitely in the streets of Palermo, and it would certainly be the best way of getting to know the city. But as your time is limited, alas, it is best, I think, as I suggested in the last chapter, to make contact at once with the epitome of Sicily's artistic history which Palermo offers you. This will allow you to make the most of your tour of the island and also of your second more restful stay in the capital just before you return home.

So we start with the Greeks? Yes, although Palermo, despite its Hellenic name, has absolutely nothing Greek about it. Founded in the 6th century A.D. by the Carthaginians, it was abandoned by them to the Romans during the second Punic War. You will nevertheless find some of the most striking examples of Sicily's Greek art—in the archaeological museum.

Personally, though, I hate starting on a town through its museums; however rich, they can never be more than cemeteries. Luckily, Palermo's National Museum has pleasant surprises in store for you in the form of its two courtyards. The first, at the entrance, is an 18th-century cloister, fresh and restrained, with elements from demolished churches and palaces adroitly set in its walls. The second, another cloister, is much more spacious, full of flowers, fountains and luxuriant banana trees.

Going by the chronological order, you should first visit the second floor, where you will see objects from prehistoric times and fine Attic vases. On the first floor you may inspect some statues, including the famous Syracuse ram, dear to Maupassant; a battalion of amusing little bronzes; and a whole army of terra-cotta figurines, too many for the striking ones to be easily picked out. On the ground floor you will meet a gigantic cornice from the largest temple at Selinunte, the powerful lion's-head gargoyles of the temple of Himera, and an excellent collection of Etruscan 'imports'. But above all you should end up in the hall which contains the metopes of Selinunte, and there feel your first keen excitement in the presence of Sicily's Greek art.

Opposite you are the four metopes from the E Temple at Selinunte, which has recently been so perfectly reconstructed that they could be put back in position there or at least be replaced there by mouldings. They date from the 5th century, the age of Pheidias, and they illustrate that age when Greek art was at its peak: strong, austere, simple, designed by mathematicians and carved by athletes, solely concerned with proclaiming what they believed to be the truth, as Socrates and Plato were doing in the same period.

However, I still prefer the older metopes, on the left side of the hall. The four small ones (including Europa in a long robe, seated on her curly-haired bull) were discovered in the fortifications, where they had been used as replacement stones after the destruction of the very ancient temple to which they belonged.

Above all there are the three metopes of C Temple, showing off to full advantage between their triglyphs and under a large piece of cornice. One is the *quadriga* (chariot) of Apollo, seen full face (quite bold for a bas-relief). A second is Perseus, with a bullhead and big eyes staring at you hard, while with a negligent hand he cuts off the still bigger head of the Gorgon. The third is Herakles carrying the writhing bodies of the dwarf Cercopes hanging head-first from a pole. These are archaic and clumsy works, but you can see the joy of artistic creation bursting forth, the sincerity of youth and the terror of the gods, as in Aeschylus.

From the Greeks let us go straight on to the Arabs. For the Roman and Byzantine occupations have left no traces at Palermo. But nor has the Arab occupation. What you are going to see is indeed largely the work of Arab architects and artists, but they were slaves of the Norman kings, who appreciated them to the full but, with an eclecticism amazing in these rough warriors, obliged them to yoke their talents with those of Christian architects from Sicily, Rome, Caen and Byzantium.

Before entering the Royal Palace, however, you will be able to see some remains of a mosque, incorporated into the small church of San Giovanni degli Eremiti. But it is more the church which will give you the impression of the Middle East, a sense of something completely and unexpectedly alien. When you discover its five red domes and its minaret tower, you feel you might be in Aleppo, and can see how far Sicily went on Oriental lines in the era of the Normans. Enter its tiny cloister, transformed into a delightful garden. Stay there till dusk, when the scent of the orange trees, mimosa and rose begin to rise, and you will feel Sicily is an idyllic place indeed.

The Royal Palace (or Norman Palace) looks rather heavy, but its 17th century courtyard and grand staircases are impressive. Above all, it contains two masterpieces of Byzantine-Arab-Norman art: the Palatine Chapel and King Roger's Bedchamber.

So much has already been said about the Palatine, that I leave it to you to judge this stupefying pantheon, where you will find a full muster of all the Mediterranean styles. The architecture is romanesque, but with broken arches resting on classical columns with Corinthian cornices. Floor, wall plinths, royal throne and chair are of inlaid marble, the style called 'cosmatesque', which is to be found at Rome and at Salerno. All the rest, walls, apse and dome, is wholly covered with Byzantine mosaics; but above the nave there is a purely Arab ceiling with pendentives and alveoles, as can be seen at Granada and Damascus.

At first you may be disconcerted by such a profusion of disparate richness. Then you will begin to admire certain details: the composition and freshness of the mosaic pictures, the nobility of the pascal chair and candelabrum. Finally you will feel caught up in the mystical atmosphere created by the dim light which makes the golds and colours gleam in their chiaroscuro. Then you will see unity coming out of diversity, a general harmonious and religious design; the whole Palatine Chapel rises like a homage, or a prayer, towards the austere images of Christ enthroned at the back of the apse, the far end of the nave and the keystone of the cupola.

Yet I think I prefer King Roger's Room (contemporary with the Chapel), which is to be found on the second floor of the palace, enshrined and miraculously preserved amidst solemn and heavy Bourbon suites. It repeats in miniature the Chapel's general architecture: high inlaid marble plinths, mosaics covering the rest of the walls and the vault. But the wall mosaics—hunting scenes, globular palms and trees, stags, flamingos and peacocks—have a free-and-easy, cheerful air seldom found in Byzantine art, which is rather in the Persian style. As to the mosaics on the arches, they have the warm colours and arabesques of an oriental carpet. It is easy to imagine Roger II meditating here on the grand design he had formed of marrying east with west in his Sicilian kingdom, to make it the most civilised and highly developed State of the Middle Ages.

You may be curious to meet this enterprising King Roger. Go and visit him, then, in the Church of Santa Maria dell'Ammiraglio, called La Martorana. It was built in 1143 by a certain George of Antioch, who was perhaps the first sailor to bear the title of admiral—a Latinization, in the Sicilian melting-pot, of the Arabic *Emir al Bahr*, commander at sea. The church makes an astonishing picture with its cloister, its campanile and its twin sister, the San Cataldo Chapel, very bare inside in contrast with the richness of the church.

This richness includes, unfortunately, some 18th-century frescoes in fruit-drop colours; and, fortunately, some 12th-century mosaics as remarkable as those in the Royal Palace. Among these is a portrait of King Roger crowned by Christ, which is not only a masterpiece but one of the most eloquent historical 'documents' I know.

If you are expecting to see a stalwart Norman warrior, a jovial giant with red hair and face flushed with brandy, you will be disappointed. You will see a flexible Mediterranean with the eyes of a gazelle and an Arab beard, clad like a Byzantine king. As M. Béraud-Villard says in his excellent book, *Les Normands en Mediterranée* (The Normans in the Mediterranean), this unexpected image helps to explain why the Norman invasion in Sicily, and the synthesis between east and west attempted by Roger, came to grief so comparatively soon. Such a synthesis may anyhow be a snare and an illusion. History seems to demonstrate that many marriages between east and west end disastrously, with the masculine element of the west slowly absorbed by the feminine element of the east—unless the former reacts violently against this, choosing to be a Caesar or an Octavius and avoid the fate of a Pompey or an Antony.

To judge from his portrait in the Martorana, Roger II succumbed too readily to the intoxicating philtres and delicious poisons distilled for him by Sicily. It is not surprising that under his successors, far lesser men, youthful Norman power was absorbed by the weakness of ancient Sicily.

Nevertheless, this invasion endowed Sicily with an art which is a fusion of Byzantine, Arab and Romanesque. That was an event in its history, indeed in the history of Mediterranean civilization, almost as striking as the flowering of Greek art on Sicilian shores.

You will not find in Palermo any certain traces of the French occupation, though in an old churchyard to the south of the town you can visit the austere Santo Spirito Church, with the square outside it where that occupation came to an end in the bloodbath of the Sicilian Vespers.

There should still, however, be some traces of Anjou and Provence in the Cathedral. For this building, conceived in the Norman era by an English archbishop, is so vast that it took centuries to complete, and almost all Sicily's successive foreign influences during the Middle Ages can be found in it. The adaptation of Sicilian artists and the regrettable revision and correction in the 18th and 19th centuries produce a composite result, overloaded with campaniles, pinnacles and battlements—although I appreciate its indisputable majesty and pleasing honey colour.

The Cathedral makes its appearance chiefly from the side, which is extremely long but fortunately broken up by an elegant porch from the Aragonese era. It has indeed a Gothic façade and porch, but you will find it hard to see them in proper perspective from the end of a narrow alley spanned by two huge buttresses. It also has an apse, which is worth seeking out as the sole remains of the primitive romanesque construction. As to the interior, it is immense and irritatingly 18th-century; it contains the austere sarcophagi in which rest the two greatest sovereigns Sicily has known: King Roger II and the Emperor Frederick II.

The historical summary of Sicilian art offered you by Palermo should now, I feel, take in a visit to Sicily's National Gallery: first of all because this has been recently installed, with good and eclectic taste, in the Abbatelli Palace, the work of a great Sicilian architect, Matteo Carnelivari. This is a fine example of the transition architecture between the Middle Ages and the Renaissance which flourished in the 15th century throughout Italy. It is also a sturdy building, designed to resist any attacks; although brightened by wide windows with pillars and by an elegant porch with a flattened arch heralding the Renaissance.

A second reason for visiting the Gallery is that it contains three of Sicily's Renaissance masterpieces: the great fresco of the *Triumph of Death*, the bust of Eleonora of Aragon by Francesco Laurana; and the *Annunciation* by Antonello da Messina.

The first of these is a frightening picture, of bizarre composition. Death is in the centre, 'a skeleton king astride an immense galloping mare' (as t'Serstevens puts it). Below on the left there are a group of poor wretches whom he ignores; in the middle 'a mass of kings, popes and prelates' whom he crushes; on the right, threatened by the arrow he is preparing to shoot, a crowd of pretty women, rich and sad, grouped round some musicians at the foot of a fountain which rises to the top right-hand corner of the fresco. Then, above and on the left, a big blackish space, in which a solitary hunter is strolling, with his dogs on a leash.

The artist is unknown, and probably not a Sicilian; more likely a Catalan or a Fleming. The latter hypothesis is naturally adopted by the Flemish t'Serstevens, who would see a self-portrait by the artist in the figure of the lute-player, 'Flemish from brow to jaw, with the slightly sad mouth of lads from Flanders.' Personally I would imagine the anonymous artist rather as the solitary hunter in the black void, walking about indifferent to the tragedy of death developing below him—the same indifference or pretended indifference of the Renaissance Epicureans who gravitated round the little courts of North Italy (like Este, for instance). The *Triumph of Death* reminds me of certain frescoes at Ferrara.

Francesco Laurana, who carved the second masterpiece, the bust of Eleonora of Aragon, is considered, although of Dalmatian origin, as the great master of Sicilian sculpture, the equal of his near-contemporary, Antonello Gagini. Gagini, a genuine Palerman, studied at Florence, however, under Brunelleschi; and you will find his works all over Sicily. Laurana is not at all well-known outside the island. The first time I saw the bust of Eleonora at Palermo, I was surprised by it; yet I knew it very well, for my mother had a moulding of it in her room. But despite her artistic upbringing she did not know where the original was, nor who had carved it; and she called it 'the Unknown Beauty'. It is indeed near perfection. I am tempted to see it as a symbolic image of the Spanish occupation, in fact of all the occupations which have succeeded each other in Sicily. How beautiful she is, the Infanta, with her lofty profile and noble bearing—but also how hard and foreign!

Antonello da Messina was the greatest painter Sicily had produced since the famous but rather remote Zeuxis. His *Annunciation* is different from the others: no Angel Gabriel, balustrade or lily; a simple portrait full-face. A gentle, dark-skinned face emerges from a dark green veil, almost expressionless. Only her hands reveal the Virgin's agitation. The left is closing the veil again in a gesture of modesty. The right is foreshortened, half raised, as if hesitating, then obeying and accepting: 'Behold the handmaid of the Lord.' This is not a foreigner seen by a foreigner, but a Sicilian— a Sicilian woman of the people—painted by a Sicilian.

Coming out of the Abbatelli Palace after contemplating this sublime work, so extremely simple as to be like a reflection of the soul, you will be faced with what may seem a harsh contrast in the Church of the Pietà. Its façade is one of the most remarkable illustrations of the baroque style, overloaded, full of flourishes designed solely to please the eye, which held sway in Sicily all through the 17th and 18th centuries. Still, I think you will admire this façade. I even think that if you have gone to Sicily full of the prejudices too often harboured against baroque, you will realise, in fact, that this style, after the Greek and Arabo-Norman, was the third miracle of Sicily's artistic history, and that it produced a profusion of masterpieces. You will be convinced of it when you have seen those at Syracuse, Catania and Noto.

That is why I recommend you for the moment, in the framework of the historical summary, to confine yourself to the façade of the Pietà, and wait till you have finished your tour of the island before seeking out Palermo's other baroque buildings. Baroque art and architecture are essentially histrionic; the façades are stage sets, the statues are almost 'acting a part'. To understand baroque, as with the theatre, one must know its conventions. To appreciate it, one must put oneself in the state suitable to the good playgoer, that is to say, settle down comfortably and with an open mind, to watch the make-believe developing before your eyes.

However, the last lesson in our Palermitan introduction to Sicilian art will start with some more baroque, a lesson to be developed all along the city's main artery. Set off, in fact, from Quattro Canti Square, which is pure baroque; you will appreciate its noble design, the four concave façades with the corners cut off, adorned with the statues of four Spanish sovereigns and of four women saints, patronesses of Palermo; these rise in tiers above four fountains.

Then you will pass the buildings which Palermo owes to Italy: the Grand Theatre, which has no less than 3,200 places; the ultra-modern commercial and banking centre of the Via Ruggero Settimo; and the Politeama Garibaldi. A use for this has at last been found, since it has become a huge cinema! Towards the north, the buildings of the new town are growing fast.

Finally, a few miles out of the town, you will reach the Park of the Favorita, where you can visit the folk-lore collections of the Pitré Museum and above all, I suggest, the so-called 'Chinese Pavilion'. I have reserved this for your 'dessert', first of all because our summary would not be complete if it did not mention the unique contribution made to Palermo by the Bourbon dynasty, and secondly because it will give you the chance to relax. For I have seen few things more clownish and eccentric than this construction by Ferdinand IV, cousin and brother-in-law of Louis XVI, son-in-law of Maria Theresa of Austria and father-in-law of Louis Philippe. With completely serious intentions, he lumped together emanations of bad taste from all ages and from all over the world.

---

31. *Chevet of Cathedral.*
32. *The cloister.*
33–36. *Cloister capitals.*
37. *Cathedral and cloister.*
38. *William II offers the Cathedral to the Madonna.*
39. *Interior of Cathedral. Mosaics in choir.*
40. *The fountain.*

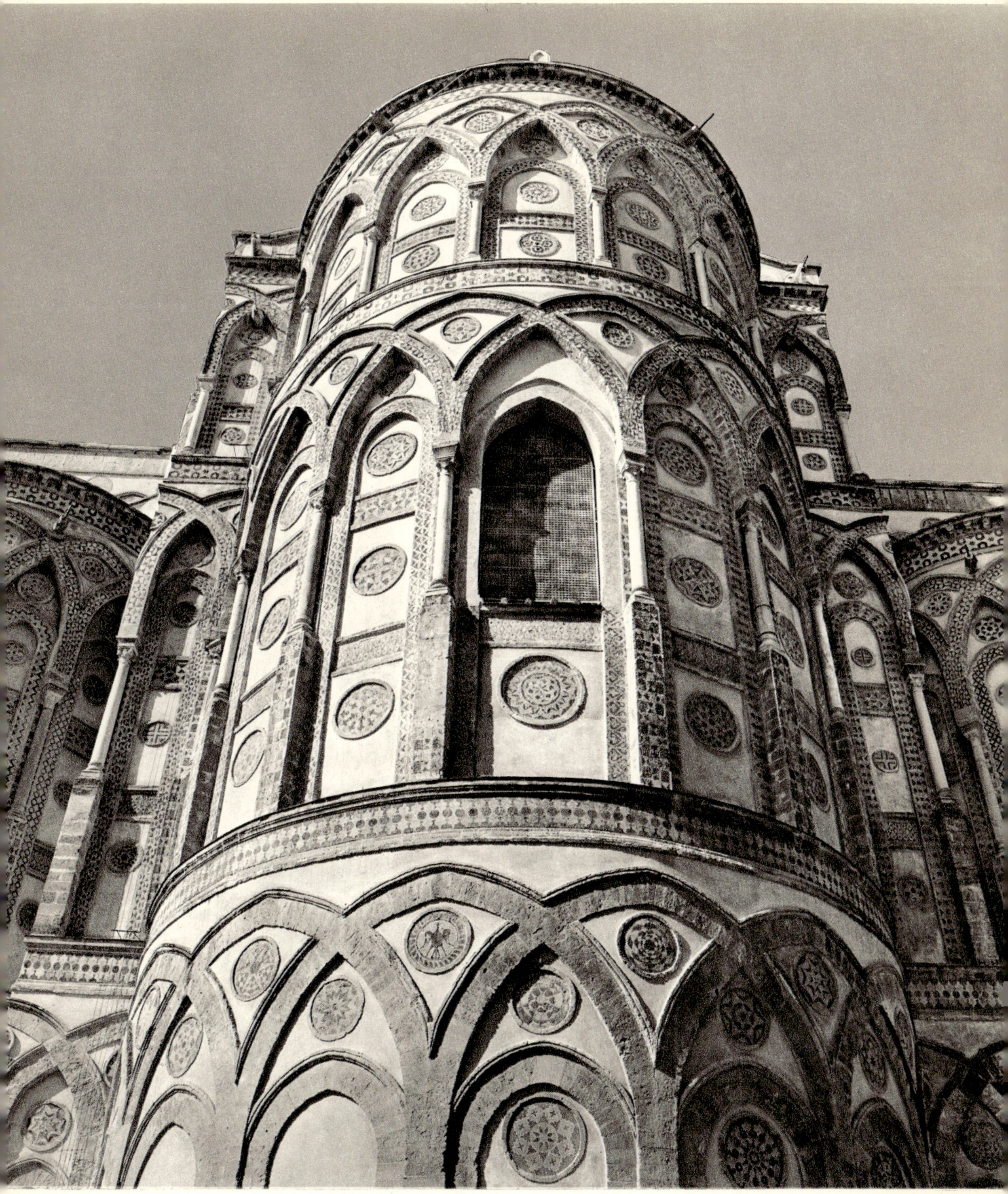

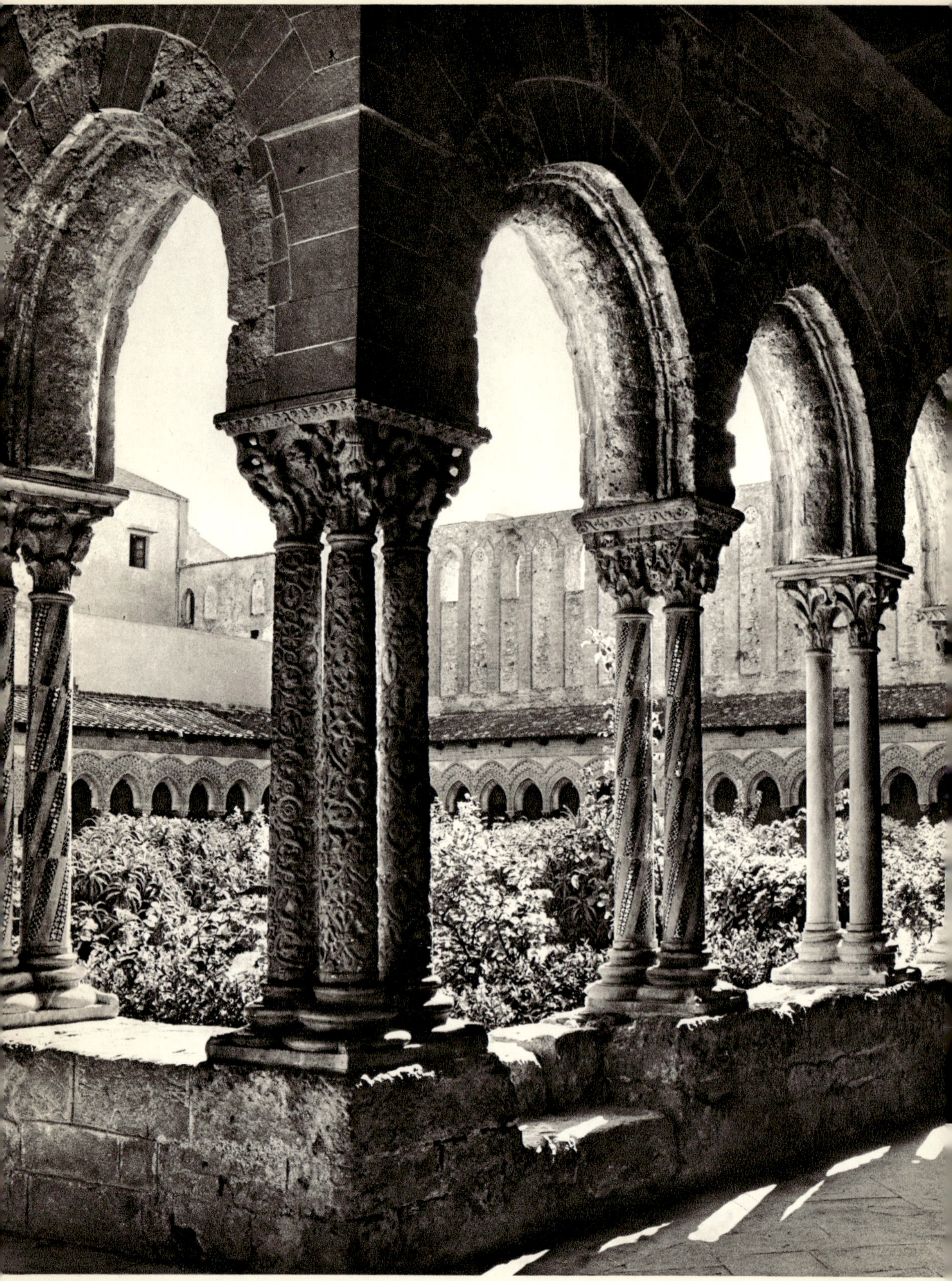

32

33

34

35

36

37

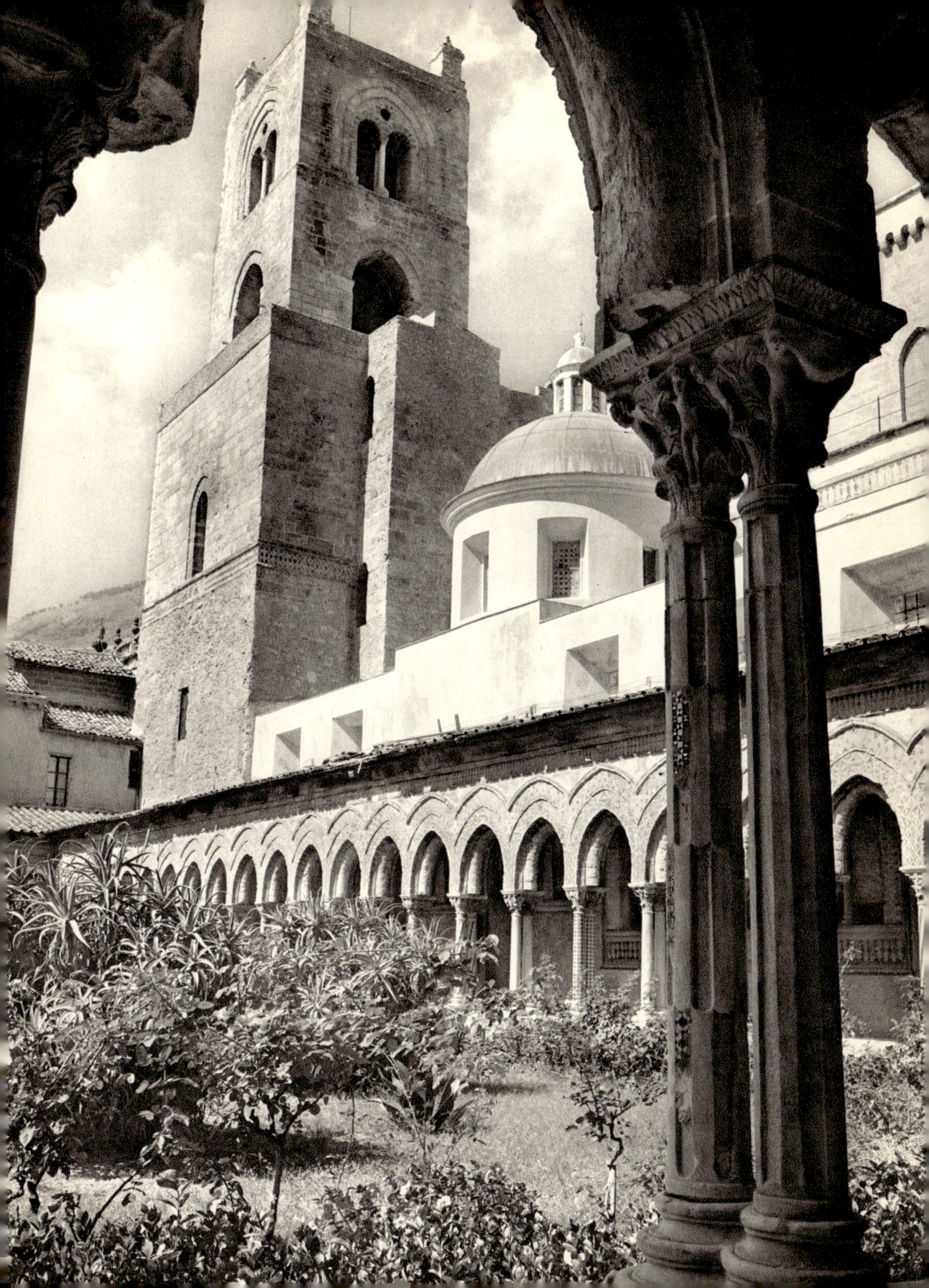

38

39

40

MONREALE

BEGUN in 1174 on the order of William II, second successor of King Roger II and Sicily's last Norman sovereign, the Cathedral of Monreale was completely built under the same impetus. Since then it has not had to suffer too much from providers of 'embellishments' and restorations. You will see it, then, on its hill five miles out of Palermo, more or less in its original purity, the masterpiece of the Byzantine-Arab-Romanesque art produced in Sicily by the Norman invasion. But it was the swan-song of that art, and while you will admire it, you may regret that the Normans could not continue any longer with their attempt to synthesise east and west. However, if you look at it attentively, concentrating especially on its celebrated mosaics, you will soon realise, I believe, that the attempt in question still brought something important to Mediterranean civilization.

The Cathedral of Monreale, like Palermo's Cathedral, makes its main appearance from the left side. This has a portico which is a 16th-century 'embellishment', but the architects succeeded in adapting it to the lines of the whole building. Under this portico there is a porch which forms the usual entrance to the Cathedral, and has superb bronze doors carved and cast by Barisano da Trani in 1178. The same combination can be found in the front: a new portico added (but very unskilfully in this case), and bronze doors, equally superb, by Bonano, sculptor of the Cathedral at Pisa, completed in 1186. The two masterpieces are only eight years apart, and yet belong to different ages: Barisano's is still mediaeval and influenced by the Byzantine tradition, while Bonano's is already in the Renaissance spirit and points forward to the Baptistry at Florence.

Walk left, under a baroque arch, to see the Cathedral's chevet. The classical norms of Italy's romanesque style are respected, an apse and two semi-circular, aligned absidioles; but the architect has given these norms new life by a decoration which is quite unique: overlapping blind arches, resting on fine pillars, framing panels with rose-windows—the whole done in brown lava on a background of orange pink limestone. The Arab influence is obvious; one thinks of the brown, pink and white stonework in the mosques of the East, but also of the multi-coloured romanesque churches in the Auvergne and Tuscany.

I suggest you leave the Cathedral's interior as climax, and first visit the cloister. This will be one of the happy moments of your tour of Sicily, for I can think of few places more peaceful and completely satisfying. The impression of serenity is established straight away by the harmony between all one's sensations: the contemplation of the perfect square, with a perfectly homogeneous architecture round it; and the silence, scarcely disturbed by the murmur of a fountain. Even when you come out of this first emotion, the harmonious effect is enhanced and developed in the details of the cloister.

It is rather like cloisters from the same period at Rome, Saint-Paul hors les Murs and Saint-Jean de Latran. Here are the same pairs of pillars, each pair differing from the others, sometimes smooth, sometimes carved or twisted, often inlaid with mosaics in bright-coloured glass and geometrical designs, like those commonly found at Rome in the style called 'cosmatesque'. In fact the cloister is signed, on a capital, by an artist who is clearly in the romanesque tradition. But here the arches are not quite semi-circular: they are slightly broken and even spear-shaped, in the Arab manner; and the south-west corner has a square kiosk where a fountain spurts, which is reminiscent of Granada.

Finally, unlike romanesque cloisters, which are generally very simple, the capitals range from pure Corinthian abstracts to the most realist romanesque symbols. It is a whole picture of the world, with its glories and squalors, of the Sicily, at once Greek and Norman, which the monks could comtemplate during their meditative walks. Here, supporting the abacus, are birds with long supple necks, lions and grotesque telamons, some of them touching back to back, bowed under the weight of the entablature. There, you can see the damned being driven to the flames by exterminating angels; Adam and Eve in Eden; processions and Biblical scenes and even King William offering the Cathedral of Monreale to the Virgin. One is left gasping by this imaginative orgy, the licence sometimes verging on the obscene, which is part of the genuine romanesque tradition. The whole Cathedral, too, though a product of the synthesis of Mediterranean styles, deriving from mediaeval Roman, Arab and even Greek art, is nevertheless a romanesque work above all through its capitals.

Now go into the Cathedral. At first you will have eyes for the mosaics alone, a solid mass covering over an acre, yet made up of cubes of coloured glass under half an inch on each side. They will leave you spellbound; but before studying them in detail, it is worth paying a brief visit to the sacrarium.

This, according to the classical plan for basilicas, has inner walls with the canon's stalls backing on to them; the walls are an extension of the two lines of Greek columns which separate the nave from the aisles. In the extension of the right aisle you will

41. *Segesta. The Temple.*
42. *Segesta. The Greek Theatre.*
43. *Mondello. The Harbour.*

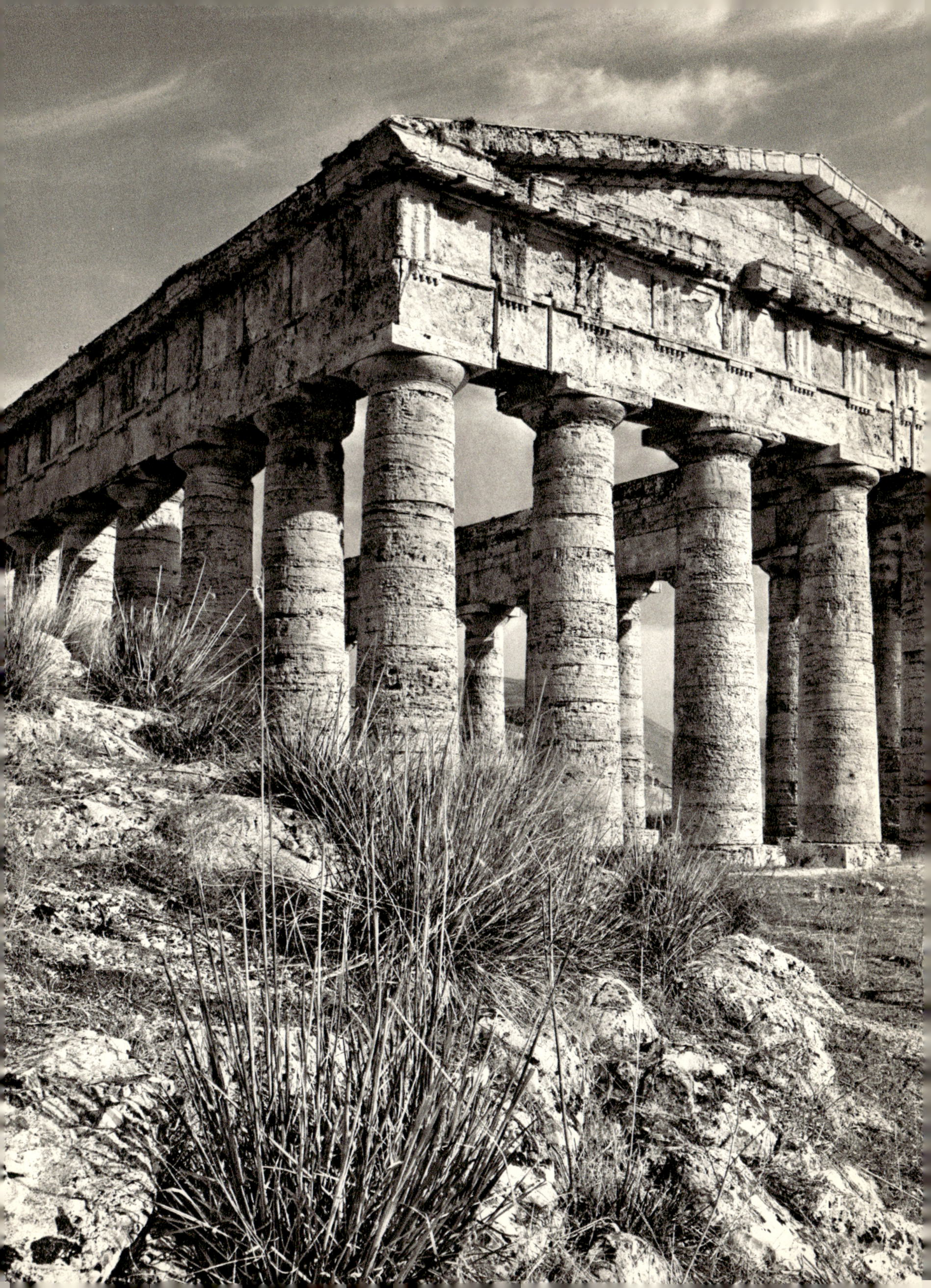

42

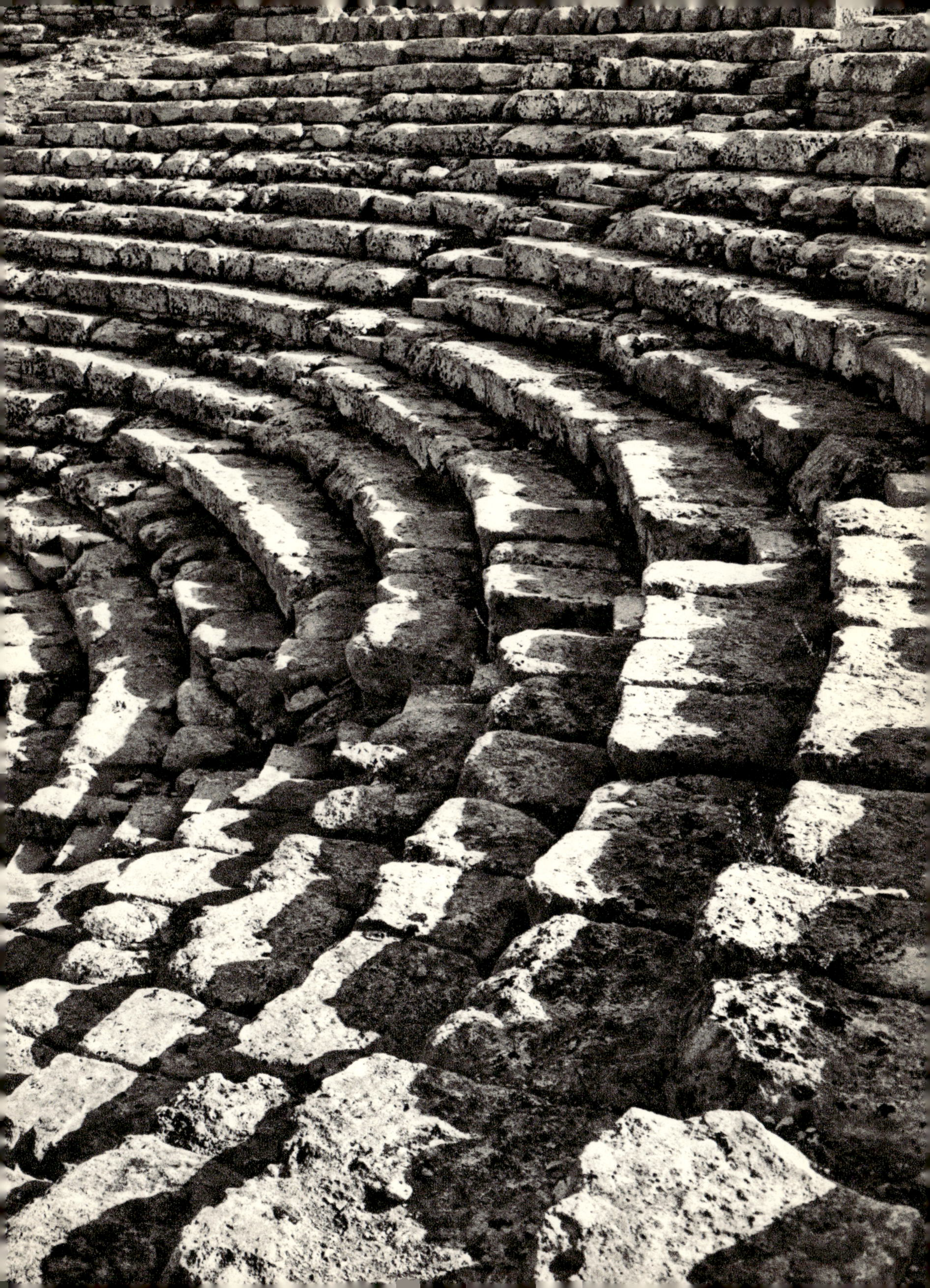

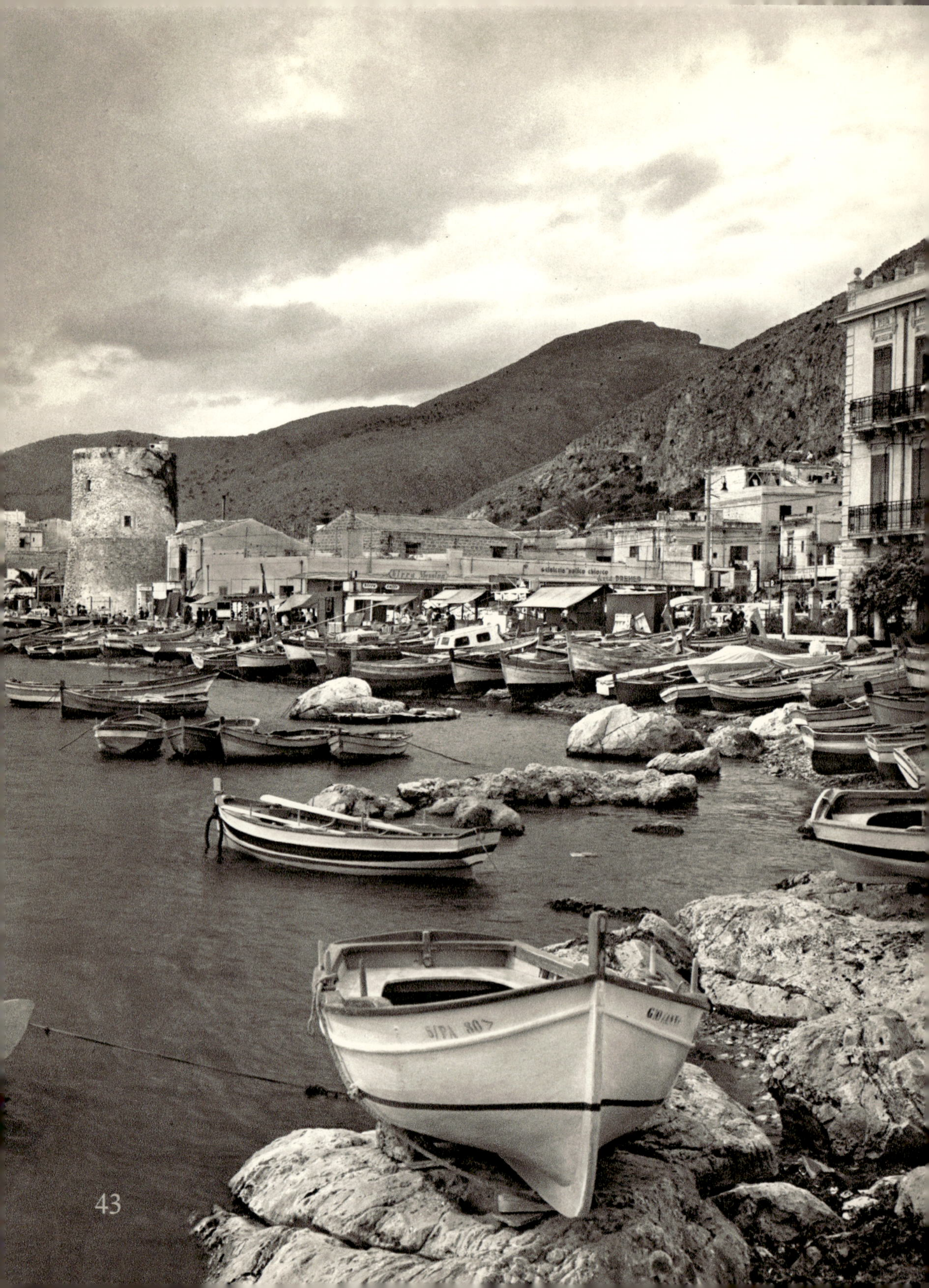

43

see the stately sarcophagi of William I and William II; on the left a modest altar with a sort of colour-print above it showing a crown at the top. This altar contains an urn which has in it some remains of King Louis IX, known in France as St Louis.

The story of how they came here is distinctly macabre. The king died of the plague near Tunis in 1270, and for fear of contagion it was thought necessary to have his body boiled. Only his skeleton was taken back to France, but at the bottom of the boiling-pot there were a few remains which devotees collected and left on their way home in this Sicilian cathedral.

Returning to the mosaics, you will need to let your eyes become accustomed to the dim light. Then the vivid colours will begin to stand out clearly on the glittering gold background.

A series of scenes runs all the way round the building, and is very logically arranged. It begins at the top of the nave on the right. First we have Genesis, with a particularly important place reserved for the patriarch Noah, as is proper in a land of navigators and vine-growers. Then comes the life of Christ and notably his preaching; finally the stories of St Peter and St Paul, which end with their portraits in the apsidals on each side at the back of the sacrarium. In the central apse, looking down on the Virgin, the whole arch is filled with a gigantic Christ giving his benediction.

He well deserves the title of Almighty, this strong young God, with eyes which follow you everywhere in the Cathedral. You come across his features not only in the Son, healing lepers, driving out of the Temple those who bought and sold, or presiding over the Last Supper, but also in the Father, creating the earth and man. As t'Serstevens writes, 'Jehovah is not here—Michaelangelo's Ancient of Days, as anguished in His work as was the artist himself; but a Christ with short black beard, powerful and peaceable, almost always seated on the luminous globe of the universe.'

The artists were probably Byzantines or Venetians—there is not much distinction, since the Venice of that age, which produced St Mark's, was the daughter of Byzantium. The pure Byzantine tradition can be seen not only in the whole but in many characteristic details: for instance, Christ is at the end of the table in the Last Supper, not in the middle; the apocalyptic angels have four overlapping wings, there are black crosses on the bishops' stoles.

But did these imported artists not have any Sicilian pupils? Monreale is thirty years later than the Palatine Chapel or the Martorana, so they would have had time to train such pupils, who may indeed have had more share in the Monreale than their masters did. Compare a mosaic from this Cathedral, Christ crowning William II, with the coronation of Roger II which you saw at the Martorana. The decline is obvious. The Christ at Monreale is stiff and gloomy in comparison with the Christ at the Martorana, enveloped in his robe which has a Hellenistic elegance.

Yet in several of the mosaic scenes from Monreale, despite their technical decline, I believe I can see something new, which is a deliberate break from Byzantine rules.

First of all, there is a new freedom. God creates heaven and earth, but He does not stand in the centre of the picture, as those rules demanded: sitting at the side, He fashions with delight His fine, iridescent, starry ball. God creates man and woman, but He creates them quite naked; this allows an anatomical study hard to render in a mosaic, on which the Byzantine artists did not willingly venture.

There is also a sense of movement. Jesus runs to drive out of the Temple those who buy and sell; he bangs with his whip on the table of the money-changers. Esau can be seen straining as he climbs the hill or bends his bow to kill some birds. Jacob is having a real struggle with the Angel.

Finally, there is a new realism. The leper and the man sick of the palsy, whom Jesus heals, are horrible sights. Adam and Eve make a sad picture as they leave Paradise. The God of the seventh day is a labourer resting after His work is finished, His shoulders sunk, His head bent, His tired, powerful hands spread out on His knees.

Such qualities mark a turning-point in art, heralding what is to follow: their freedom, movement and realism are in the spirit of Giotto's frescoes, although he was born a century later. These mosaics, clearly derived from the old art of Byzantium and Ravenna, show that, although the Normans failed politically in their attempt to marry east and west, artistically they succeeded in producing a fusion of Byzantine, Arab and Norman which paved the way for the Renaissance.

SEGESTA

THIS morning you are off to Segesta. Let us assume you have not visited Greece or Paestum, and will be seeing a Doric temple for the first time.

You are lucky to be starting with this one. It never fails in its effect whether one discovers it from the side, far down the valley, reaching it by the Calatafimi road; or approaches it from the front by the ordinary road, to see first its triangular pediment, then the six columns of its façade, gradually rising from the mound on which it stands, completely alone, against its austere backcloth of mountains. Perhaps afterwards it will give you some disappointments: like all its kind, it will seem to you too long for its height; you will also regret, with Berenson, that its columns have not the usual very slight entasis (curving line) and above all that they are not fluted.

It is not, in fact, and probably never was, a temple like the others. But it *is* Doric, and I believe once you have entered its precincts, when you see its columns in their perfect harmony and proportions, standing out against the blue sky, when your curiosity and excitement are stilled in the silence and solitude, you feel full of the 'total satisfaction of heart and mind induced, for the man born and bred in our Mediterranean civilization, by contemplating Doric perfection.'[1]

There are three roads leading from Palermo to Segesta. Each is so beautiful in its different way that I must refrain from recommending one above the other. All three reveal one of the finest land- and sea-scapes in the Mediterranean, the Gulf of Castellanmare.

The coast road, a motorway as far as Punta Raisi airport, is Sicily at its most magnificent. True, it passes some dirty suburbs coming out of Palermo, and some run-down fishing villages on the Gulf of Castellanmare. But for its whole length it is right by a resplendent sea, starting with the narrow strip of coast which has the cliffs of Mount

[1] François Cali. *L'Ordre grec*. Arthaud.

Palmeto overlooking it on the left. As you leave Palermo, there are a succession of luxuriant gardens, with 18th-century villas rising in their midst—one of which was chosen for shooting the film of *The Leopard*; thick olive groves, and green valleys where the water runs between forests of reeds.

The mountain roads do not give such an impression of opulence. But the middle one, before reaching the desert plateaux of Montelepre, goes through a lovely pine forest and then offers a glimpse of the village of Carini. Although very poor in itself, in the Greek era (when it was called Hyccara) it bore the most richly-kept courtesan in history: the famous Lais.

The last, and fastest, road goes along by Monreale Cathedral, crosses some rocky hills and, then reaches the fertile undulating plain round Alcamo. Alcamo is a big country town of over 50,000 inhabitants. It retains the name of its Arab founder and was the birthplace of Cuillo, the first Italian poet before Dante to write in the vernacular. The town is somewhat grim-looking, but animated enough and contains several churches worthy of interest.

Here you come up against the Sicilian contrasts I have mentioned before. On the prosperous coast road by the glittering Gulf you pass a fishing village, Trappeto; it has nothing special to detain you, and yet is important in modern Sicily, because it was chosen by the great philanthropist Danilo Dolci to draw the world's attention to Sicily's poverty. The middle road takes you past Montelepre, which has in its cemetery the pretentious mausoleum of the bandit Giuliano, local product of that same poverty. On the third road you see Partinico, which in my view typifies these over-populated small towns of Southern Italy, with their dusty streets crossing at right-angles, too wide for the cottages at the sides. It is amazing that Partinico is still in the same state as when it was the electoral borough of an Italian prime minister —Victor-Emmanuel Orlando, who made the Versailles Treaty with Wilson, Lloyd George and Clemenceau.

But another contrast: directly after these wretched towns and villages in the middle of a rich countryside, you are suddenly faced by pure reason, balance and beauty— in the Temple of Segesta.

There is wealth too: the past wealth of a small city which found enough money to build such a temple; and the present relative wealth of fields and pastures extending to the foot of the mountains, covered in spring flowers, with scattered sheep guarded by large white dogs, generally much fiercer than those which t'Serstevens managed to make his camp watchdogs. No doubt they would claim to be distant nephews of the legendary dog Crinisios, who met the strange fate of being turned into a stream by the nymph Egesta after fathering on her a human child. This child, under the name of Akestis, became the founder of Segesta.

So far we are in the realms of Theocritus, whose spirit is very much in evidence in the country round Segesta. But 'the plot thickens' with Virgil, who would also be at home in such country if he had confined himself to writing poetry about the countryside; the trouble is that as poet laureate he had to glorify military leaders as well. In his eagerness to satisfy the Emperor Augustus, collecting everything which might support the thesis that Rome had Trojan origins and that the Julii were descended from Venus—he seized on Akestis. This son of the dog Crinisios and the nymph Egestis was turned by Virgil into a sort of Homeric Garibaldi who left his distant Segesta to defend the liberty of Troy; after failing in that enterprise, he returned home to organise a refuge there for fleeing Trojans; and soon welcomed Aeneas, on his way from Carthage to Latium, relieving him of his 'passengers' a—old people and children, warriors weary of adventures, and women suffering from sea-sickness.

These legends, as is often the case, explain very well the history of Segesta. It appears to have been founded about 630 B.C. by a mysterious small tribe, no doubt Sikelian, the Elymians, who in the previous millenium had come from the East—from Asia, Phoenicia, or quite possibly from Troy. For centuries, indeed, its citizens wore mourning on the anniversary of the Fall of Troy. Segesta intervened several times in the affairs of Greek Sicily, and its quarrel with its neighbour, Selinunte, was the occasion for the disastrous Athenian expedition against Syracuse in 416–413. But it never considered itself a Hellenic city and always insisted on its claim to Trojan origins. As Carthage was the city of Queen Dido, who had sheltered Aeneas, Segesta was under Carthage's protection and remained in existence in the middle of the Carthaginian zone of Sicily. Later the claim to Trojan origins proved even more rewarding, gaining Segesta the friendship of Rome. Thanks to that it prospered, and then survived, at least until the barbarian invasions.

This history, starting from legends, seems to me to explain the temple's singularities. The columns are not fluted, as we have noted. But look also at the stylobate, the base, that is, on which the temple rests: you will see there coarse tenons carved into the mass, which were used to secure the cords while blocks of stone were being put into place. Now, the Ancients were not in the habit of forgetting these unaesthetic tenons once the building was finished, and would carefully level them out. And, although they sometimes built the columns before fluting them, they always did this later. What is the answer? That the Temple of Segesta was never finished? That the small town, ruined by the war which it had itself set in motion, did not afterwards have enough money to complete the exorbitant work it had undertaken? Such is the verdict of some archaeologists.

But there are other unusual features about the temple. Look up towards the architraves within; they do not have those holes into which the beams supporting the roof would be fixed. Again, you may have been surprised, when you went through the colonnade, to be on a quite flat surface, like a tennis court, without the least trace of *naos*, that inner sanctuary in classical temples which contains the statue of the god and also supports the framework. 'It is certain,' says t'Serstevens, 'that in the construction of temples, the *naos* had to be built before the colonnade, so that the stones did not have to be taken between the shafts, which were only about seven feet wide. Also, without *naos*, how would the architects expect to support the framework of the roof?

For no assemblage of beams at that period would have been able to cover at one go some eighty feet from one frieze to another.'

From these observations other archaeologists have concluded that the Temple of Segesta was never a temple, but a sort of peristyle, designed either to frame an altar without *naos* or even, if it was placed behind the altar as was customary, to provide a colossal setting for that altar and an ambulatory for the devotees. The devotees of whom? The neighbouring Aphrodite Erycine, mother of Aeneas, who was worshipped at Segesta under the Roman Empire? Artemis, whose statue here was sneaked away by Verres? More probably a local divinity, half Sikelian, half Asiatic, perhaps the nymph Egestis and her dog husband, whose effigy, strapping and with tail high, we find on all the city's coins.

We should perhaps adopt a little of both explanations. But leave the matter to the archaeologists, and do not be too scornful of these Segestan hybrids who lacked the Hellenic concern with perfection, for whom Greek art was doubtless merely decoration, not the emanation of their whole being. If the temple here is the first Doric temple you have seen, you will understand how Aristotle could say that Doric harmony brought perfect satisfaction to the soul.

Drive up a fine new road, to the top of a steep hill, overlooking the temple on the east, and you will arrive at Segesta's second attraction, the Greek theatre. This is pure Greek; the Elymians took no liberties here with Hellenic rules. From the top there is a wonderful feature common to Sicily's other Greek theatres, a backdrop supplied by Nature, visible above the 'set'—in this case the vast and brilliant panorama of the Gulf of Castellanmare.

It is a good idea to walk down to the temple. This will give you a fine view of it from above, and also of the ruins of the ancient city—what there is of them. For all you will see are a few stumps of stone, in striking contrast with the well-preserved temple and theatre. All through their history so many generations of men, claiming Trojan or Sikelian origins, served Carthage and then Rome with devotion. It is a shade ironical that two 'Greek' buildings are all that is left of their city.

44. *Alcamo Marine.*
45. *At Trapani.*
46. *Balestrate. Weighing of grapes.*
47. *Balestrate. Sicilian cart.*
48. *Erice. The Castle.*
49. *Between Trapani and Marsala. Lifting couch-grass.*
50. *Salt-marshes near Trapani.*
51. *Castelvetrano. The Ephebe of Selinunte.*

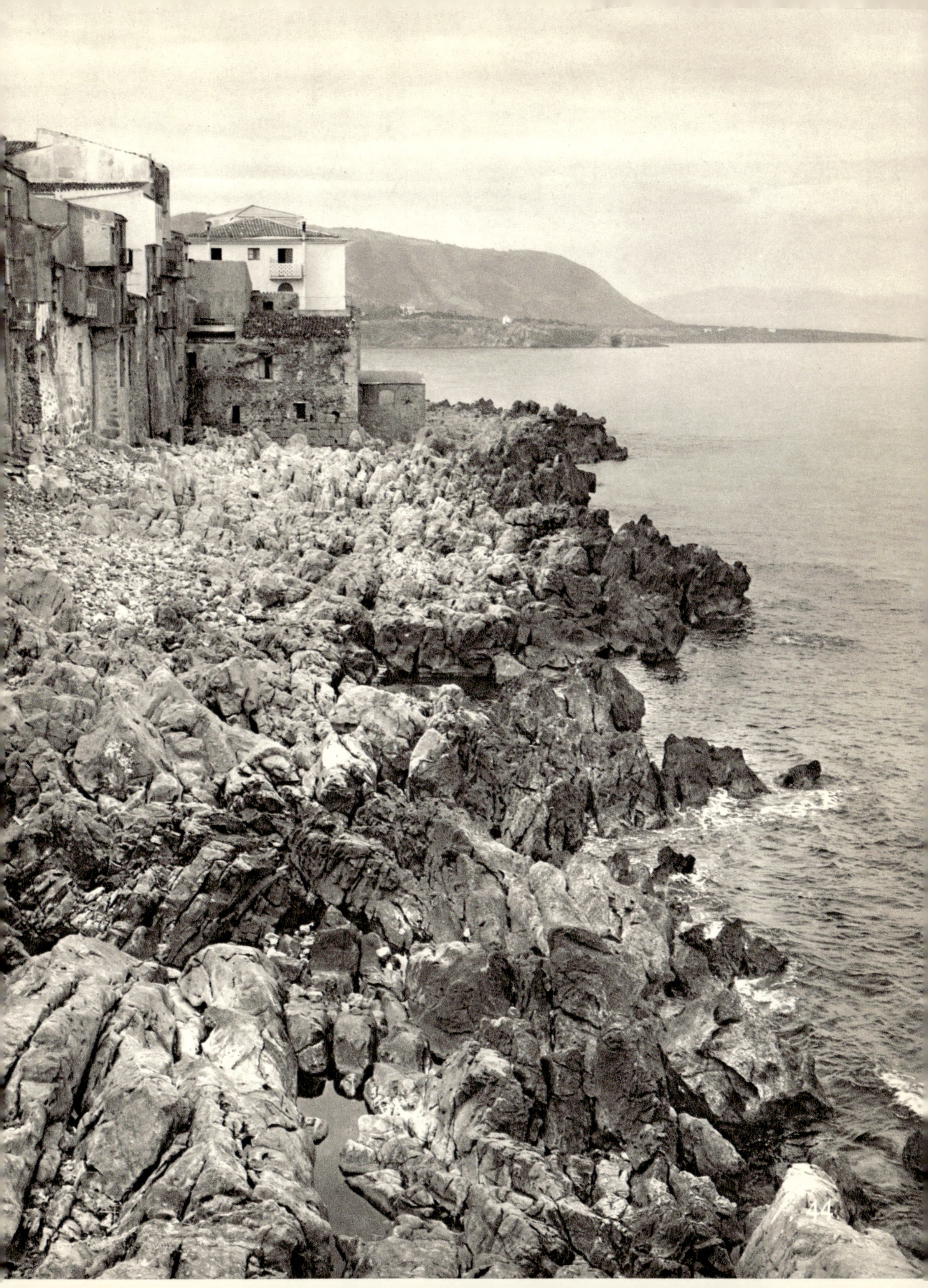

44

45

46

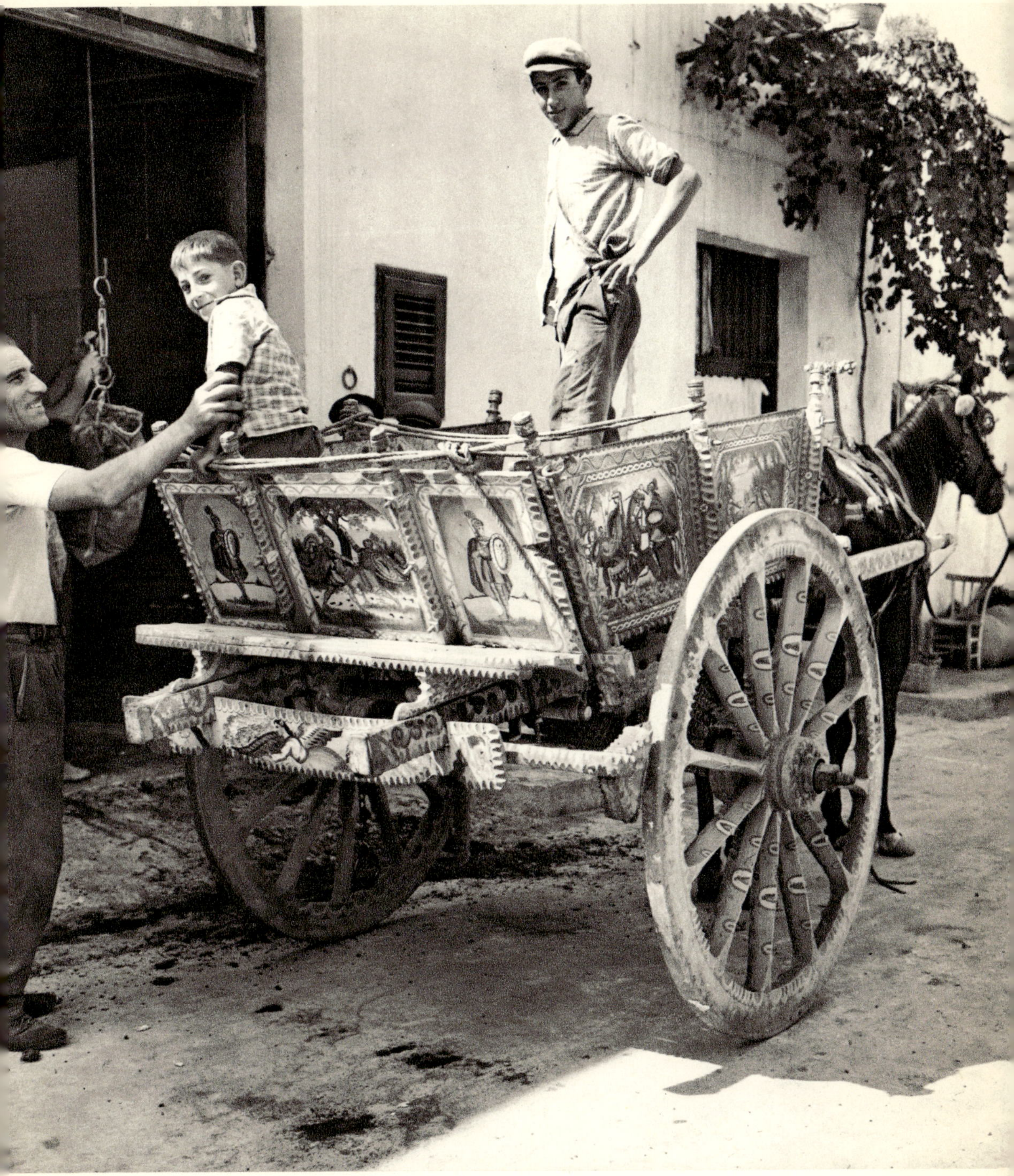

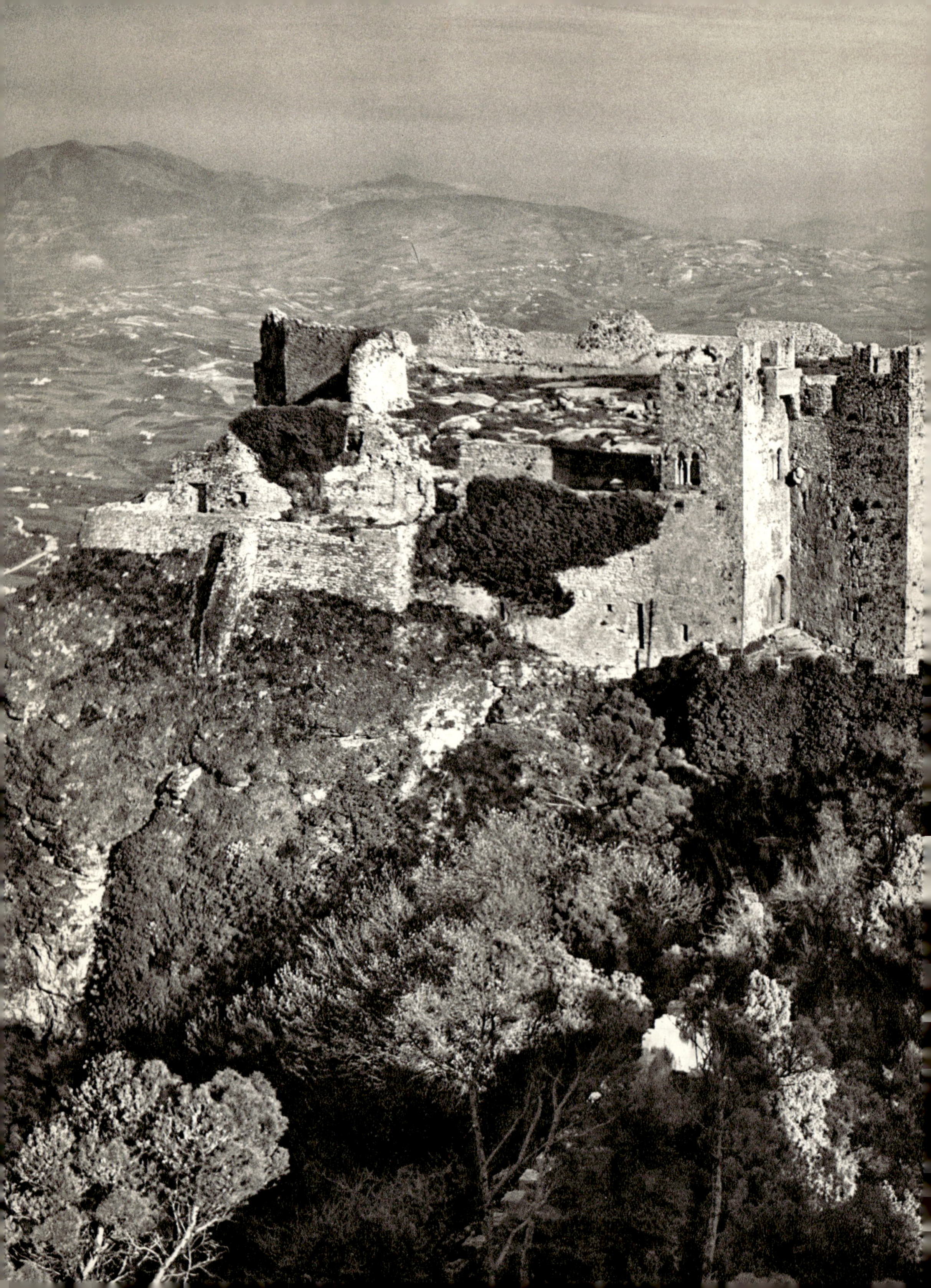

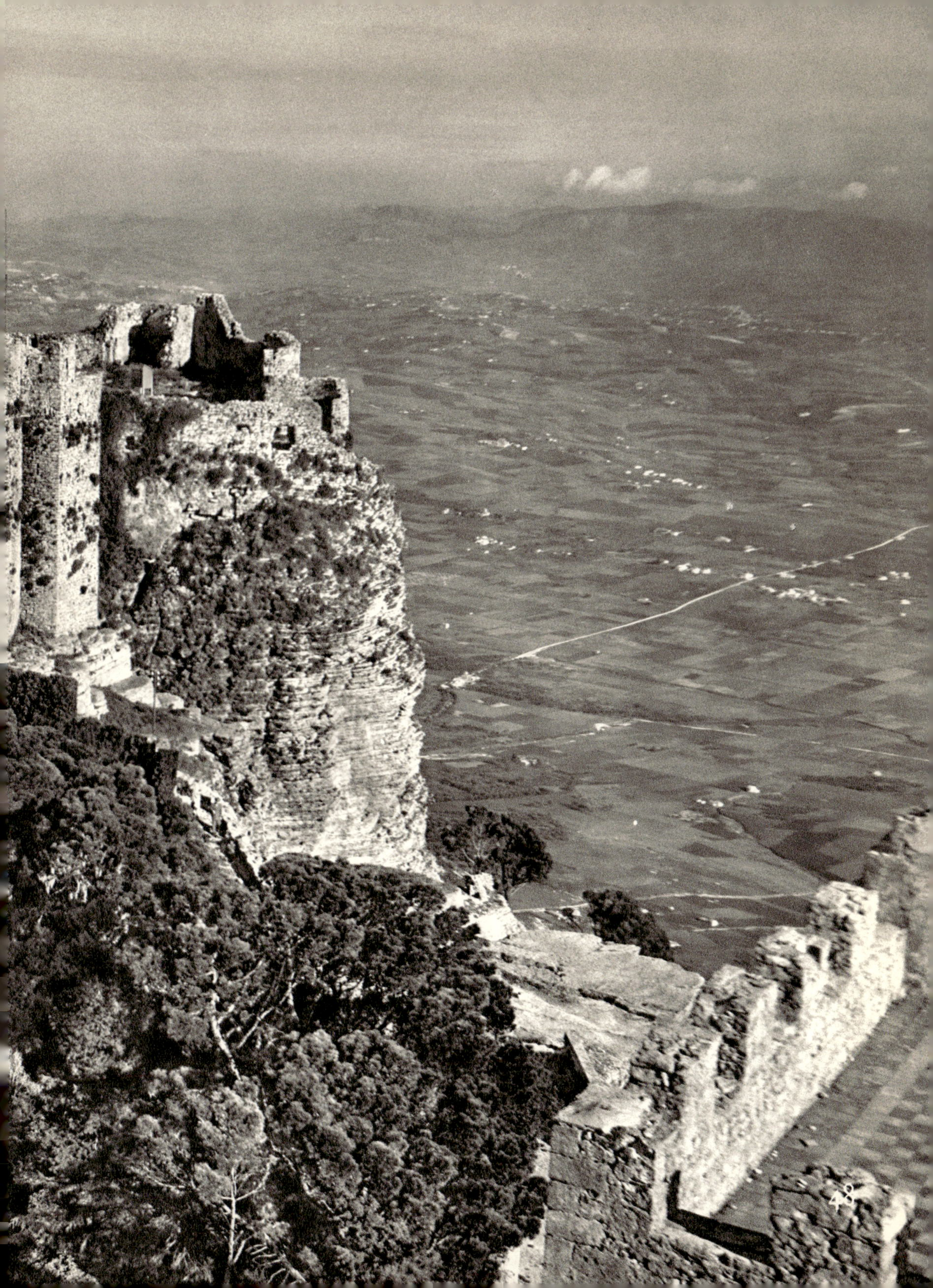
48

49

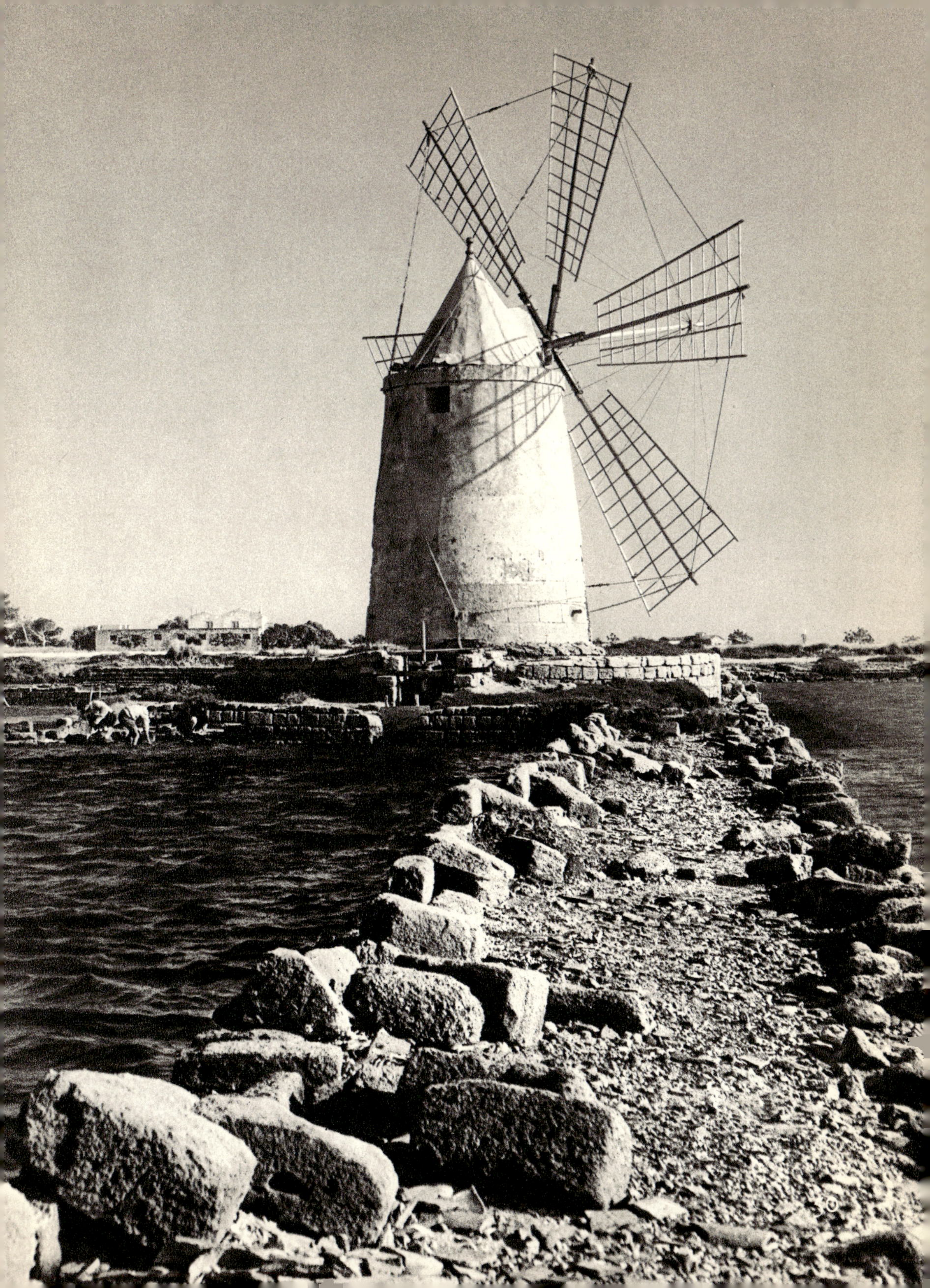

51

THE WEST COAST
ERICE—TRAPANI—MARSALA—CASTELVETRANO

THE west coast of Sicily is often neglected by travellers. Flat, intensively cultivated, bounded by salt marshes, it has few scenic charms. It passed directly from Carthaginian to Roman domination, and contains no vestiges of Greece; there are, however, some interesting Norman and baroque buildings at Trapani, Marsala and Mazara del Vallo. Today this coast is chiefly concerned with tunny-fishing and the production of dessert wines for export; but in classical times it was one of the main poles of attraction in the Mediterranean, because of the famous shrine of Venus, on top of Mount Eryx: Venus, 'daughter of the bitter wave', and therefore kindly to sailors. The priestesses tending the shrine were of a very particular kind called 'hierodules'; they sacrificed to the goddess by acting as prostitutes for the devotees; pilgrimages there, as can be imagined, were made very assiduously!

'Passing sailors came to Eryx,' writes Gaston Boissier, 'to pay homage to Venus with all the ardour and excesses of life-loving people in constant danger of death.' A great store of broken jars has been found on one of the slopes of the mountain, with handles bearing Greek, Latin and Carthaginian inscriptions. Probably sailors from many countries who climbed Eryx brought their wine with them and drank it up there in cheerful company. The 'hierodules' helped them to spend the money they had laboriously amassed on their arduous voyages, and some of these women soon made their fortune. Cicero mentions one of them called Agonis, originally a slave, then emancipated by Venus, who had become very rich and was envied in particular for the slave musicians she owned.'

Travellers today should not expect any such amenities! All that is left of Venus in Erice is a delightful little head by Praxiteles in its museum. Where her temple stood, there are the ruins of a massive feudal castle. Some scholars believe they have found traces of her cult, as brought from distant Asia Minor by Aeneas and his fugititive Trojans, in the strange costumes which the local inhabitants wear for the procession of Santa Maria di Custonaci (it takes place the last Wednesday in August).

In summer the air on the heights of Erice is cool and refreshing after the sultry heat of the coastal plan. The museum mentioned above contains a splendid *Annunciation* by Antonello Gagini, and on the church there is an astonishing 17th-century St Martin emerging from his baroque niche on a galloping horse. You can admire the church's Aragonese porch and campanile, but do not go inside it, even to see the curious Chapel of the Crucifix, if you wish to avoid the spectacle of what Berenson called 'a restoration in Louis-Philippe Gothic.'

Take a walk in the small streets, meticulously paved with cobblestones separated by slabs of white marble. The municipality, concerned with its reputation among tourists, keep these streets up so carefully that they seem a shade artificial. The public gardens give you the same feeling, but they are pleasantly leafy, and from here or the terrace of the church there is a fine view. On your right you have the headlands of Monte Cofano and Capo San Vito, descending sheer into the sea; on your left the plain and the salt-marshes, which merge with the sea; straight ahead of you the sea itself, with the Egadi Islands lying a little way out like three stone battleships; and on a clear day you can see the coast of Africa on the horizon.

When driving down to Trapani, stop on the edge of some pinewoods, to look up at Erice and its castle, perched on their colossal cliff.

Seen from above, Trapani is a cramped white town, looking rather Middle Eastern, on a horse-shoe spit of land jutting out into the sea. At closer quarters the first impression persists: if you stop at the fish market you can feel how close you are to Africa. The north-facing shore, curving inwards, has its houses built directly on to the water. The southern shore, however, reminds one of an Atlantic port, with its docks, moored boats and channel, and beyond them an ill-defined embankment of mud and salt-marshes.

Inside the town there are several interesting sights, mediaeval and baroque. Among the former there is the arabesque rose-window of Sant'Agostino; and the Palazzo de la Giudecca, in the Catalan style, although very dilapidated, has two notable architraves and a squat tower with walls worked in nail-heads. The baroque buildings include the Collegiate Church, the Cathedral and the Town Hall, a narrow three-storey triptych of columns and statues, with a huge clock at the top of each shutter.

As a sea-port Trapani is naturally cosmopolitan. The Church of Santa Maria del Gesù contains a typically Florentine Madonna by Andrea della Robbia. The sacrarium of the Annunziata is rather forbidding, but when you have gone through a fine monumental arch, you will be welcomed by the serene smile, very un-Sicilian, of another lady from Tuscany, the 'Madonna of Trapani'. She was brought one day from Pisa, it is said, direct from the studio of Giovanni Pisano.

The road out of Trapani is dull, and does not even give you a view of the ruins of Motye, first Carthaginian settlement in Sicily, which are in an island on a lake.

Before long you will be at Marsala. This has many memorials to Garibaldi's landing on 11 May 1860, but nothing left to evoke the fortress of Lilybaeum, a Carthaginian strongpoint which held out against the Romans for ten years, or the great Arab port of Mers al Ali.

The town hall square at Marsala is quite fine, but I prefer the one in the next town, Mazara del Vallo. This is a charming 18th-century square which would make a good setting for *The Barber of Seville*. The warehouses of the big wine merchants, looking on to the promenade along the sea and the harbour, are full of character. They are generally surrounded, like fortresses, by high walls with a big door, sometimes flanked by turrets. They give an impression of vine-growing power reminiscent of Bordeaux or Oporto; and several of them, as at Bordeaux and Oporto, were founded by Englishmen.

At Castelvetrano you will see for the first time one of those big country towns so numerous in Sicily, where the peasants would rather crowd in together than live on farms or in villages; they are ready to travel miles every day, in carts or on mules, to go and cultivate their fields. The result is a sort of collection of urban farms, very individual and very dirty, but generally well aligned on the sides of over-large streets in which sheep roam. I remember visiting one of these peasants whose farming was done near Selinunte and who had discovered there a much more remunerative activity, in the sale of archaeological finds, which he had dug up himself or bought from his neighbours. I was amazed when I saw him pull out from under his bed an Ionian statuette of a smiling girl which seemed to light up his hovel at once. I bought the statuette, and we sealed the bargain by drinking some wine together. I might have been a bit worried had I known that at that very moment the famous Salvatore Giuliano was perhaps concealed a few yards away, in the hide-out where the following year he was betrayed and killed.

The centre of Castelvetrano, happily, has quite a different atmosphere, with its vast irregular squares and its churches. There is the Chiesa Madre with a sober Renaissance façade; St John the Baptist, which has an impressive statue of John the Baptist by Antonello Gagini; and San Domenico. This last church shows the emergence, at the end of the 16th century, of an art which was to develop strikingly in baroque Sicily, the art of stucco sculpture or rather stucco modelling.

In the main square of Castelvetrano one of the most moving ceremonies in Sicilian folk-lore takes place on Easter morning: the 'Dawn Office'. Two statues are set up at either end of the square, one of Christ, the other of the Madonna, hidden in a vast mourning cloak. At the hour of the Resurrection, an Angel carried on a man's arm runs to bring the good news to the Madonna. But she cannot believe it, and the Angel has to repeat his embassy three times. The third time Mary, at last convinced and exultant, dashes towards her Son, throwing down her sad cloak, from which a swarm of sparrows suddenly flies out.

Castelvetrano has unfortunately lost its main 'sight', a bronze *Kouros* (boy) with enamel eyes, known as the Ephebe of Selinunte. The municipality kept him in an office in the Town Hall, where he could scarcely be seen to full advantage, but his presence certainly brought good business to the town. But he has now disappeared, I am told, whether fraudulently bought by some collector or foreign art gallery, or even by an official from the Italian Ministry of Fine Arts who felt this splendid youth would be better placed in a gallery at Palermo or Rome, and is waiting to exhibit him when the population of Castelvetrano are resigned to their loss. I dare say Interpol are on the tracks of the Ephebe, and when he eventually turns up, he will be worth your inspection.

There is something else worth seeing on the outskirts of Castelvetrano, and that is a little Norman church called La Trinità di Délia. In the town there are plenty of small yellow plaques showing you the way; only they stop when you get out into the country, and you may easily go off course and find yourself at the artificial lake of Delia. This will anyhow show you an example of the great irrigation works carried out in modern Sicily, and also a Theocritus scene with green fields, purple hills and flocks of sheep.

Retracing your tracks, you will see quite close to you a large new farm. Make straight for it, and in its garden you will find the Chapel. It may not seem very original if you already know Greece or Calabria, but have a good look at it all the same: a simple block of stone; three facades almost without ornament except for an archway on each, framing narrow windows; behind, three semi-circular double apses; the whole surmounted by a round cupola. Inside there are four columns supporting the cupola, and round it bare arches, slightly broken but romanesque; at ground level the modern tombstones are lit by candles stuck to the floor.

When you withdraw a little and look at this shrine in the shadow of the palm-trees which surround it, you will think at first that the Arab world is really not far away, on the other side of the Strait of Sicily. Then, attending chiefly to the architecture, you might think of Byzantium and Mistra. But in the end you will realise that the essential thing about this modest church is that it is romanesque. The art of Caen and of Pisa dominates and absorbs that of Cordova and Byzantium, keeping only their outlines and fusing them into this little masterpiece of simplicity.

SELINUNTE

52. *E Temple and, in foreground, stones of F Temple.*
53, 54. *Ruins of G Temple.*
55. *E Temple.*
56. *Metope of C Temple: Apollo's Quadriga (National Museum at Palermo).*
57. *C Temple.*
58. *Selinunte. The beach.*

52

53

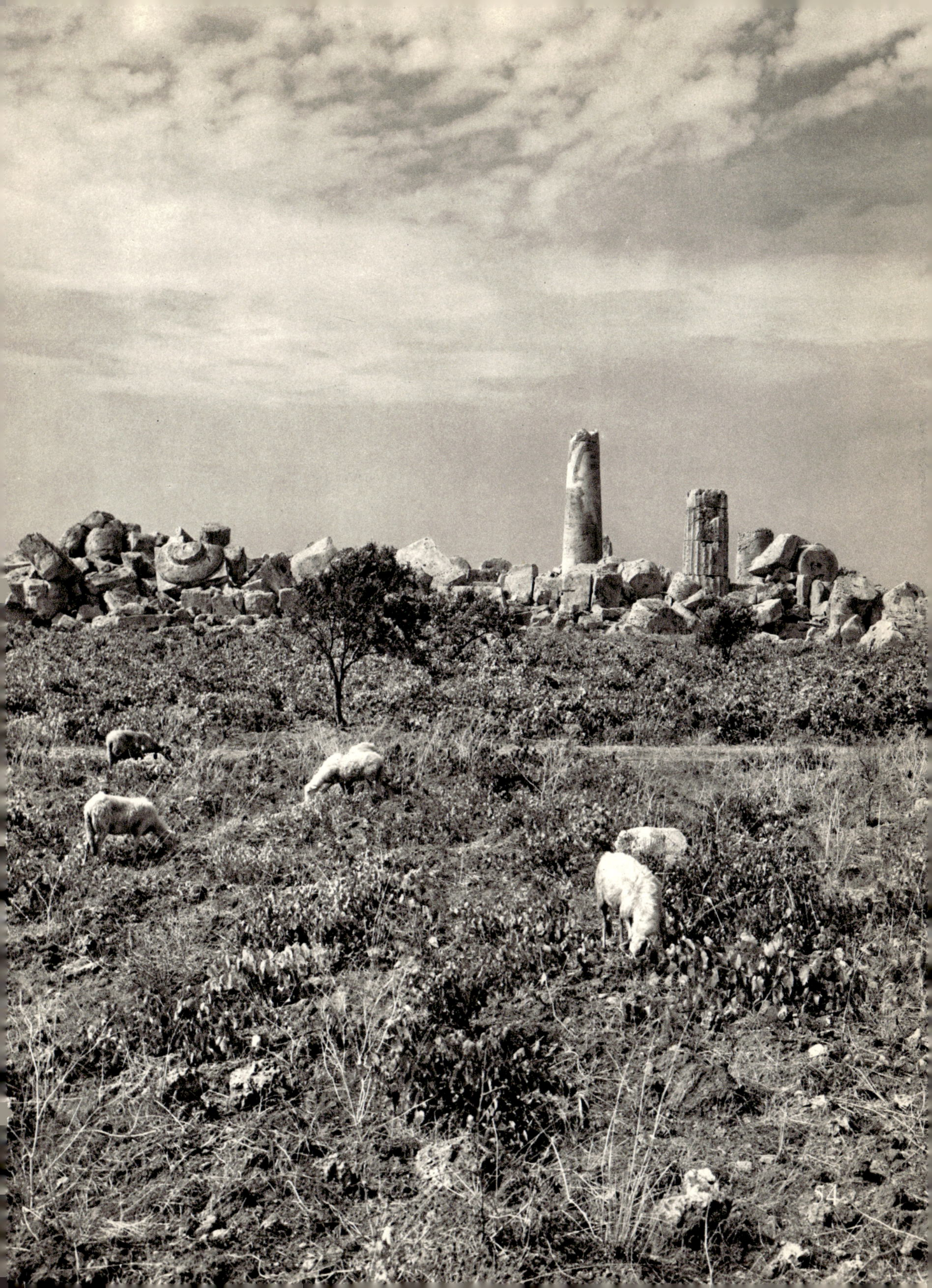
54

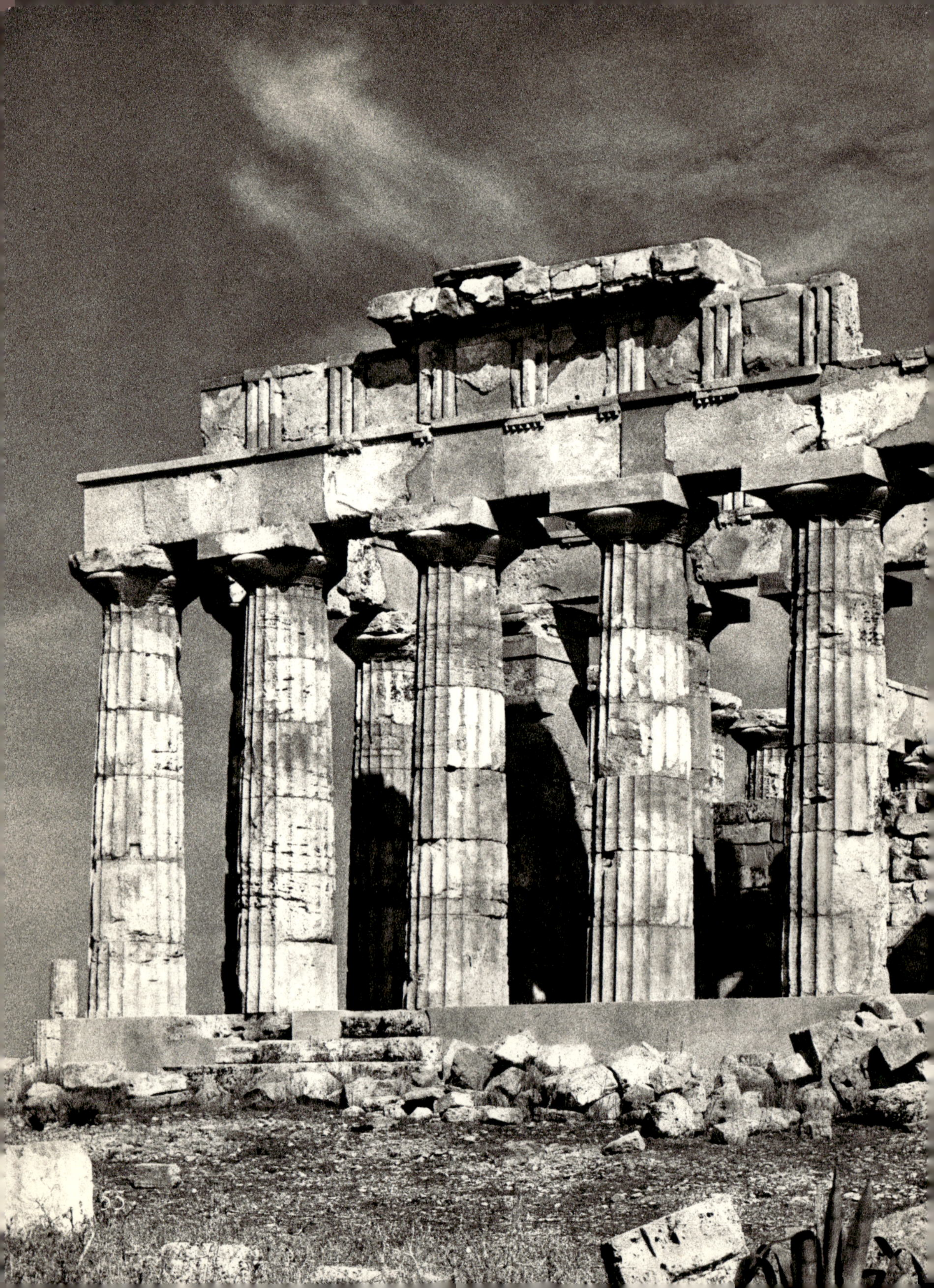

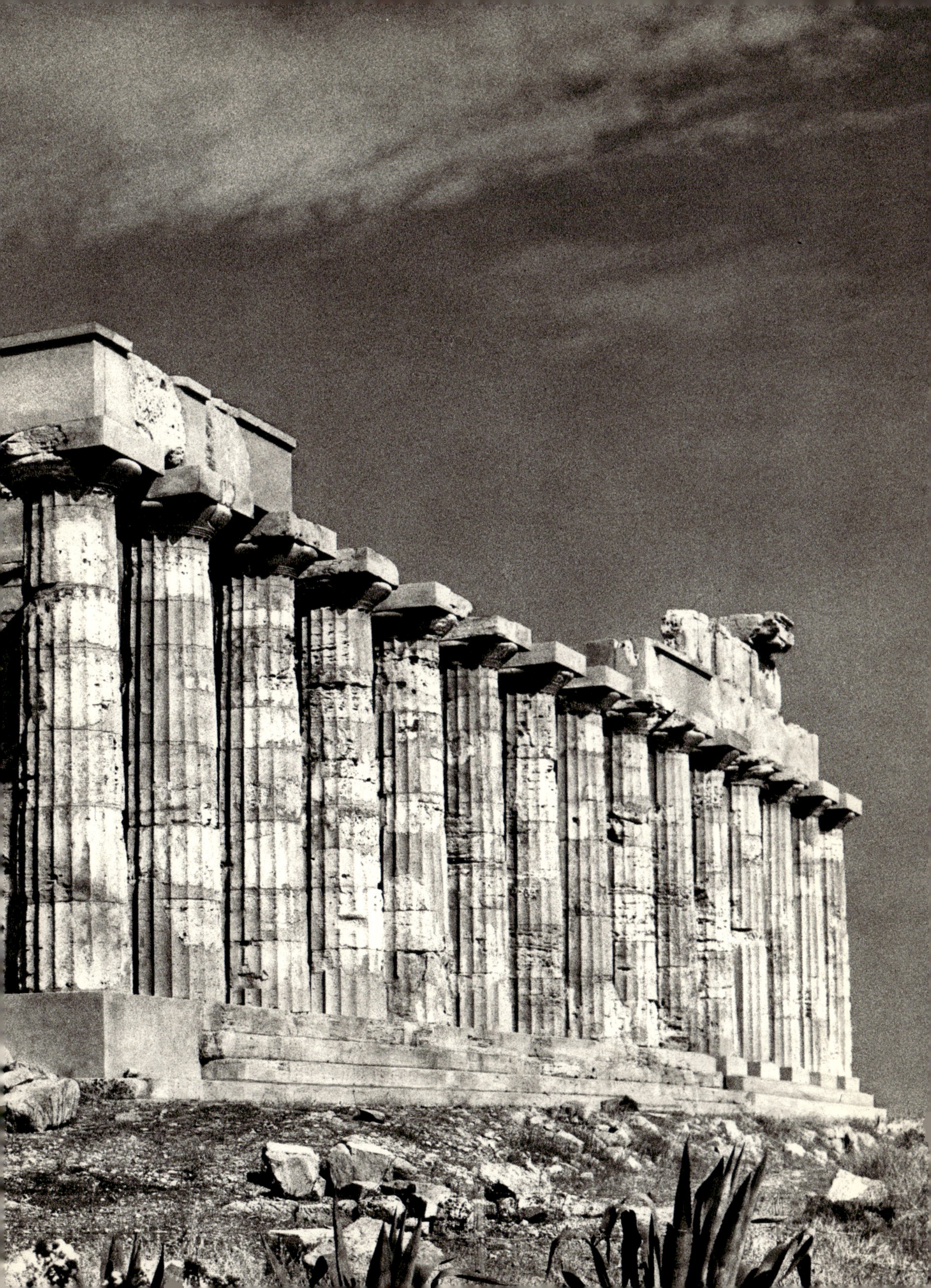

56

57

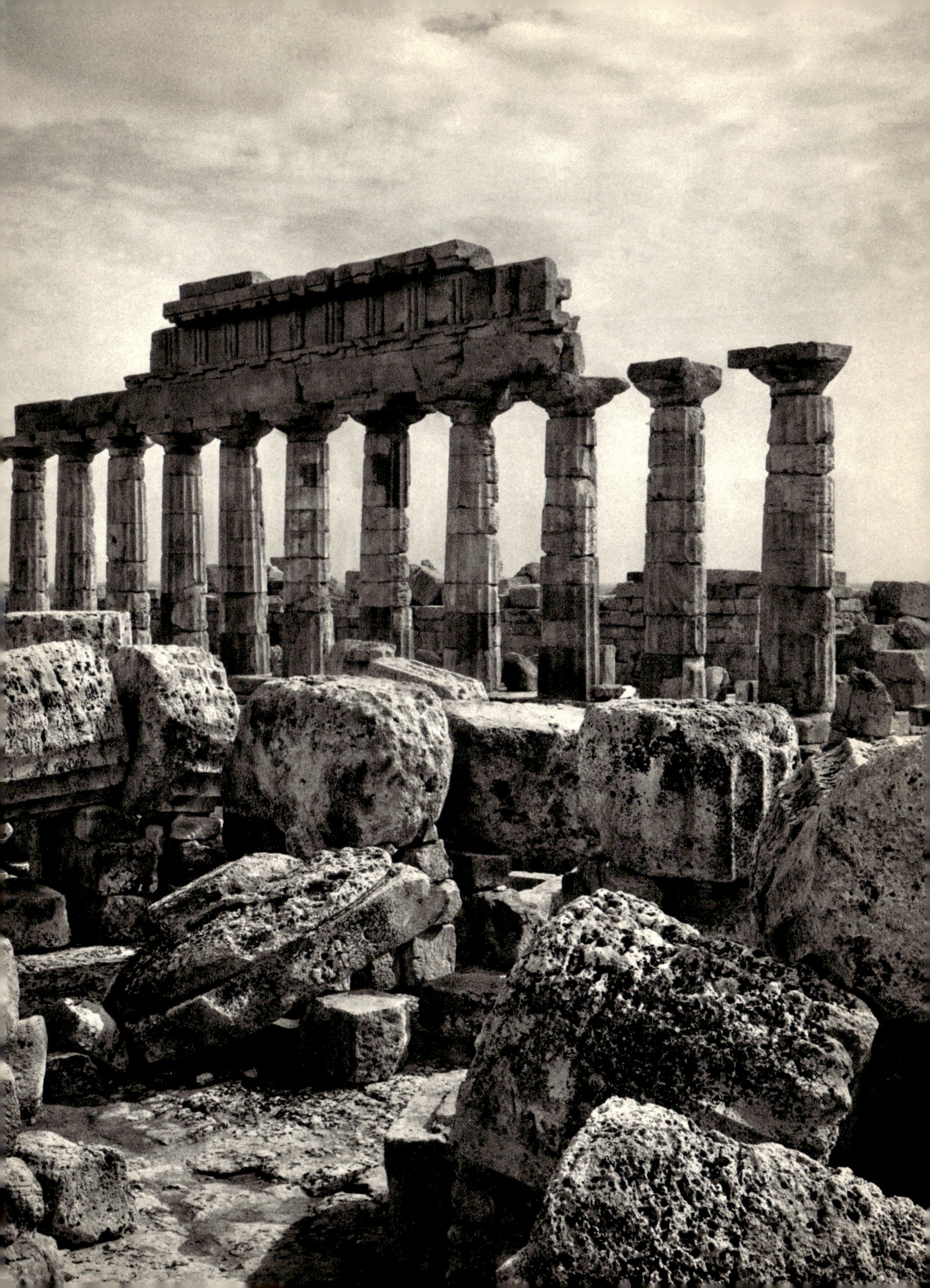

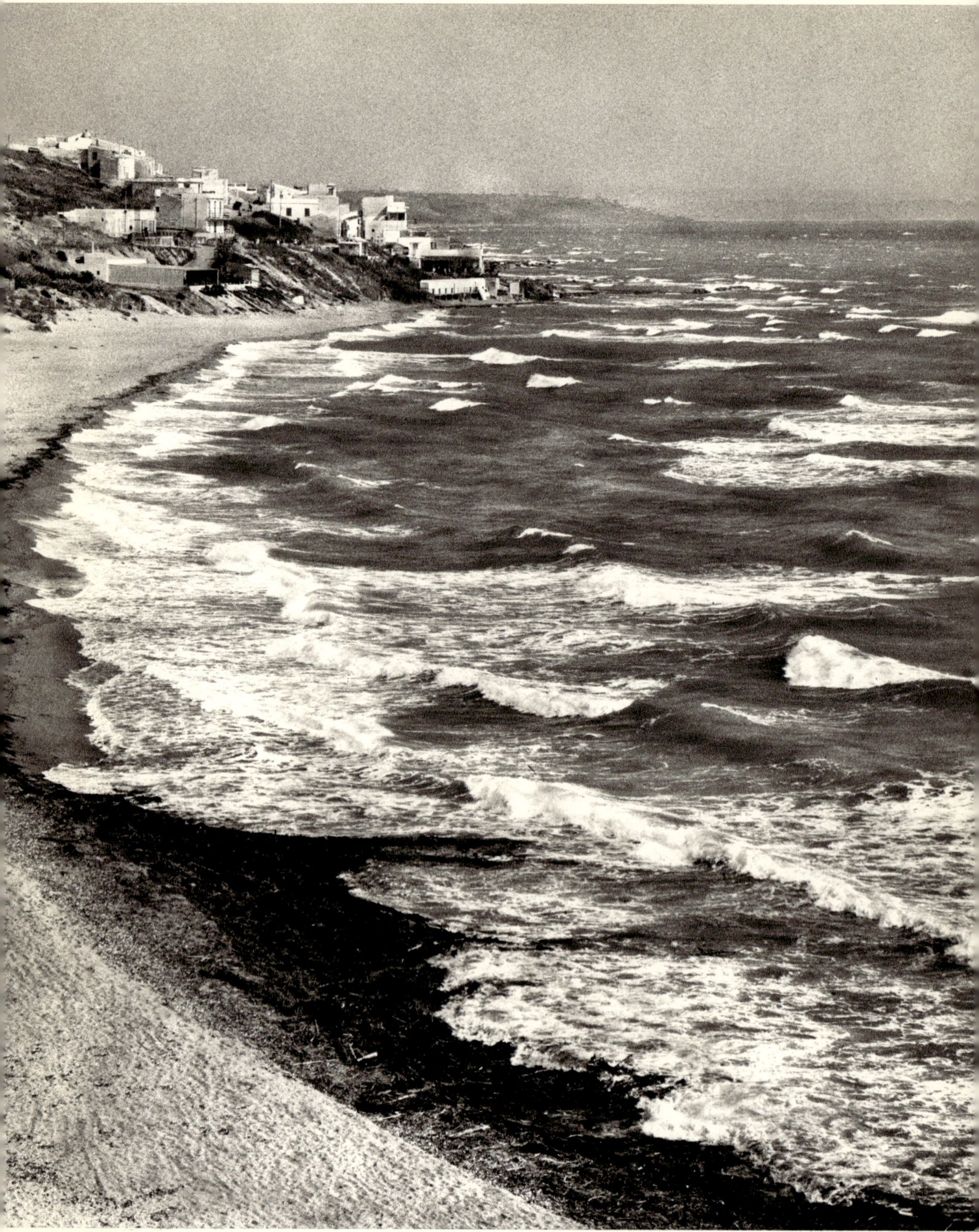

I FIRST heard the name of this ancient city pronounced by my father. I was only just ten, and my imagination began constructing a vision of grandiose and tragic ruins. For some reason the name conjured up the red and black colours of fire, blood and mourning; and by chance I first discovered the site in the red and black light of a stormy evening.

It had just been raining hard, and looked likely to do so again. Huge black clouds rose from a leaden sea. Three highish hills dropped steeply down into the sea, sheltering between them the twin harbours of the former city. Without stopping at the remains on the eastern hill, the first you pass on entering the archaeological zone, I made for the central one to see the only colonnade then standing, that of the C Temple, restored in 1925–7. I did a quick tour of the remains of the five temples on that hill; they lie along an esplanade at the end of an acropolis overlooking the sea. Then I returned to the eastern hill, where the biggest temples had been, and climbed to the top of the colossal ruin of the enormous G Temple—the building of this was so ambitious that it was left unfinished. At that moment the sun broke through on the horizon like a ball of fire, between the black of the clouds and the black of the sea, revealing a glory of red rays, tingeing the bare hills with dark purple, picking out in the distance the colonnade of C Temple as in a shadow theatre. Toiling against the wind, three large herons flew past in single file . . . .

It was very much the picture I had imagined as a boy, and that image has remained with me ever since, although I have been back to Selinunte several times, and always in superb weather.

I have bathed on the beach of pink sand which has spread into the site of the eastern harbour. I have seen all the remains on the central hill, of A, B, C, D and O Temples, the houses on the acropolis, Carthaginian, Hellenistic or Roman, and the imposing walls round the acropolis itself. By walking some distance north of this central hill, I have come to the vast plateau of Manuzza, site of the actual city in the Greek era, of which nothing is left today. I have crossed the valley of the eastern harbour and the river where the wild parsley grows; this parsley (*selinon* in Greek) gave the river Selinus (now Mondione) and hence the city its name, and also the symbol for its coins.

The western hill seems to have been the hill of the dead. On it I have visited the sanctuary of Demeter Malophoros where it is thought that funerals stopped, before coming to the neighbouring 'cities of the dead'. I have returned to the eastern hill, and climbed at leisure amidst the chaos of G Temple, which was one of the greatest of the world after those of Artemis at Ephesus, Apollo at Miletus and Zeus at Agrigentum. The tambours are eleven feet in diameter, the capitals fifty square feet; altogether, these fragments leave you with the feelings of mingled admiration and repulsion inspired by anything gigantic. F Temple was rased, alas, in the time of the Spaniards, who were building bridges there. The columns of E Temple had been lying in such a neat row on the ground, one tambour behind another, making me wish this temple could be restored—and it recently has been. So I have had the satisfaction of seeing it erect in all its Doric purity, displaying on its cliff-top the perfection of its lines and the orange hues of its stone, against the blue background of the sea.

Yet none of these memories of Selinunte, not even the sight of E Temple resurrected, has wiped out my boyhood image of a doomed city—which indeed is well suited to its history.

Dorian colonists from Megara Hyblaea founded it about 650 B.C., at the western end of the Greek zone, in direct contact with the Carthaginian zone. The founders intended, in fact, to make it a sentinel of Hellenism, another Sparta, a tough, soldiers' city, always ready to check the hereditary enemy. But during the 6th century their descendants quickly grew rich and soft, preferring to build temples and beautify their houses rather than prepare for war. Finally they decided to come to terms with Carthage as the best way of continuing this agreeable existence. In 480, on the same day as Themistocles was fighting the battle of Salamis, with the fate of eastern Hellenism at stake, Gelon, tyrant of Syracuse, fought the equally decisive battle of Himera to save western Hellenism. With him were all the Greek cities of Sicily; except Selinunte, which sided with the Carthaginians.

It continued to 'collaborate' with Carthage through most of the 5th century. The democratic party remained loyal to the Greek cause, but the dominant aristocratic party, despite many warnings, put their trust in Carthage, as Diodorus relates, until the eve of disaster. In 416 (as mentioned above) a dispute between Selinunte and Segesta provided Athens with the occasion for attacking Syracuse, and by 410 the quarrel between these two neighbouring cities grew so fierce that Carthage decided to intervene—on the side of Segesta.

A Carthaginian army came to besiege the city of the three hills, took it in 409, fired and sacked it, slaughtering its inhabitants or dragging them off into slavery. It rose from the ashes in 405 under Hermocrates, but after that was an unimportant city, subject now to Syracuse, now to Carthage. For strategic reasons Carthage destroyed it again, this time completely, during the first Punic war. It disappeared from the map; and if some modest Roman and Byzantine remains had not been found there, one might have thought it had remained since 250 B.C. in the same abandoned and deserted state as we see it today.

At Segesta I mentioned the striking contrast between the city, totally destroyed, and the temple and theatre still standing—the theatre in comparatively good condition and the temple very solid, defying the centuries. But at Selinunte, apart from the two recent restorations all, is rubble. The ruins reflect an impressive faith, wealth and creative power, but I am more impressed by the destructive power revealed in their present desolation.

Except for the gigantic G Temple, attributed in an inscription to Apollo, we do not know to which gods the temples were dedicated. Taking into account the metopes found there (which you saw in the Museum at Palermo), scholars think that C, F and E were the temples, respectively, of Hercules, Athene and Hera (or Dionysus); D was the temple of Zeus; while O and A are too inchoate for any guess on whose they were. No doubt most of the city's inscriptions were systematically destroyed by the Carthaginians, so there are very few left. Nor are there many references in literary works—perhaps Greek writers felt that the history of Selinunte did little credit to Hellenism, and they preferred to avoid it. Because of our ignorance about the temples, they are still commonly referred to by these letters of the alphabet.

How were the temples actually destroyed? By one or more earth tremors, most archaeologists believe. They occurred long after the sacking and firing of the temples by the Carthaginians; if not in the hour when Christ died, as local legend has it, at least in the Christian era. The idea of an earth tremor running from south to north seems very plausible to anyone who saw the lateral colonnades of C and E Temples before restoration. The one on the north side lay neatly by the temple, one column beside the next, one tambour behind another. The colonnade on the south side was spread out in disorder on the stylobate, according to the resistance each tambour happened to meet when falling on the inner walls of the *naos*. The date of the collapse is defined for C Temple at least, because its quarry-stones flattened a small Christian oratory in their fall.

But the earth-tremor hypothesis is rejected by some, notably t'Serstevens. He observed that except for those of C and E Temples the colonnades are spread about in complete disorder and in all directions; and that the cracks and minor subsidence usually produced by tremors and earthquakes are nowhere to be seen on the stylobate. He concludes that the destruction was human, and may reasonably be attributed to the Carthaginians rampaging in victory: 'these thousands of men bent on destruction, overturning the colonnades right to the last tambour'.

The trouble about this is that there is another Doric temple from the same period, of identical construction and equivalent dimensions, which we know was destroyed by men; and its ruins do not look at all like those of Selinunte. During their revolt of A.D. 115–6 the Jews scientifically destroyed the Temple of Zeus at Cyrene, first undermining the columns at the base, then making them fall through a system of cords worked by winches. The building came apart like a ripe fruit, and although the columns lie in rows on the ground, exactly as at Selinunte, they are all facing outwards on both north and south.

The Carthaginians, however much they were rampaging, would scarcely have tried to overturn tambours eleven feet in diameter with ordinary levers. They were good sailors, and would certainly have used pulleys and winches with cords, if these were needed. Still, they had doubtless done very considerable damage; and without roofs to protect them against the elements the temples would gradually have become more and more worn. One day they might well collapse during an earth tremor, or even of their own accord as some slight extra subsidence destroyed their precarious balance. When I look at the ruins of G Temple, I cannot help imagining the tremendous and terrible spectacle it must have presented, up there on the bare hill, in the actual moment of its collapse.

At Piana degli Albanesi.

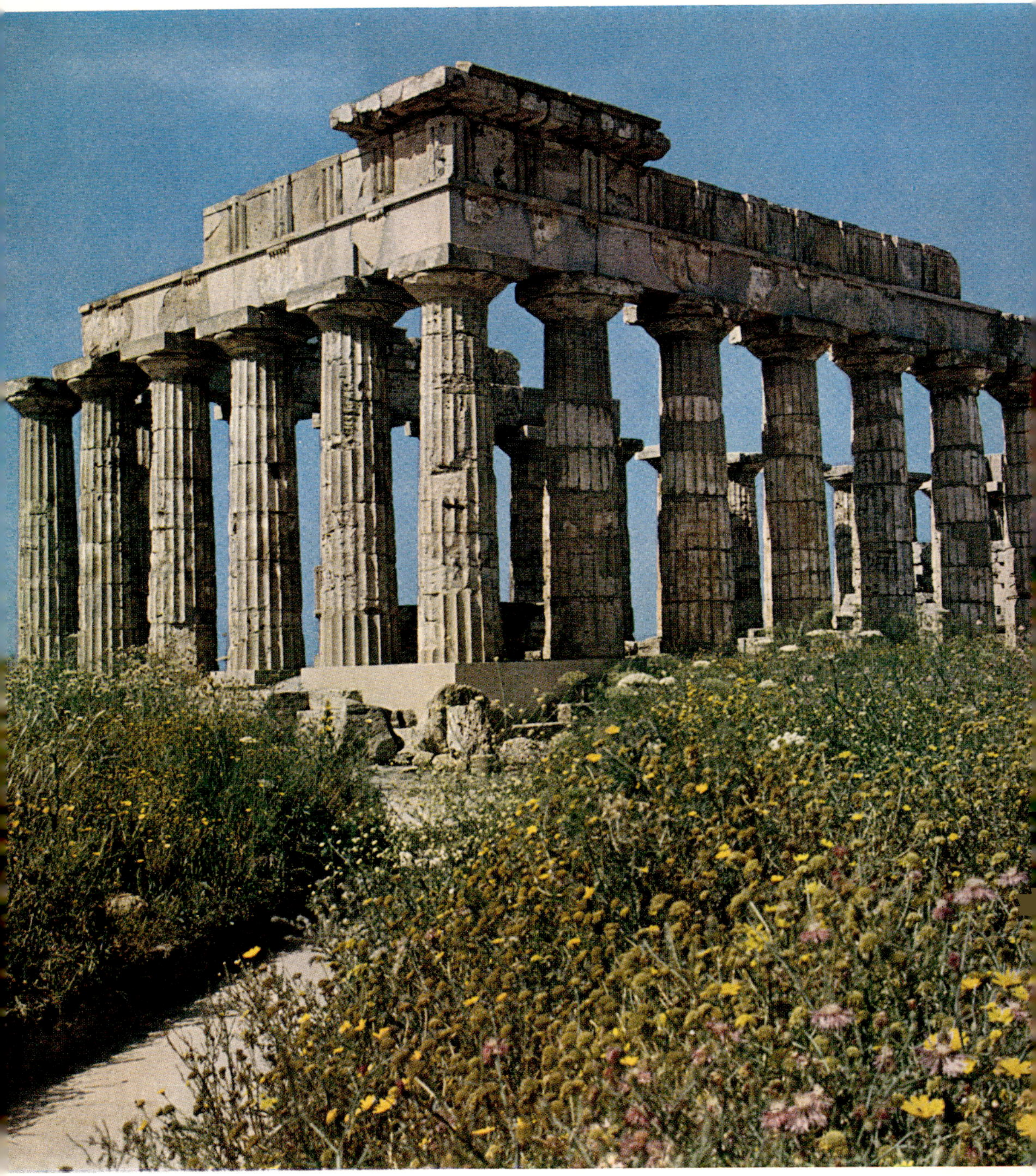

FROM Selinunte to Gela you might almost be in Africa. You will, in fact, be driving through the south-western zone of Sicily, which is only sixty odd miles from Cape Bon. The coast-line is shaped rather like the Tunisian coast opposite, and winds from the Libyan desert often sweep across the Sicilian Channel. Do not expect to find palm-trees or minarets, but stand in mid-summer on a stony hill-side and look at the sparse stubble, remains of a meagre harvest of wheat or barley, some of it burnt to supply the only manure available. With the sun blazing down, turning the stubble fields orange and brown, real desert colours, you could easily imagine yourself the other side of that channel; surely at any minute the silhouette of a camel will appear on the horizon coming over a sand-dune.

This makes the drive more interesting, but the first part of it, from Selinunte to Agrigento, is rather annoying because of the road's course. Like many of its kind in southern Italy, instead of quietly following the coast, it has to find a way of climbing into the interior, passing through remote villages or small towns like Menfi and Ribera. The former has the remains of a Frederick II castle; the latter, though of no great interest in itself, has produced an Italian prime minister: Francesco Crispi was born there in 1819.

The only time this road goes briefly along the coast, it takes you to Sciacca, a small town of 30,000 inhabitants with some fine and unusual buildings. I am perhaps specially fond of the place because they have a light red wine there with a splendid strawberry bouquet I still remember. Two of the gates in its 14th-century walls are remarkable for the sense of military power they give and even more for the architectural contrast between them. The Porta San Salvatore is Renaissance, almost baroque, and with its overloaded construction and the proud armorial bearings at the top, it looks Spanish. But it is Sicilian in its decoration, showing two of the cheerful-looking tail-in-air griffons the Normans liked so much, with tracery in Arab style around them. The Porta San Calogero, on the other hand, is simply made, from sixteen enormous blocks of stone supporting an even more enormous keystone.

Sciacca also has the Church of Santa Margherita with its graceful porch. This is no longer Gothic, although it cannot yet be called Renaissance; it is attributed to the illustrious Domenico Gagini. Among Sciacca's palaces the strange Palazzo Steripinto, from the Catalan period, is notable: its façade is entirely in nail-heads, like the Palazzo dei Diamanti at Ferrara. Then there is a very ruined castle, which still looks impressive, however, and recalls the fifty-year war between Barons Luna and Perollo, Sicily's Montagues and Capulets.

Finally, there are the thermal baths. One is right in the centre of the town, on a vast terrace overlooking the harbour and the glittering sea. The other is on top of the steep hill above the town, Monte San Calógero, and this has the remains of installations from ancient times.

For Sciacca is perhaps the world's oldest spa. According to legend it goes right back to Daedalus, that early inventor and airman. He built the Labyrinth at Crete on the request of King Minos, but then produced a wooden cow for Queen Pasiphae, in which she could respond to the advances of Poseidon who was disguised as a bull. When Daedalus heard the use his device had been put to, he felt that as innocent accessory to this deception he would no longer be *persona grata* with the King. So he made wings for himself and his son Icarus, and hastily took flight. The foolhardy Icarus, unfortunately, went too near the sun; it melted the wax by which his wings were fastened and he crashed into what came to be known as the Icarian Sea.

Daedalus, however, set up a long-distance record as the crow flies, by reaching Sciacca, where he discovered the hot springs and was fortunate enough to cure the rheumatics of Cocalus, the local potentate. After that Daedalus lived like a lord, and began to forget his troubles with Minos. But one day, as he sat on the terrace outside the baths, sipping his wine with the strawberry bouquet in the company of his new master's charming daughters, Minos with his galleys appeared on the horizon, evidently still seeking vengeance. Daedalus gave instructions to the Cocalus girls, then went into hiding. They proceeded to the harbour to welcome the angry Minos, assured him that their father's army was hot in pursuit of the infamous Daedalus and would soon bring him back with feet and wings bound. Meanwhile, they suggested, he should avail himself of one of the local amenities to refresh himself after his long crossing. Minos accepted the suggestion, and when he was safely lying in one of Daedalus's baths, the obliging daughters of Cocalus came up and drowned him in it.

Despite this violent method of settling with an enemy, the baths of Sciacca kept their reputation, and they are still much frequented by those in Sicily who suffer from rheumatism.

59. *Irrigation by canals between Selinunte and Menfi.*
60. *Menfi. The Castle.*
61. *Sciacca. The Cathedral.*
62. *Sciacca. The Harbour.*

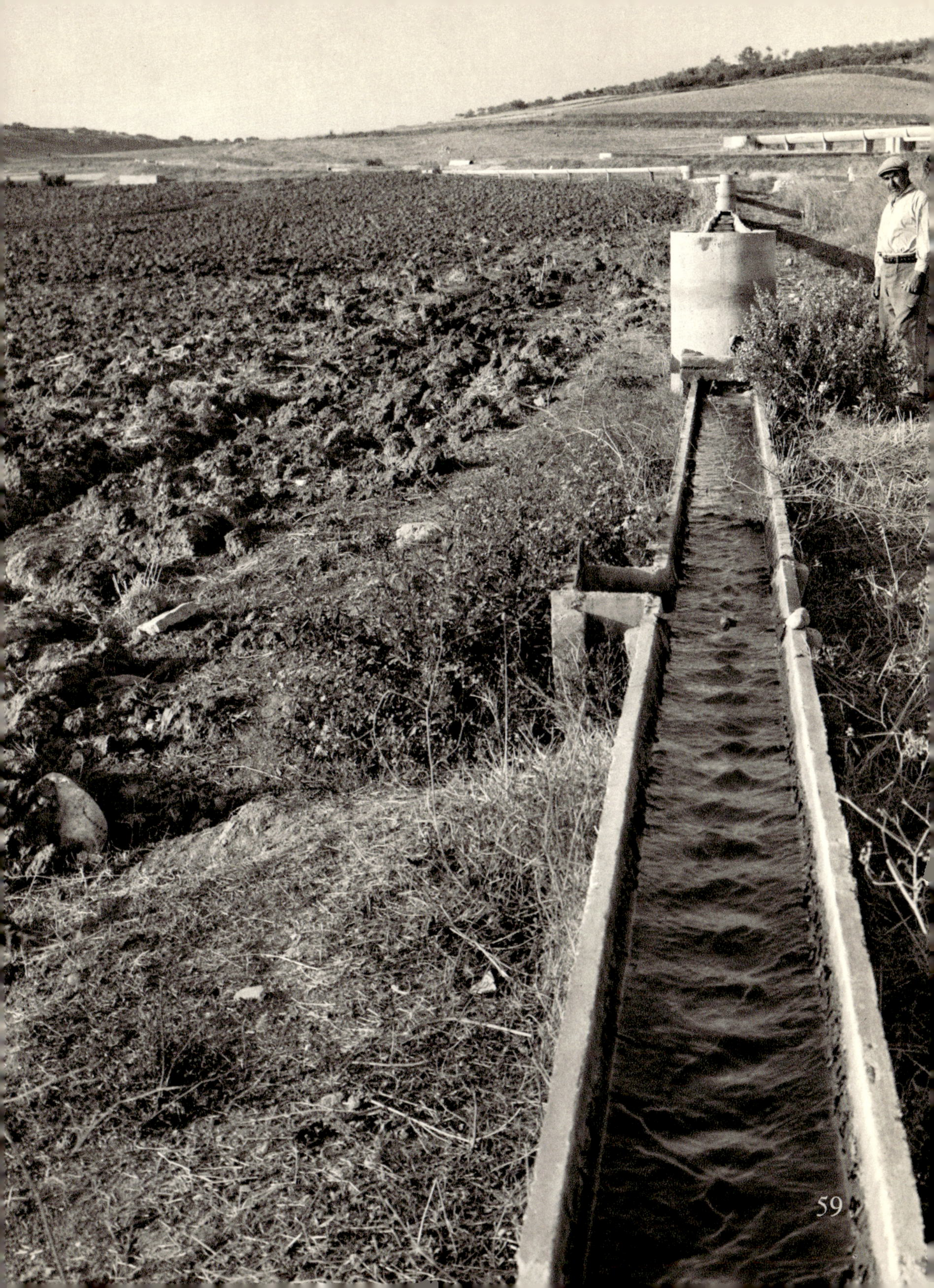

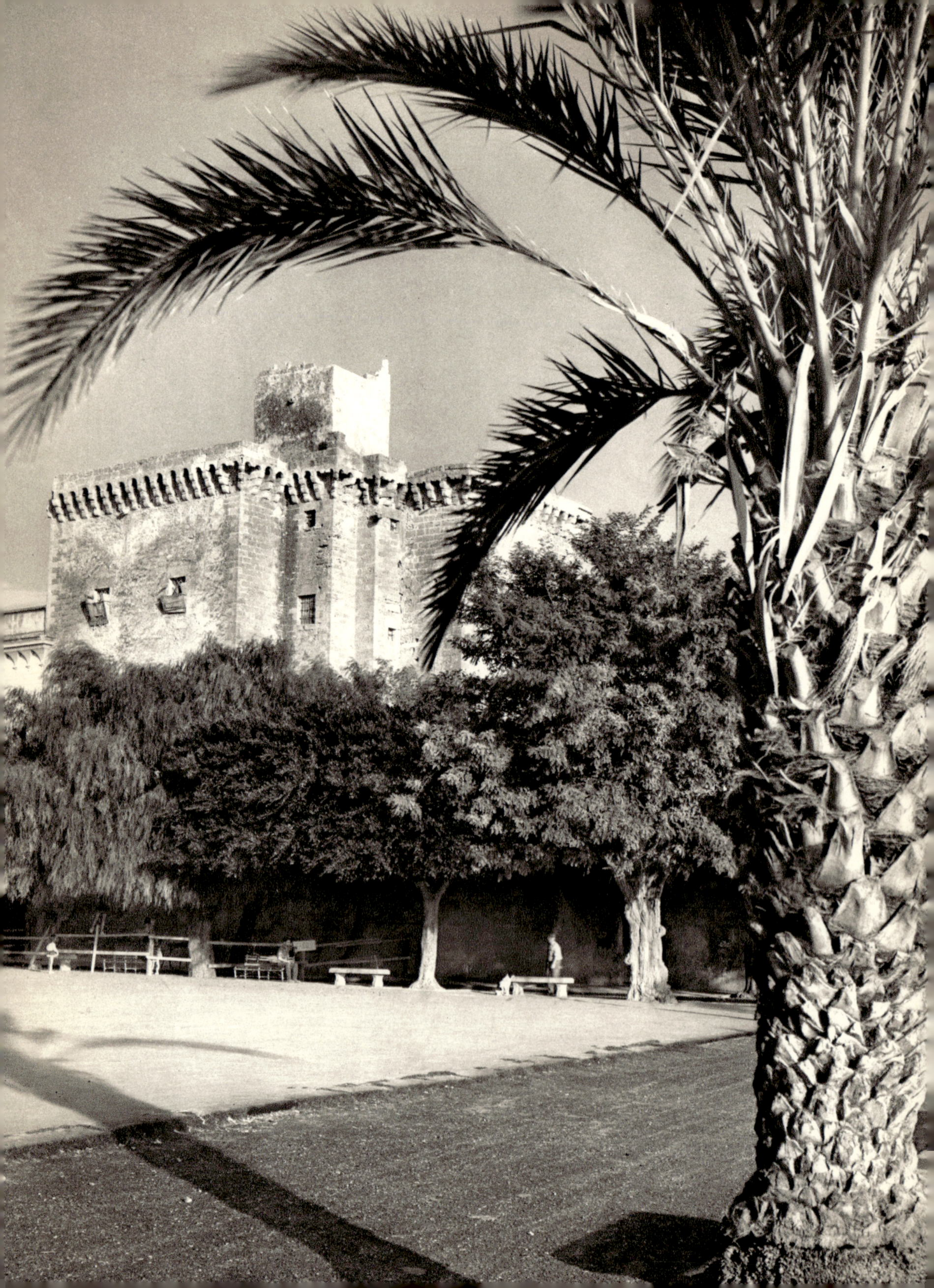

61

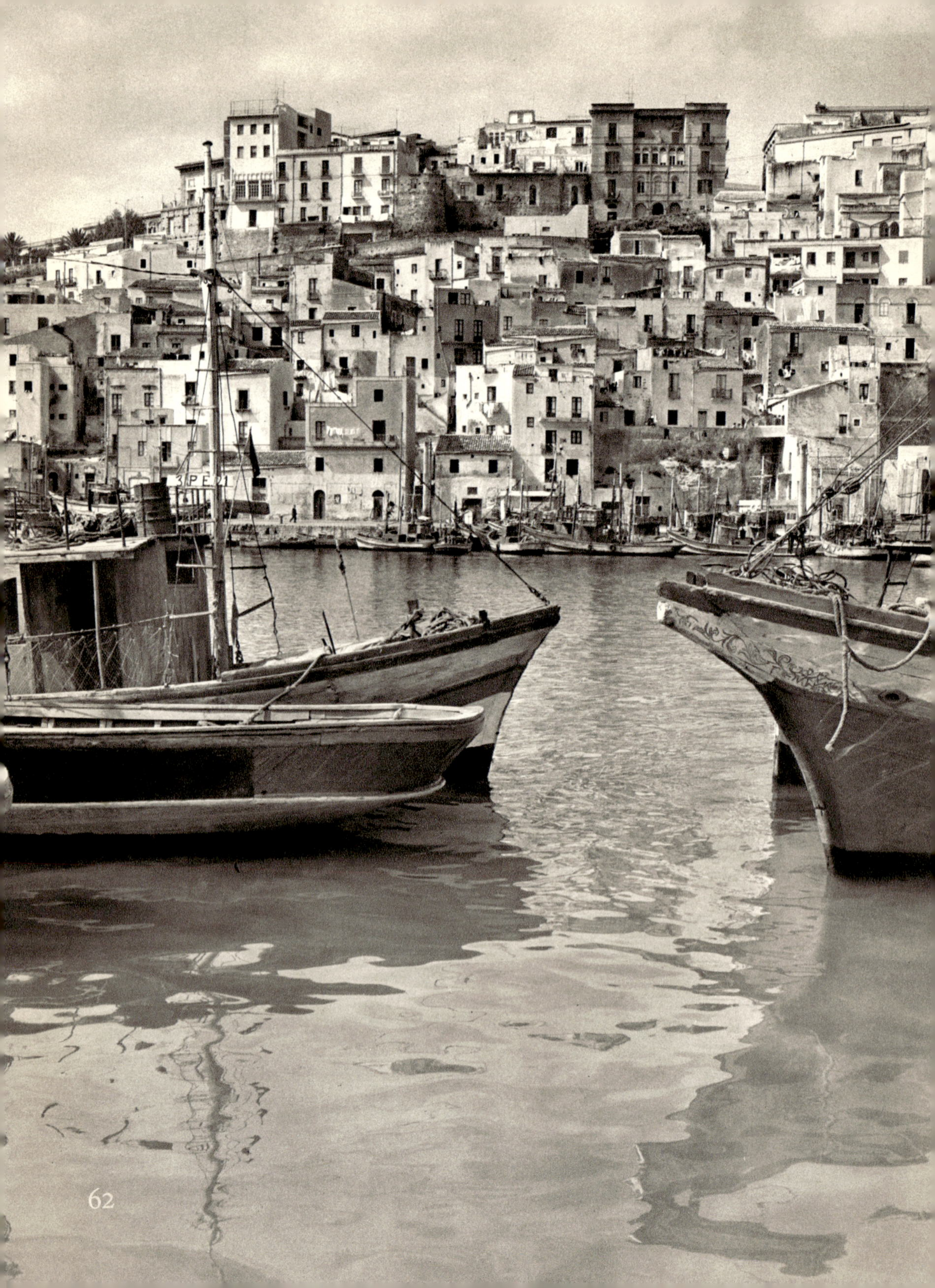

AGRIGENTO

A GRIGENTO gave me a rude shock last summer when I returned there for the first time in ten years; although I had taken some care to renew my acquaintance to the best possible effect. I was arriving from the west in the evening, but did not immediately use the town's only entrance, the Porta Aurea. I passed that without even looking up from the road, and drove along on the other side of the river Akragas (from which Agrigento took its name). I meant to approach it as the Ancients did when they landed on the shore nearby and discovered, in front of and above them, what Virgil called 'the majestic line of its escarpments crowned with mighty walls'. Above all, I wanted to see its sacred-hill temples gilded by the setting sun.

At first my plan succeeded perfectly. Everything went so well, indeed, that I could have told myself, like Goethe's Faust: 'Oh moment, stay, you are too beautiful.' But alas, it wouldn't stay, I knew. The sun would soon have disappeared, nor had I a hotel room booked. So I set off back towards the town, excited at the prospect of staying there once more. Then came the shock.

Ancient Akragas occupied a vast plateau, bounded to east and west by the deep valleys of the Hypsas and the Akragas. It rose in a gentle slope from the hill of the temples, the first eminence you reached coming from the shore, to another hill, much higher, with two separate peaks. The Acropolis was on the right-hand peak, the present town is on the left-hand one.

I hadn't been able to see these before because the hill with the temples was in the way. The Porta Aurea is a deep trench cut into that hill, Passing through it, I suddenly stopped in amazement. Up there on the left-hand peak, and even on the right-hand one, previously deserted, Agrigento showed me a completely new face.

I saw a mass of modern buildings, some almost sky-scrapers, and they looked as if they were all on fire, as the setting sun lit up their wide stained-glass windows. I remembered two famous early 'pyromaniacs' from Akragas, the tyrant Phalaris (who burnt his victims in a brazen bull) and the philosopher Empedocles, for whom fire was the first of the four elements.

A few hours later I felt reconciled to these buildings, now a mass of glittering electric lights, as I sat near them on the terrace of the public gardens. After all, I was back in Agrigento, which offered one of the finest views in the world: I could reconstruct it from memory with the aid of the moon, reflected far out at sea. Besides, I had enjoyed a stroll in the tortuous Rupe Atenea, and found the old part of the modern town quite untouched. Finally, I had dined with some Agrigentines, who explained the apparent transformation of their city.

Agrigento was having a boom. Not because of the sulphur mines. Oh no, certainly not. For a long time now, alas, foreign customers had found sulphur supplies, in the United States and at the wellheads of natural gas, which were cheaper than those of Sicily. The island's mines were still operating, the docks at Porto Empedocle were still submerged in a suffocating yellowish fog; but that was only to keep alive miners who wouldn't or couldn't find work elsewhere. Italy was the only market for this sulphur, and the industry was heavily protected.

Agriculture, then? No—agriculture was always the same. The almond-trees in February still showered their white blossoms over the plateau, and the vines still produced wines which were delicious but unsuitable for export. Corn still grew, sparsely enough, on the stony or clayey soil; but that would never cause a boom. Tourism was an important source of revenue, but didn't vary much from one year to another.

Then what was it? Speculation, of course, and building works. As in many parts of Western Europe, industrial and agricultural investments, useful to national development and life, failed to attract capital because they brought only 5% interest, but it was attracted by investments in real estate which were largely sterile yet brought in 25%.

Anyhow, the sky-scrapers were no more shocking than the late-19th-century railway station below, which I could see from the terrace. As I now realised, this was merely a pretentious façade, cluttering one of the town's main squares, with a very paltry building behind it. The sky-scrapers too were only a façade, and left behind them a small Sicilian town which remained unchanging.

As you pass the ruins of the great Greek city before you come to this, you may easily neglect the modern town, which does not have many interesting 'sights'. But it is worth taking a stroll, or rather a climb, in its labyrinthine small streets. On a summer's day, walking up them is pretty tiring, so I suggest you find a taxi to get you to the high point of the town—the Cathedral.

This is of Norman origin, but its rococo frills have been removed so as to give better effect to its ceilings of painted wood, which has the eagle with two heads of the Emperor Charles V hovering in the centre. The Cathedral *Treasury* contains

63. *Temple of Hercules.*
64. *Temple of Castor and Pollux, and view over the town.*
65. *One of the telamons supporting entablature of the Temple of Olympian Jupiter.*
66. *General View. In background, from left to right: Temple of Concord, columns of Temple of Hercules, and a stretch of the panoramic road.*
67, 68, 70. *Temple of Concord.*
69. *Detail from sarcophagus of Phaedra in Cathedral.*
71, 73. *Temple of Lacinian Juno.*
72. *Trunk of olive tree used as seat.*

63

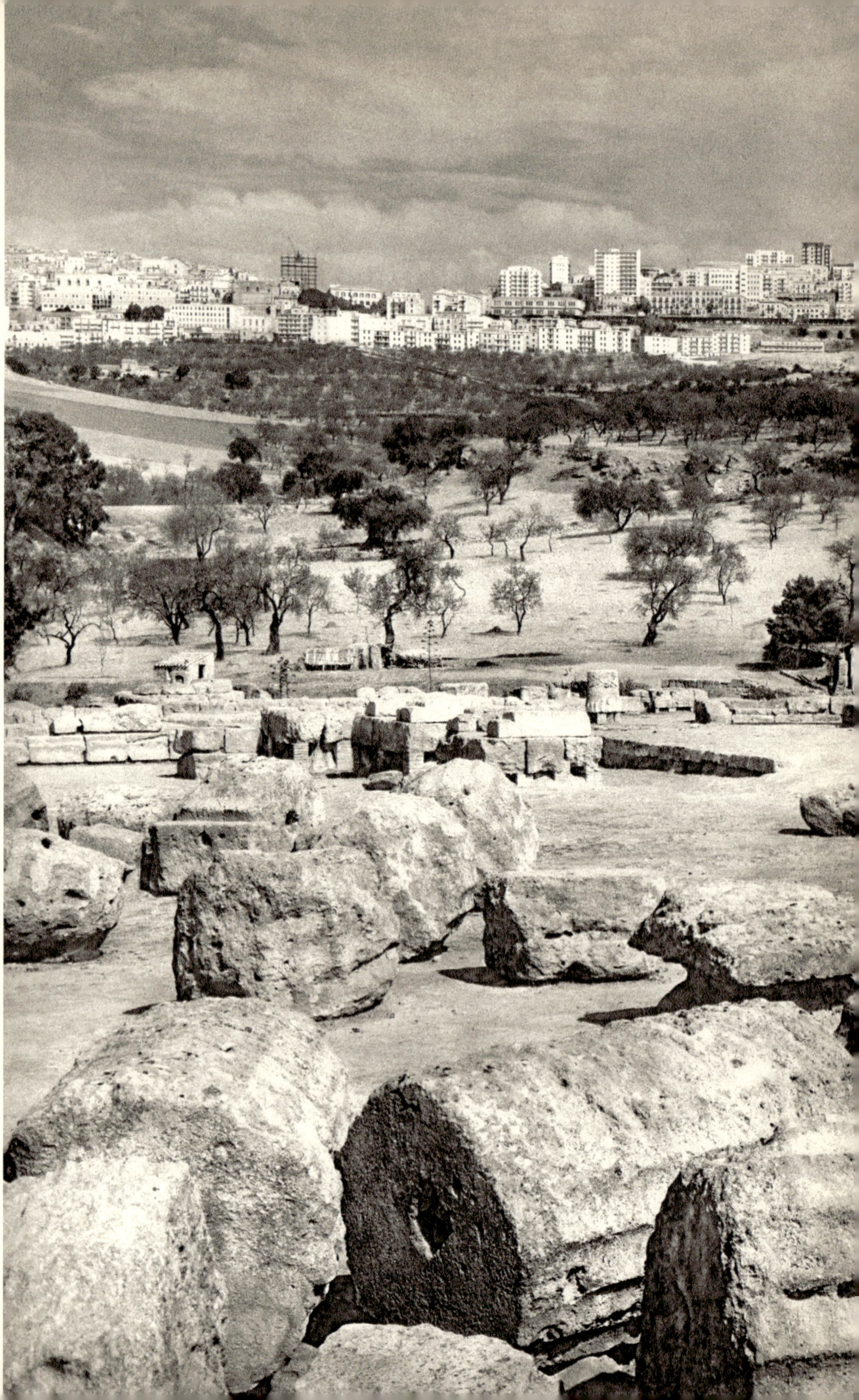

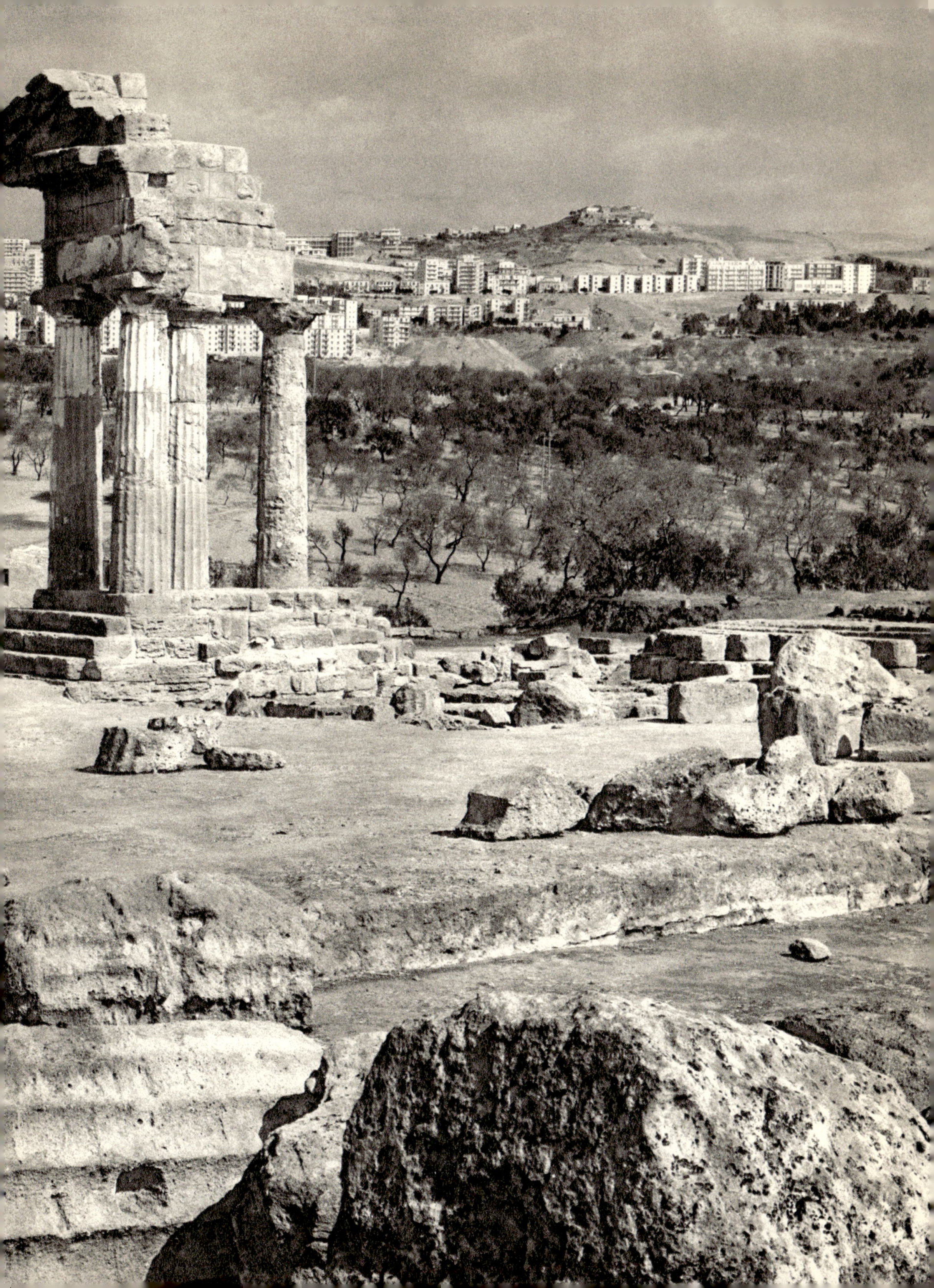

65

66

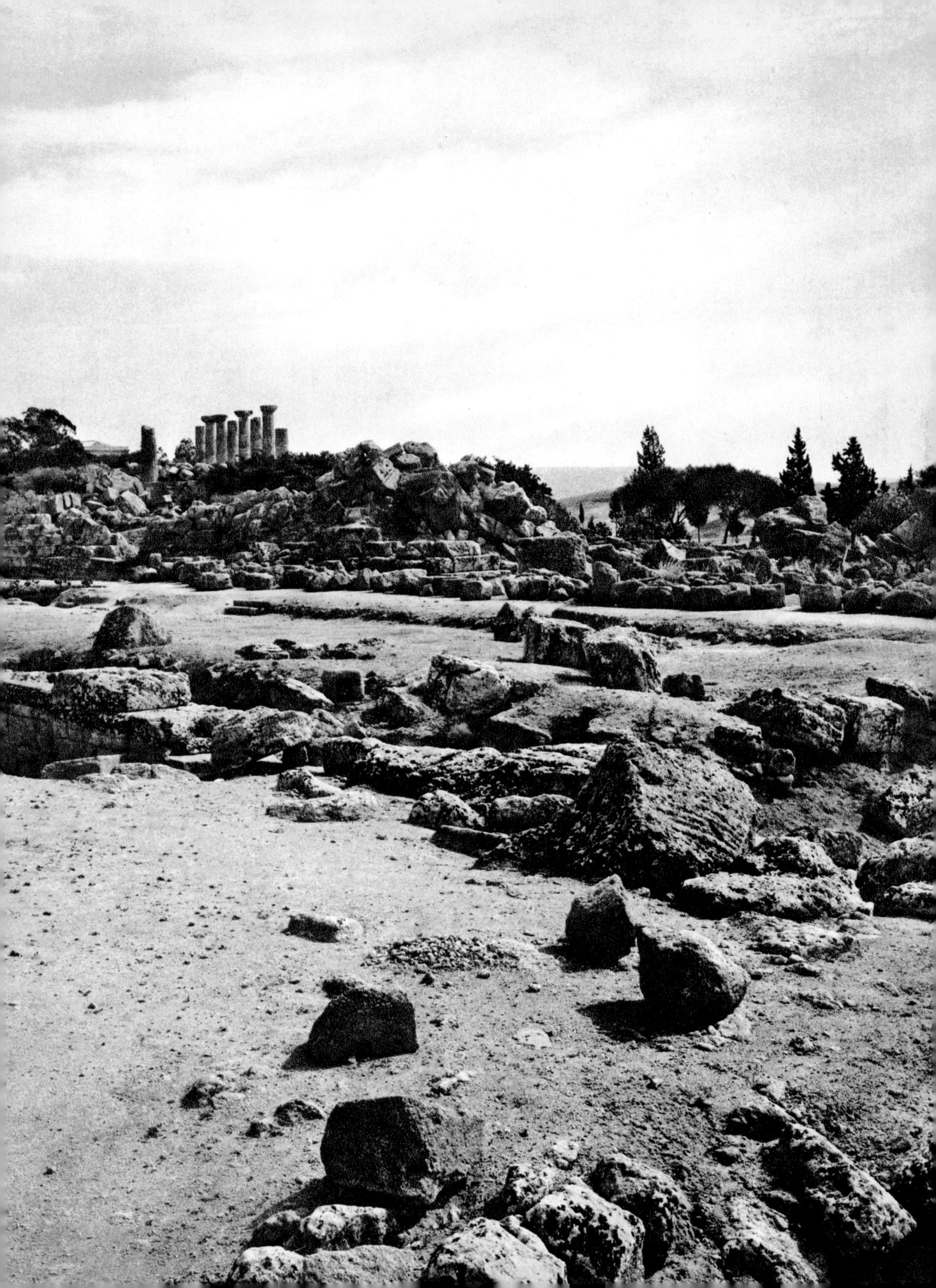

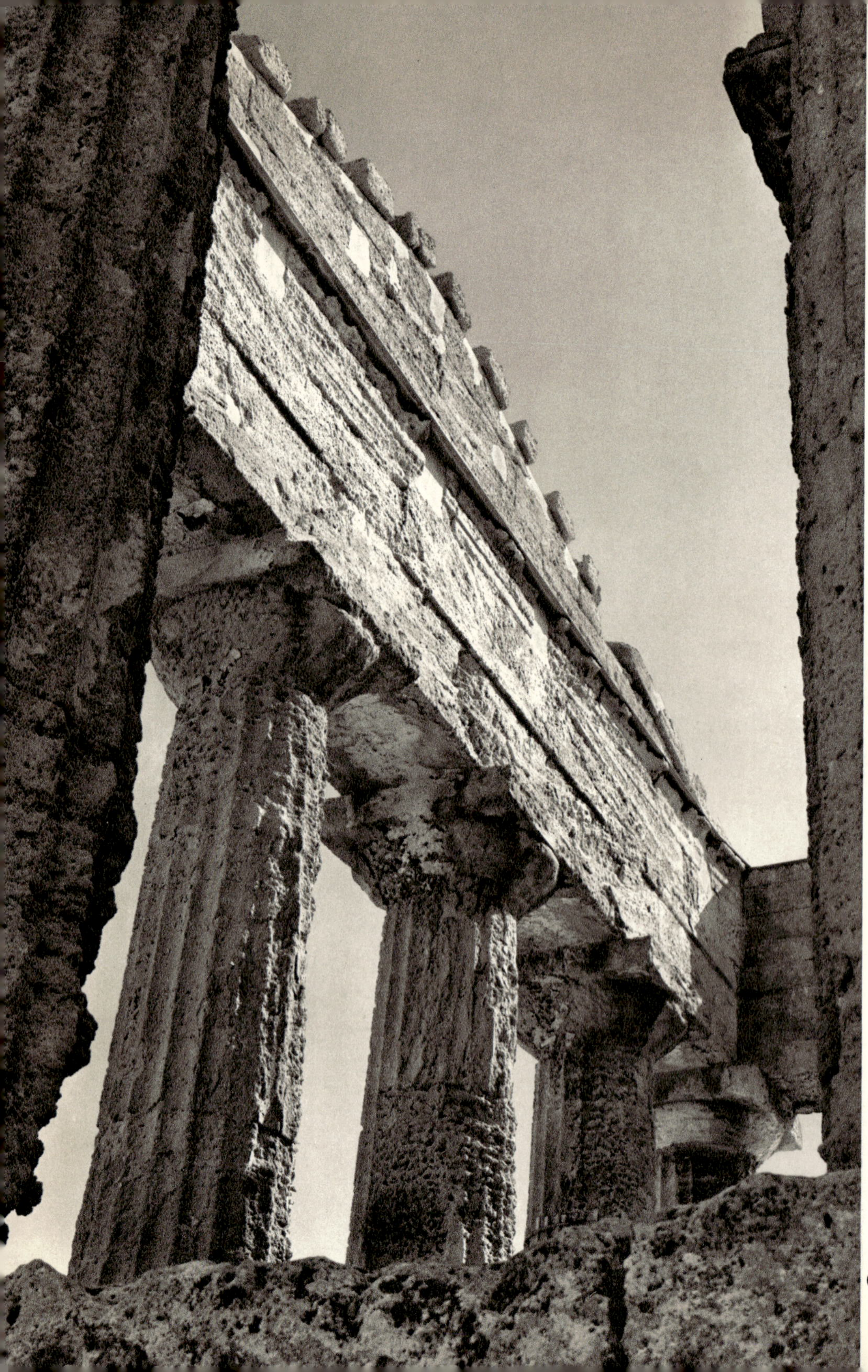

68

69

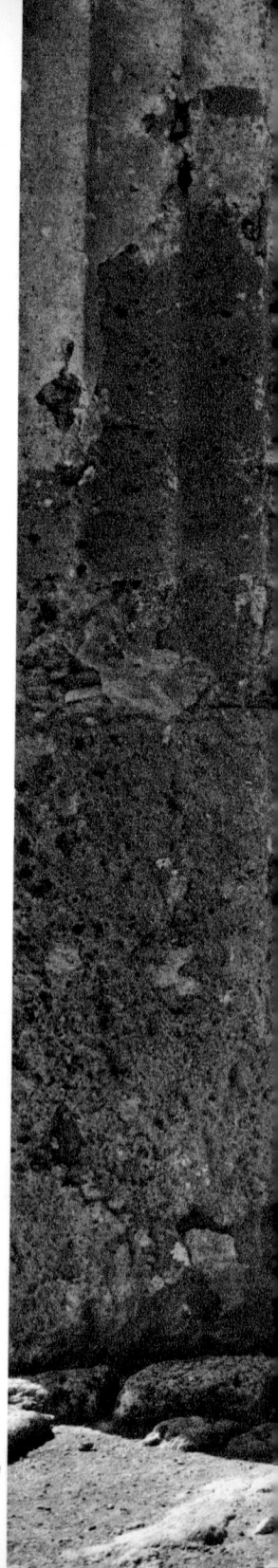

70

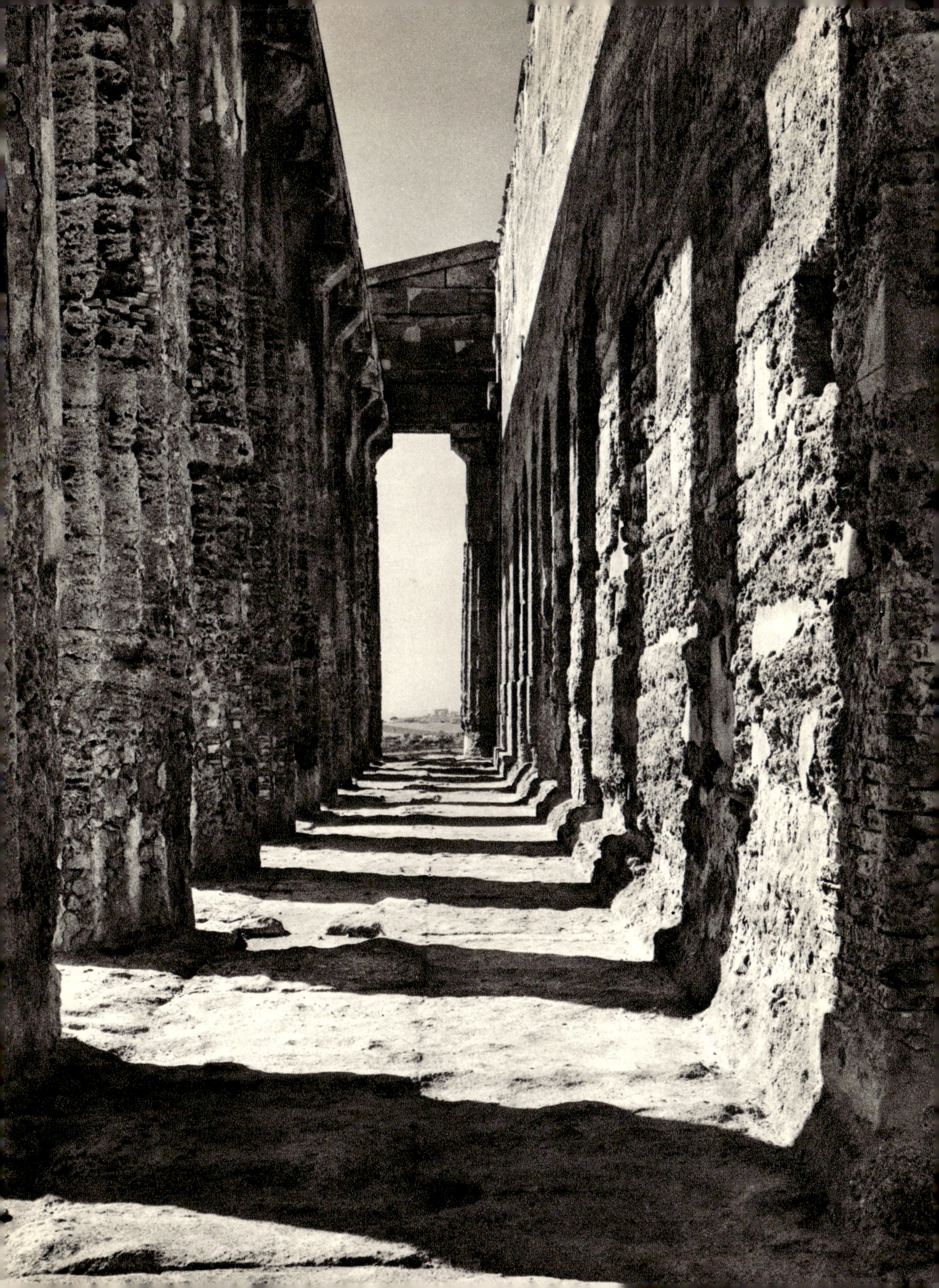

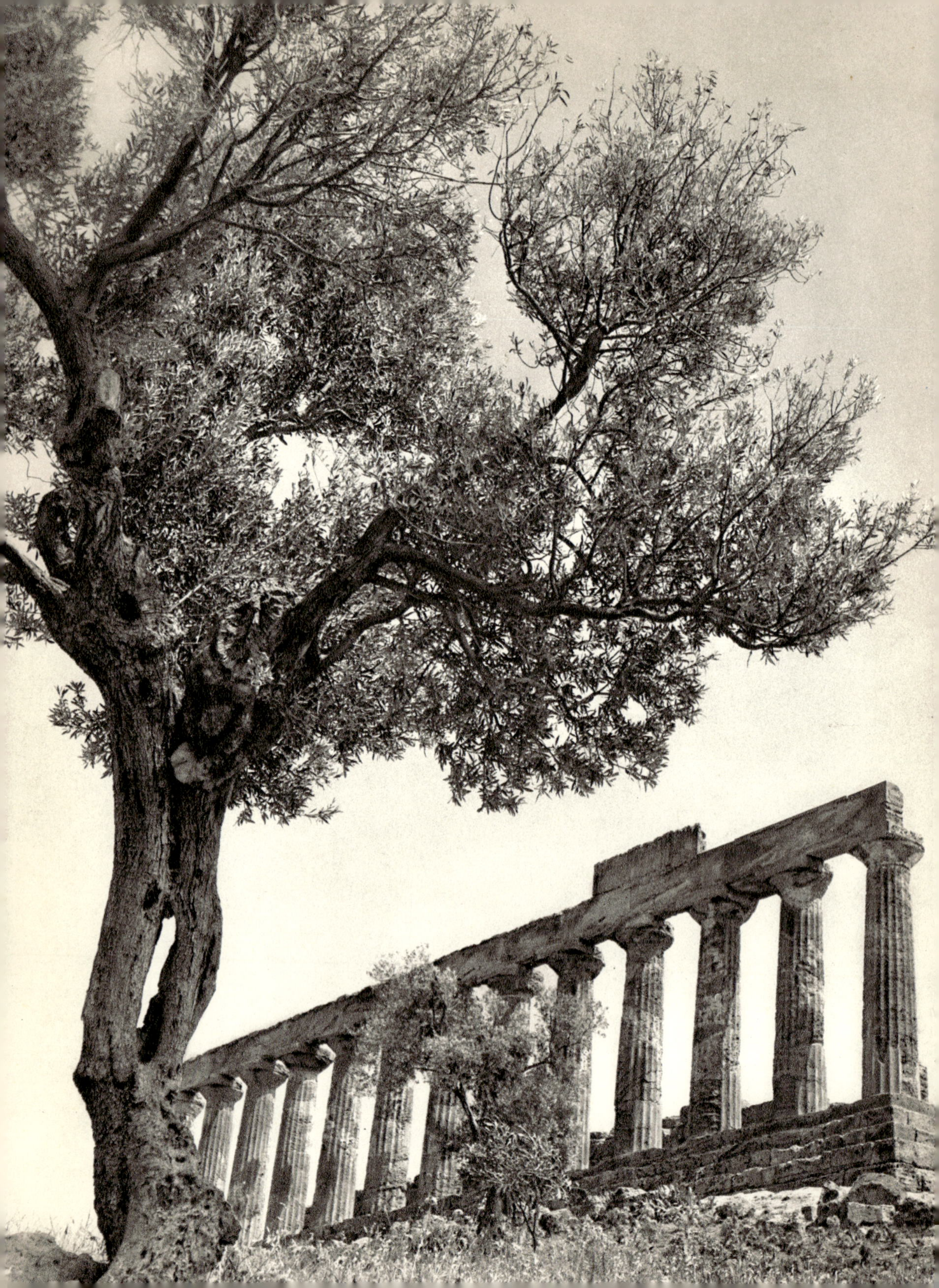

71

72

73

fine Limoges enamel reliquaries and a well-known sarcophagus of Phaedra, which delighted Goethe, although people nowadays are inclined to look down on this Roman copy of a Greek original. I must admit to finding her very graceful as she swoons into her ladies' arms when her stepson Hippolytus rejects her advances.

You get a good view of the bare countryside from the Cathedral Square, which is a pleasant spot; you will like the sturdy campanile overlooking it and the baroque façade of the seminary. Walking down the steep little streets, you will see various interesting places, such as the 18th-century Lucchesiana Library; the Church of Santa Maria dei Greci, which is fitted out in a Doric Temple; the so-called Hypogaeum of Purgatory (a Hypogea is an artificial cave); and the Museum, where there is an Ephebe almost as celebrated as the one at Selinunte, only it is in marble. Traces of the immense wall of the ancient city have been found everywhere at Agrigento except in the church of Santa Maria; and as the Hypogea was once a reservoir, which would have been inside the city walls, we may assume that these walls went right round the site of the modern town.

When you get down to the Rupe Atenea, I suggest you buy yourself a drink, and sit on the terrace outside a bar, just watching people pass. They will almost all be dressed in dark clothes, whether townsmen in tight-fitting suits or peasants in wide capes. They might come straight out of the pages of Pirandello, and change as little as their town.

Having finished this part of your tour make your way to the terraced walk along the right-hand peak, where the Acropolis used to be. Since ancient times this walk has been called Athene's Rock. On it you will pass a small romanesque church, with walls incorporating the remains of a temple dedicated to Demeter and her daughter Persephone. You will also get a fine view, and be able to take in at a glance the lay-out of the ancient city you are about to visit.

On your right and your left, on the other side of the Hypsas and the Akragas, there are bare, sun-scorched hills; in the background a large expanse of sea. In the centre the plateau is covered with almond and olive trees; but you can imagine it bristling with houses and enclosed by walls. You can still pick the walls out; they go down along the Akragas, returning along the Hypsas, and in between they skirt the crest of the sacred hill with the columns and ruins of the temples.

Walking down towards them, you should glance at the small Hellenistic building traditionally called the Oratory of Phalaris; the crude romanesque and even Cistercian church of St Nicholas, unexpected in this Greek setting; and a terrain recently excavated, where important traces of the city's urban zone have been found. These prosperous middle-class houses, from the Hellenistic and Roman period, have little interest except that they bring out two essential characteristics of ancient Akragas: its opulence and the remarkable town-planning methods used when it was being built.

The plan revealed by excavations and aerial photography consists basically in rectangular blocks of houses, each block the same size, separated by streets intersecting at right angles. This shows a Hellenistic technique, but there are reasons for thinking that the plan of the early city had a similar lay-out.

Akragas was the youngest of Sicily's great Greek cities. Its foundation, in fact, by colonists from the neighbouring city of Gela, goes back only to 581 B.C., half a century after Selinunte and a century and a half after Syracuse. It was first of all governed by the aristocratic party, that is to say by 'tyrants': the abominable Phalaris, and then the remarkable Theron, who in alliance with Gela won the battle of Himera against the Carthaginians in 480.

This victory, the enlightened government of Theron and his successors, and the continued alliance with Syracuse, reinforced by marriages, gave Akragas a century of prosperity. It filled its walls, built in the previous century, which are seven and a half miles in diameter; built its great temples; and became in the words of Pindar, to whom it long gave hospitality, 'the most beautiful of mortal cities'.

According to Diogenes Laertius, it had 800,000 inhabitants, obviously an exaggerated figure; according to Diodorus 200,000, though this may apply not merely to the city but to the whole of its territory. Pietro Griffo, author of the most recent guide to Agrigento, thinks there were a little less than 100,000 inhabitants; and if we accept this estimate, it was still a big city for the age.

The people of Akragas, moreover, seem to have been very rich. They mustered three hundred chariots with white horses in harness to welcome Aegenetes, victor in the Olympic Games, and eight hundred for the wedding of the daughter of Antisthenes. Gelias, one of the rulers of the city, lived in such state that at a moment's notice he could 'put up' five hundred knights from Gela who had been caught in a storm. The people of Akragas earned an unusual tribute, in fact, from either Empedocles or Plato (it is attributed to both), that they 'eat as if they were to die next day, and build as if they were to live for ever'.

This prosperity did not last, however. In 406 the Carthaginians returned to the offensive, and after a long siege they took Akragas. Having seen Selinunte, you can imagine what happened to 'the most beautiful of mortal cities'. Although repopulated by those of its citizens who had escaped the disaster, it never recovered its former greatness. It was still quite an important place, however, during the Hellenistic period and under Rome, when it experienced the benefits of the *Pax Romana* but also at one point the extortions of Verres. Its importance progressively declined until it became the small town it is today. Still, it was luckier than the other Greek cities, for it kept its temples.

Leave your car in the park opposite the Porta Aurea, and walk east, past a hollow full of vegetation. You will come to the Temple of 'Vulcan', which has only two columns still standing, but from here you will get a fine view on to the sacred hill.

If you haven't too much time, go first to the sanctuary of the 'Chthonic Divinities' (earth gods) at the foot of the four columns of the 'Castor and Pollux Temple'. These are the pure Doric columns which appear on all the tourist posters and make a perfect subject for photography, with their large fragment of architrave and traces surviving there of ancient paintings. Only, as a matter of fact, they were reconstructed quite arbitrarily in 1836, and the temple they belong to was never dedicated to Castor and Pollux! There was a vast sanctuary there, containing several temples and several altars, both round and rectangular; and this was doubtless the religious centre of the city. It already existed in pre-Hellenic times, and with Athene's Rock was probably one of the places where the divinities of primitive Sicily gradually became confused with those of Greece under the name of 'Chthonic divinities' and took on the characteristics of Demeter and Persephone.

Walk on towards the east, and you will next come to the ruins of the temple of Olympian Jupiter, which are massive but chaotic; they may remind you of G Temple at Selinunte. The Olympieion at Akragas was a little vaster than that, as we have seen, and in all the Greek world its size was only exceeded by the temples of Ephesus and Miletus. Like the G Temple it was never completely finished, and today there is not a single piece of wall standing.

As soon as you arrive on its immense platform, you will be drawn immediately to a collection of carved stones placed together like the tambours of a collapsed column. Lying on the ground, they take up nine yards. When you go nearer you will recognise them as a telamon designed to carry a heavy load on his head and his folded arms. No wonder with telamons like this that during the Middle Ages the Olympieion was called 'the palace of giants'. You may find him pretty shapeless; but he and one enormous capital, together with some tambours and bits of architrave, are all you have from which to picture the colossal building that was the pride of Greek art, although like its equivalent at Selinunte it did not have the classical form of Doric temples.

Its peristyle, for instance, was not open on the outside, between the columns; it was closed by a wall reinforced with embedded columns and also, in the spaces between, by telamons—their contribution was essential to support the weight of a crushing entablature. What an effect it must have produced when you looked at it from the city below!—this mass 120 yards long and eighty foot high, with semi-columns so large that a man could easily get into each of their flutings, with its twenty-five foot telamons standing on a base of the same height, the whole thing covered in ivory or ochre stucco, set off by brilliant paintings.

It is hard to make such an imaginative reconstruction from practically nothing. That is why the temples you are now going to see will touch you more, for they are in a better state of preservation.

Not much better, you may say, when you see the Temple of Hercules, close to the Porta Aurea. There are only eight columns left of this, and they were raised in 1924; but they are enough to give an idea of what it might have been like—until the comparatively late date when it was violated by Verres, who removed the statue of the demi-god. Going back to the end of the 6th century B.C., it was the oldest Doric temple in Akragas, and was extremely big for the period. A liking for outsize things, by-products of wealth and vanity, seems to have been natural to the people of Akragas.

At the end of the Via dei Tempi you will be faced by the 'Temple of Concord' perched high above you. At Segesta, Selinunte and, till now, at Agrigento you will have hoped to gaze on a perfect Doric temple perfectly preserved: here it is. It is not the vastest, nor the most ornate. Inside, it has walls with arches between them, built in the period when it was turned into a church; that, however, ensured its preservation. The interior, indeed, is only a skeleton which has lost its stucco outer skin, a skeleton of coarse limestone encrusted with shells, although in the sun it turns beautiful colours: pink at dawn, ochre at noon, orange at dusk. The exterior, however, is complete: the pediments are intact, so is most of the entablature; the columns of the peristyle are all present in their original place on the base with its four steps. 5th-century Greek art is there before you in all its purity. Make the most of it, you are seeing one of the most perfect buildings ever produced.

From there follow the crest of the hill, where there are some traces of the ancient wall and the remains of a Byzantine 'city of the dead'. By a gradual rise you come to the last of the temples of Akragas, that of 'Juno Lacinia'. This attribution is pure fantasy and the building is pretty badly damaged, with only its north side intact and a few columns besides, some with and some without entablature. No matter; what counts is its situation, at the highest point on the sacred hill, which makes it seem as if it were floating in the air.

Your tour of Agrigento will no doubt have taken you a whole day; so arrange to reach Juno at sunset. Take a rest, sitting on the steps of the stylobate, and look at the opposite view to the one you had this morning from Athene's Rock. In the east the hills are still bare but no longer sun-scorched. They are turning that pinkish-purple which is the colour of dusk in neighbouring North Africa. In the south the sea darkens, so does the coastal plain, where you can just pick out the little Temple of Aesculapius and the so-called Tomb of Theron—this is in fact a Roman funerary monument in the form of a square tower with pilasters on the sides. In the north the plateau covered with almond and olive trees, where the great city used to be, grows brighter the further you look up the slope—towards the present small town with its modern buildings. Eastwards the wall goes along the spine of the sacred hill to the Temples of Concord and Hercules. Above you, finally, the last patch of light lingers over the capitals of the columns of Lacinian Juno.

All Sicily is there, round you in the falling night: land and sea, Greece and Rome, Doric temples and electric-lighted buildings, with the queen of the Olympian gods presiding over all.

FROM AGRIGENTO TO SYRACUSE
GELA—RAGUSA—MODICA—NOTO

O N the road from Agrigento to Syracuse you will see very different aspects of Sicily, from ancient Gela, which is also the centre of the modern oil industry, to the completely baroque town of Noto. But first you pass through Palma di Montechiaro.

I had been through this town several times on previous visits to Sicily, without noticing anything much there except a fine baroque church and a great deal of poverty. But since then I had read *The Leopard* and discovered that this small town was founded by the author's ancestors, the Tomasis of Lampedusa. I wondered whether it had served as model for Donnafugata—a delightfully ironical name, which is really that of a village in Ragusa province—and if so, how I could have missed seeing the large and mysterious manor where the Prince and his family used to spend the summer. So I determined to be more attentive, and here I was, back in Palma—but still didn't see anything manorial. By contrast I once more gained an impression of great poverty, and even saw a sign of under-development which happily is uncommon in Sicily: a group of fine-eyed children playing in the dust, and among them a small boy completely naked. The 'Leopard's' ancestors must indeed have been very bad lords of the manor.

Coming out of such a place, I was glad to return to the sea, with a view of the headland of Licata at the top of a hill. This big town derives from the ancient Eknome (Ecnomus), where the Roman fleet defeated that of Carthage. Its harbour is still lively, but of no particular interest. It ends in a narrow, longish bridge, on which I found myself behind a herd of goats so disinclined to hurry that I had plenty of time for a chat with the goatherd. They were goats from the town, and every day he brought them to graze in the fields; in the evenings they would go back to the houses, or rooms rather, where they lived with their owners.

Eventually, after driving along by the beaches where the Anglo-American force landed in 1943, and round the feudal manor of Falconara, I began to be able to pick out the Acropolis of Gela.

There are few hills more in keeping with one's idea of an acropolis. It rises abruptly and in complete isolation between the sea and a vast semi-circular plain. But the nearer I came to it, the harder I found it to recognize. I had seen it in the post-war years, potholed, gutted, ravaged by the air raids. I found it now, covered with new houses, factories, service stations, standing out against an immense grey and yellow cloud of industrial smoke.

Approaching the town by the western end of the long street which follows the crest of the Acropolis, I noticed a board recommending me to visit the excavations at Capo Soprano. I knew that archaeological discoveries had been made recently at Gela, but had not expected to find here this fine fragment of a Greek fortress, carefully restored and protected by a glass screen: several layers of well-cut stone at the base and countless rows of closely fitted bricks on top. Such a technique is poor enough, betraying the haste and improvisation of a reconstruction carried out with inadequate resources. Yet seeing this wall, one is grateful to those who discovered it and to the sand-dunes which preserved it in such a condition.

From there I drove through the whole agglomeration, which is quite large, down a superb promenade wide open to the sea with blocks of shiny new houses on the other side, to reach the Museum, equally new and very well arranged. There are fine items of pottery and sculpture here, both indigenous and from Greece, which have been discovered in excavations or in holes dug for one reason or another in this hill crammed with relics of ancient times. Then I crossed a public garden, where the infrastructure of two Doric temples have been cleared and one column raised. Eventually I came to the end of the Acropolis and stopped with a gasp.

What made me gasp was the suffocating stench of oil and the sight below me. There was an immense refinery, bristling with silver tanks, gaudy spheres and pipes, high torches plumed with flames, vomiting up the smoke which I had seen from a distance behind the hill. To the right, in the sea, tankers were loading up along a wharf which looked endless. Further out there was an artificial island supporting the very modern derrick of a submarine drill.

Such, then, was the latest 'incarnation' of this city, whose history is full of deaths and resurrections. Founded in 688 B.C. by Dorian, Cretan and Rhodian immigrants, Gela grew so fast that a century later it had enough men available to found Agrigento, and a century after that to provide Syracuse with a new ruling class and one of its most illustrious tyrants, Gelon. Its vigour was perhaps exhausted after that, for it does not reappear in history till 424. Then, however, it was the moral capital of Sicily's Greeks. It was there they held the congress at which they proclaimed themselves independent of their Greek motherlands.

This first resurrection, or at least revival, did not last long. In 405, a year after Agrigento, Gela was carried away in the Carthaginian tidal wave. A second

74. *Porto Empedocle.*
75, 76. *Palma di Montechiaro, village used as model by Tomasi di Lampedusa for his novel* The Leopard.
77. *Gela. Oil wells.*
78. *Near Ragusa.*
79. *Gela. Morning street scene.*
80. *Coping of funerary* stele *from Gela (Syracuse Museum).*
81. *Ragusa. Church of St George.*
82. *Ragusa. General view.*
83. *Noto. Church of St Dominic.*
84. *Noto. The Cathedral.*
85. *Noto. Baroque balcony.*

74

75

76

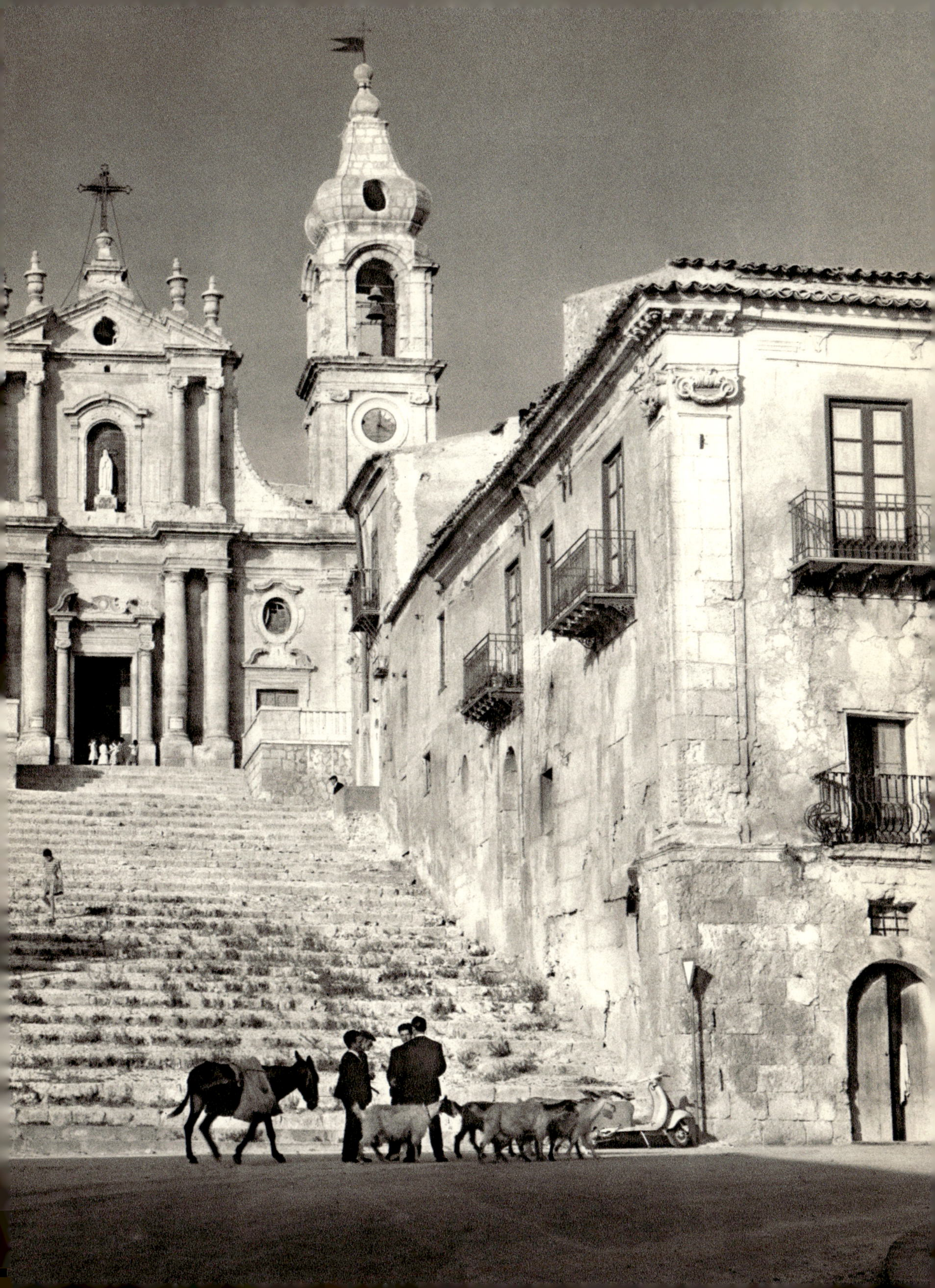

77

78

79

80

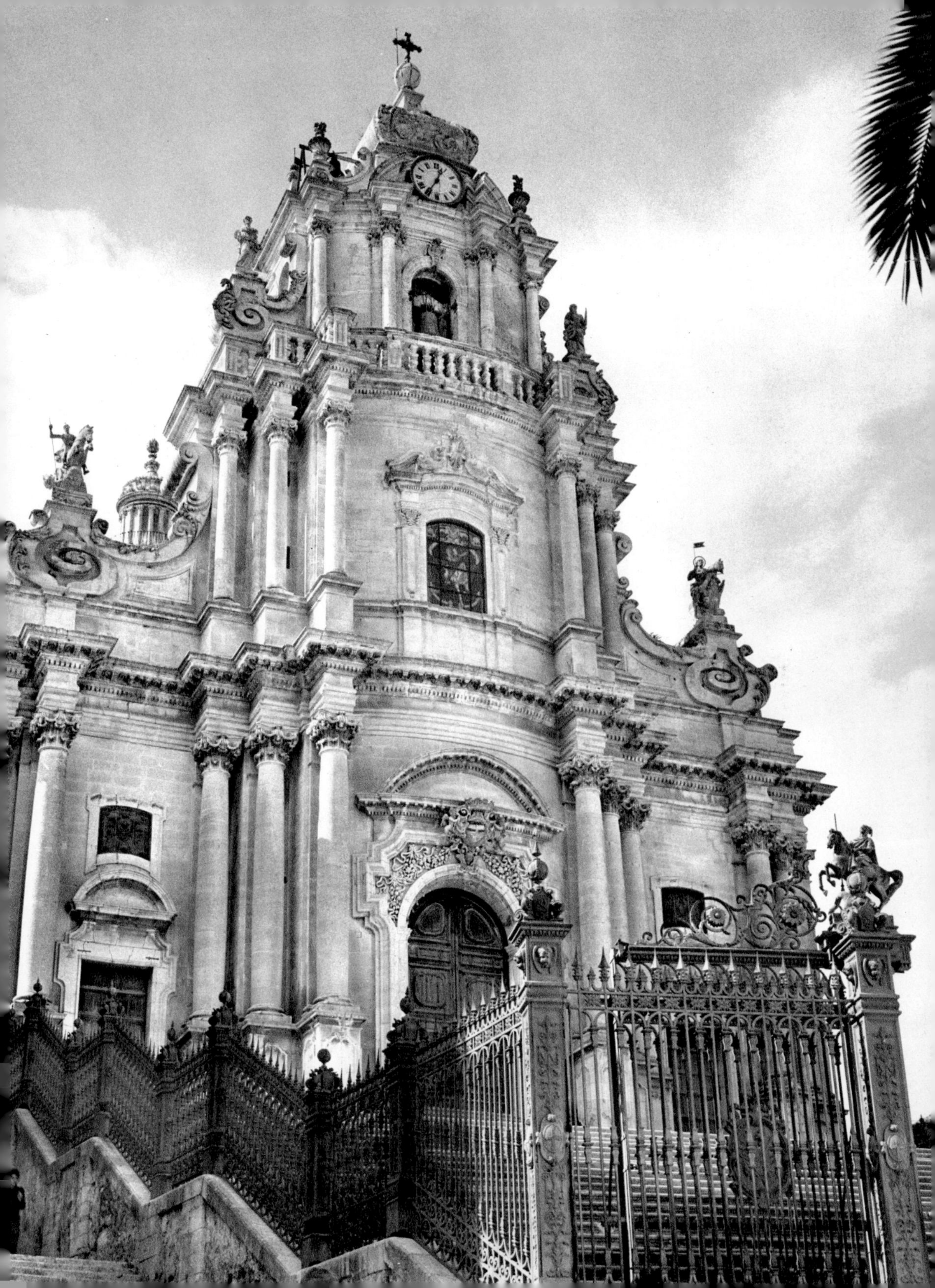

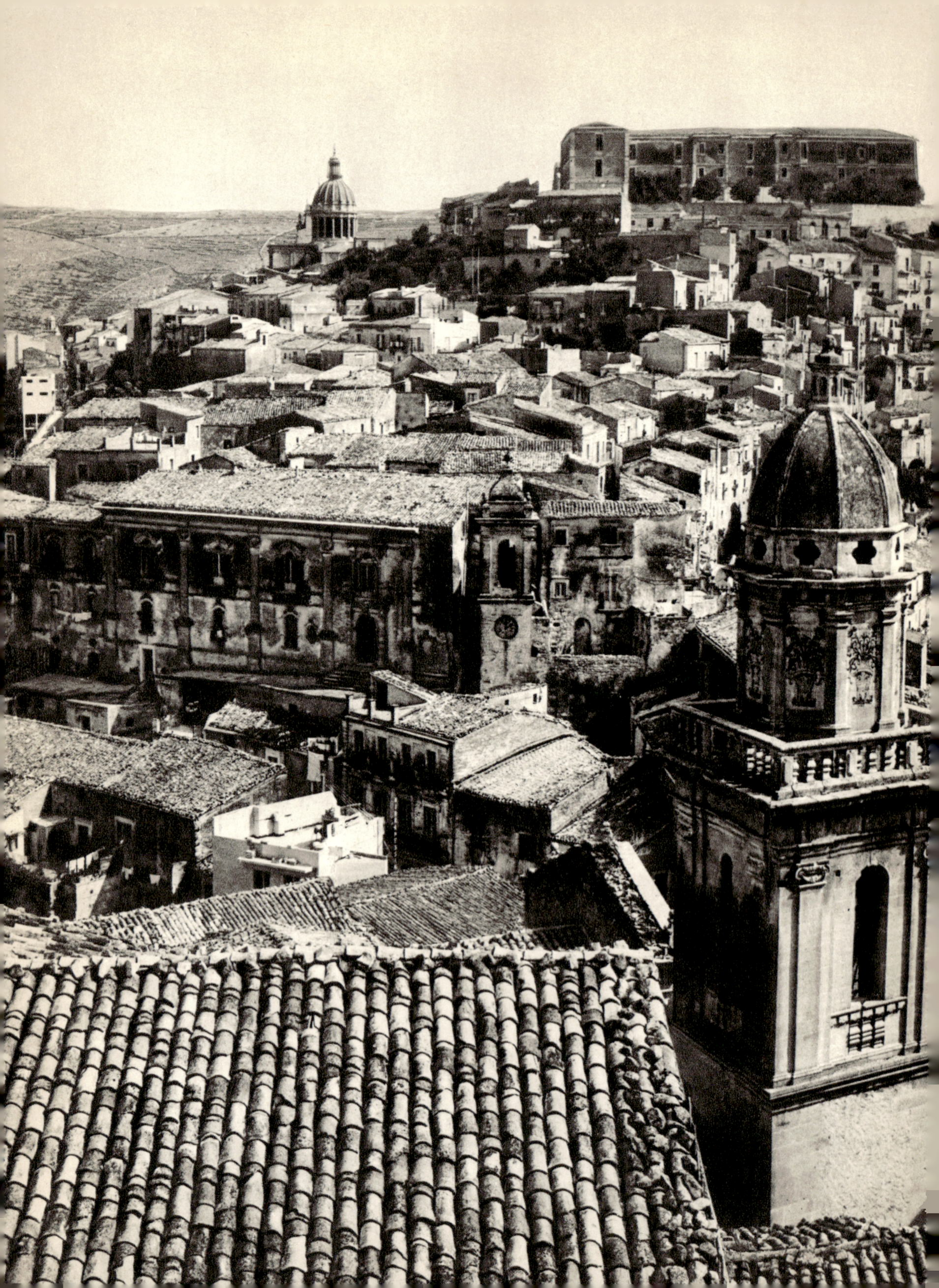

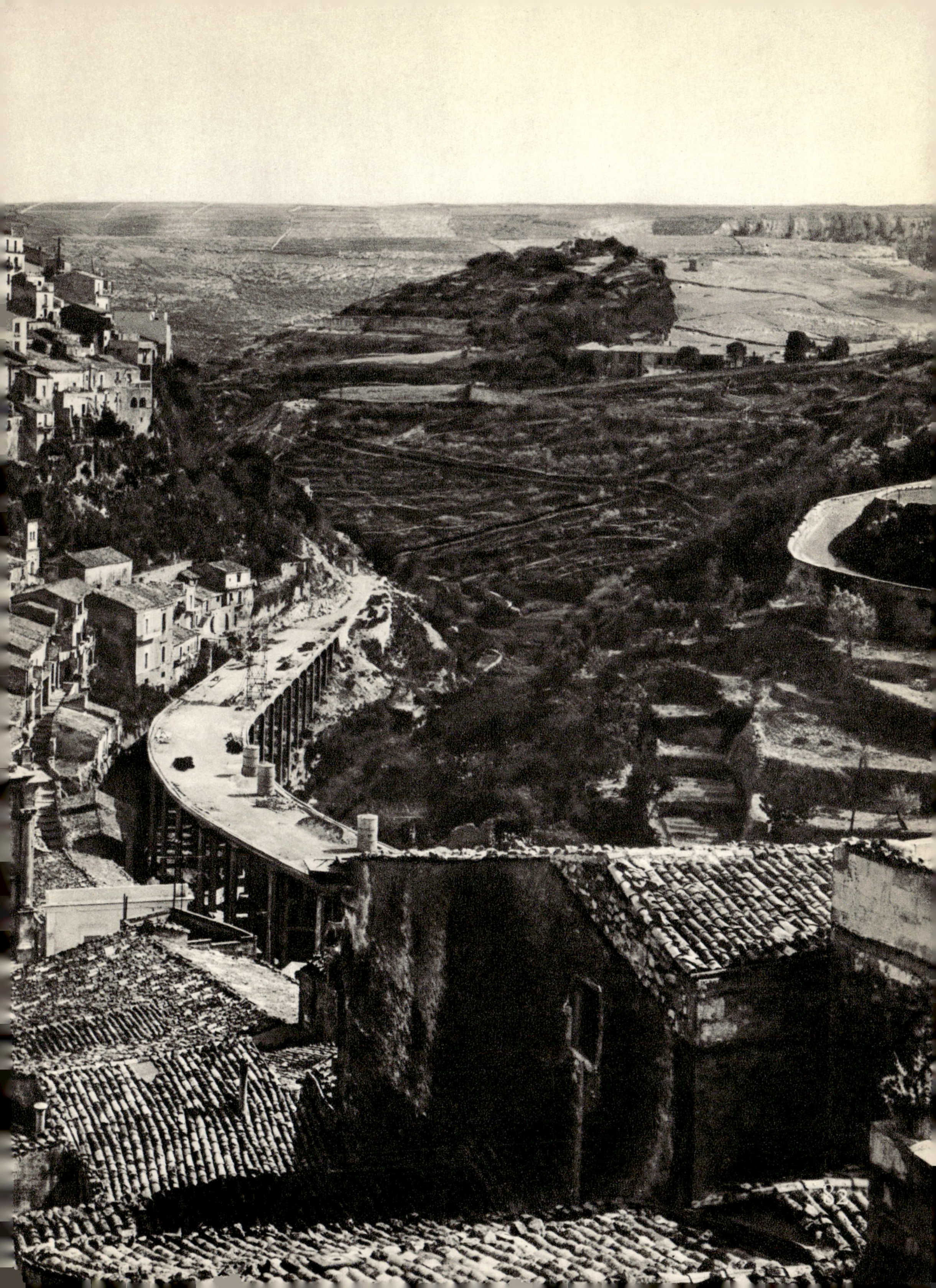
82

83

84

85

resurrection occurred quite soon, and by 338 the city had recovered sufficiently for its sovereign, Timoleon, regent of Syracuse, to authorise the rebuilding of its walls, as they may be seen at Capo Soprano. But the walls did not succeed in protecting Gela during the wars of the 3rd century, and it disappeared again more or less completely. This time there was no resurrection until A.D. 1230, when the Emperor Frederick II, struck by the strategic position of the Acropolis, re-established a citadel there. Gela became a big agricultural centre, but had no special history until 10 July 1943, when it was once more destroyed by the battles after the Anglo-American landing. A few years later oil was found there, and it had its fourth resurrection.

Sitting below the Doric column and looking at the refinery from the Acropolis, I could not help thinking how one of Sicily's oldest cities had in this chance way become one of its most modern towns. Still in the realm of chance, so often productive of archaeological discoveries, I imagined a drill going into the ground one day in search of an oil well and hitting on a famous funeral inscription which has never been found—to Aeschylus, founder of Athenian tragic drama. But the inscription says nothing of drama and poetry, only about his services to the Greek cause in war: 'This stone covers Aeschylus, son of Euphorion. Born an Athenian, he died in the fertile plains of Gela. The celebrated wood of Marathon and the long-haired Persians will testify that he was brave; they saw him fight.'

You may have been surprised not to have met more signs of the Spanish domination, seeing that it lasted for exactly three centuries. It left a greater mark on the Sicilian character perhaps—a haughty pride even in poverty and under oppression—than on the island's physical features. The Aragonese sovereigns, Castlian viceroys, and even more the Sicilian aristocracy under Spanish influence, did have many churches and palaces built or transformed. They employed Sicilian architects without making them follow masters or techniques from Spain; on the contrary, indeed, when during their dominance Sicily produced a great architect, Filippo Juvara, he was brought to Madrid to build the Royal Palace there.

Sicily was never more than a colony for the Spaniards. That is no doubt why the south-eastern region, which we shall now be entering, makes me think not only of Spain but still more of my image of Spanish America. For most of the civil and religious buildings in the region date from the era when the Spanish domination, passed on through the Jesuits, held sway in Mexico, Peru and Paraguay as well as Sicily.

How does it happen, you may ask, that a region civilised for thousands of years no longer contains buildings earlier than the 18th century? The answer is a terrible earthquake which ravaged it on 11 January 1693. The Spanish viceroy presided over the reconstruction, and as usual entrusted it to Sicilian architects: Vaccarini for Catania and Gagliardi for Noto. Vaccarini was born at Palermo, right in the centre, that is, of Spanish dominance in Sicily; and Gagliardi had received his training there. The result is a remarkable unity in the Jesuit-baroque style, of the Spanish or Spanish-American type.

Vittoria is the first town in the 'Vale of Noto' that you pass coming from Gela. In its main square, beside a charming little neo-classical theatre, you will at once notice a baroque church with a curious façade. It is tall, narrow and slightly convex. There is a sort of pyramid tower in three storeys. The bottom contains five panels, including the porch (at the centre). The middle storey has three panels, and the top has one, with a triangular pediment. There is little ornament; pilasters between the panels, a balustrade on each storey, volutes to make the storeys look more connected. This is the first example, among many you will be seeing, of the Gagliardi style; and it is one of the most modest.

Imagine such a façade amplified several times, enhanced by clusters of columns, massive works and lively statues, and set at the top of a huge flight of steps which has a long narrow square rising towards it. There you have the façade of San Giorgio at Ragusa. Personally I find it superb—but you may consider it merely a monstrous wedding cake! Anyhow, go and see it, for at least it will take you into the curious town of Ragusa, capital of the Vale of Noto.

Avoid the new Ragusa, which is rather dull, and I should also advise you to leave your car at the foot of the old town (which was the Greek Hybla). For it stands on an acropolis so steep that the streets here too are like flights of steps. On these streets you will pass several interesting palaces and churches, such as the old San Giorgio Church with its Catalan Gothic porch which withstood the earthquake. The streets will also give you sudden glimpses of the countryside, vast and austere, although the oldest civilization imported into Sicily, that of the Sikelians, once developed here. And when you have resumed your route to Syracuse, turn back for a general view of Ragusa's Acropolis, dominated by its churches and barracks, with houses hanging on to the very edge of the precipices surrounding it. The view might make you think of Toledo.

After going through a region of asphalt mines and oil wells, you come to Modica, which has another San Giorgio. Its façade, to my mind, is Gagliardi's masterpiece. You reach it by a long flight of steps which becomes more and more impressive as you reach the end of it, and see the church gradually growing before your eyes. The architect has purified his conception of the central, convex bell-tower in three storeys, by eliminating any break between the second and third storey. Thus the tower rises all in one piece, set off by the usual clusters of superimposed columns. It looks right down on the lower storey, which is severe, with five classical panels, each having a porch in the middle. This describes a reverse cross, like St Peter's, which faces the large ordinary cross erected at the spire of the tower. Very theatrical, no doubt, as usual in Jesuit baroque art, but what 'theatre' and what art!

You will admire the art even more when you see how it has inspired the design and architecture of a whole town. This is Noto, heir to ancient Netum, a Sikelian village, a Greek city, a Roman colony strong enough to resist Verres, and then a mediaeval fortress. Nothing is left of all these but a mass of ruins. The town, in fact, was so completely destroyed by the 1693 earthquake that its inhabitants decided to rebuild it five miles away, on the side of a hill which has a distant view of the Ionian sea.

They made it what t'Serstevens calls 'the noblest town in Sicily'. The mediaeval town had a traditional reputation in scholarship and the arts, producing among others the illustrious Carnelivari, the 15th-century architect of the Abbatelli Palace which you saw at Palermo. The new Noto maintained this tradition: the noble and erudite monk, Landolina, planned the whole town in one piece, a wonderful unity of conception, and the work was carried out by the team of a single architect, Gagliardi.

Facing you is the Corso, which runs through the town from end to end. It is a dead straight, level street cut in the side of the hill, with three successive squares on the left which rise by impressive flights of steps to various examples of baroque architecture. The first square, its gardens arranged round a Renaissance fountain from the mediaeval town, leads to the church of San Domenico, one of Gagliardi's smaller-scale works but very pleasing. The steps from the second square lead up to the Cathedral, a more classical and severe baroque with two lateral towers; those from the third, Immacolata Square, to the church of the same name, which has an even more severe façade, and to the less solemn lines of the Salvatore Convent.

If you carry on to the end of the Corso, you reach the gate that brings you out on the Syracuse road. But if you have more time to spend in the town, allow yourself the pleasure of seeing what Berenson called 'the most inspired of Laurana's Madonnas' in the Church of the Crucifix, and of strolling in neatly designed streets with other baroque buildings on them; convents, churches and palaces—with rounded iron balconies supported by consoles in the form of lions or dragons. Altogether, if you were not already converted to a liking for baroque, I hope you will be by now!

The Fire of Etna

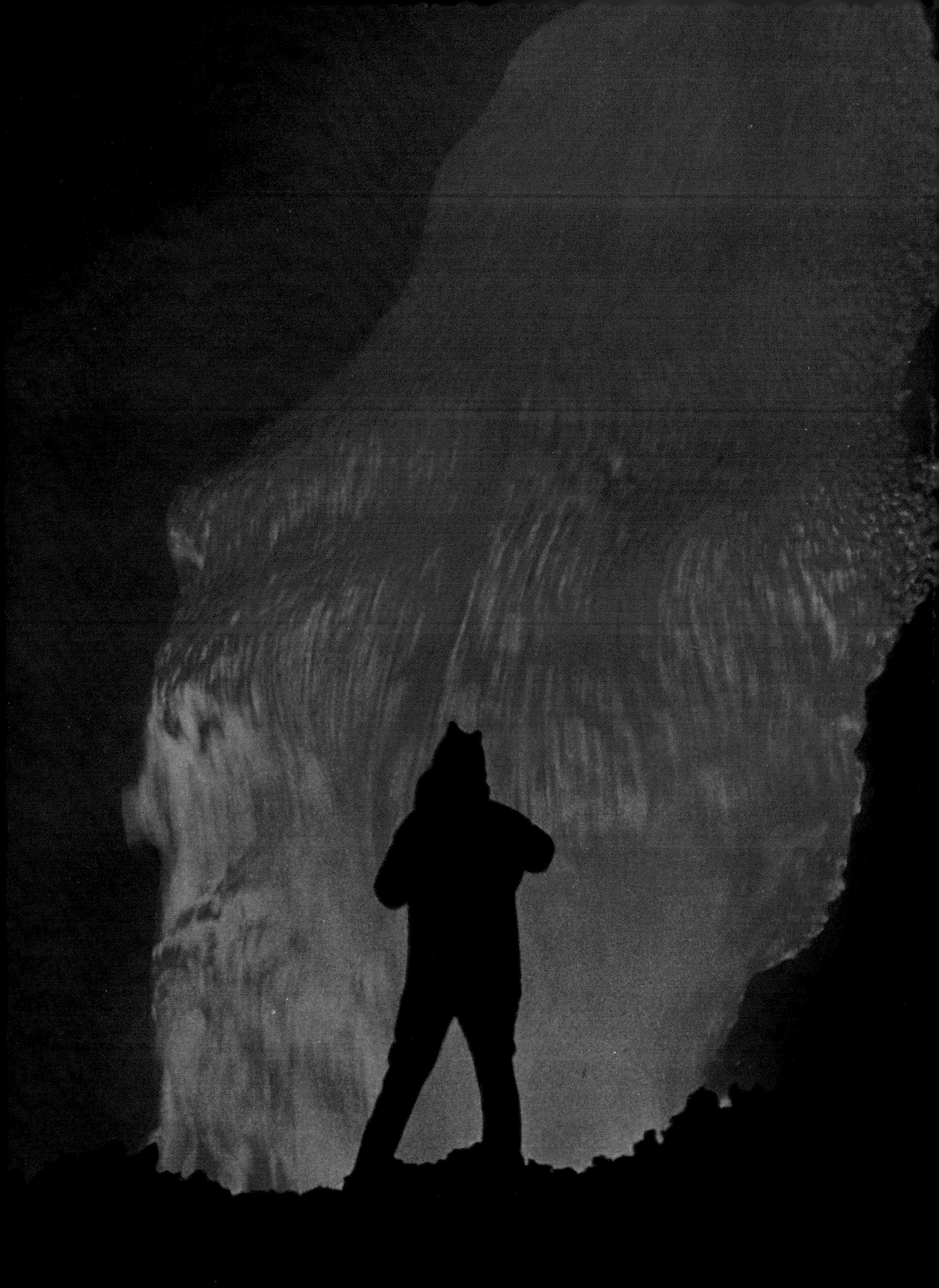

SYRACUSE

THE finest way of coming to Sicily is by sea to Syracuse. I am convinced of this since I was lucky enough two years ago to pass through the illustrious road known as the Porto Grande, the larger of its two natural harbours. Syracuse is perhaps my favourite of all Sicilian towns; and when I had stayed there before, I often wished I could come in from the sea.

So I was expecting a good deal; although when the moment came, I let myself be distracted by the sight of a fleet of fishing boats returning to Catania; they were leaning on their red lateen sails and seemed to be having a regatta. When I turned back towards the land, it was already close. Still, the panorama then was revealed to me just as I had imagined it.

To my right were the roads of Augusta, covered in a fog of oil fumes. In the centre, much clearer, was the flat top of Mount Climiti, and behind it the Hyblaean Range, forming a wide line of darker blue between the blue of the sky and the blue of the sea. To the left, still clearer and obviously Greek, I saw the limestone hill of ancient Syracuse, and in its peninsula of Ortygia the town proper, springing directly from the water like Venus Anadyomene.

Then we entered the harbour, leaving on one side the peninsula of Plemyra, with its fine bare lines, violet against the light; on the other side the Maniace Castle and the walls and houses of the sea front—in all conceivable shades of yellow, but turning orange the nearer the sun came to the horizon. Soon we came to the causeway and canal connecting the Porto Grande with the Porto Piccolo (small harbour) and the island of Ortygia with the mainland. Our boat docked here amidst the ritual Mediterranean agitation.

Unfortunately, if you are travelling from northern Europe, it is not so easy to enter Sicily at Syracuse; although like Palermo it could offer a basic introduction to the island's political and artistic history.

Naturally the Greek period is dominant. We have already come across Syracuse in history many times through her dominance over other cities like Segesta, Selinunte, Agrigento and Gela; so I will merely give the essential dates and facts.

The city was founded in 733 B.C. by colonists from Corinth. It grew rapidly, despite the difficulties caused by the habitual rivalry between aristocrats and democrats. In 485 Gelon made himself tyrant and formed a coalition of Greek cities round Syracuse, defeating the Carthaginians at Himera (480). For about half a century there was a golden age, when Syracuse stood out as the capital of western Hellenism and a centre of all Greek culture, frequented by Aeschylus and Pindar, and when many famous buildings were erected. In 415 the Athenians landed, besieged the city and had their fleet trapped in the Grand Port; their army was routed, and the survivors were sent to the City's *latomie* (quarry pits). In 405 Carthage renewed her offensive, but Dionysius I successfully withstood it. Timoleon restored democracy in 343. In 317 the tyrants returned, first Agathocles, then Hieron II. There was a second period of artistic predominance and fertility, during which Syracuse produced her greatest poet, Theocritus. In 212 the city was taken by the Romans, despite the inventions of Archimedes.

After that, although it became the chief town in the Roman province of Sicily, Syracuse declined in importance until recent times. It was, however, the first point where Christianity reached Europe; St Paul passed it on his journey to Rome and to martyrdom. For three centuries it remained the capital of the Byzantine province. It was occupied by the Saracens in 878, but witnessed the last appearance of the Greeks in Sicily, when retaken by the Byzantine general, George Maniace, in 1038. The Normans rather neglected it, but it recovered a little owing to the favour shown by the Emperor Frederick II and then the Spanish viceroys. There are indeed hardly any traces of the Saracens and Normans, whereas the Swabians (Germans), the Aragonese and the Spaniards enjoyed beautifying it in their fashions. The Spaniards had to rebuild it after the 1693 earthquake, and they have left on it the seal of baroque.

Although it again had to repair many ruins after the last war, Syracuse is today the fifth largest town in Sicily, with nearly a hundred thousand inhabitants. How many were there in the 3rd century B.C.? Some scholars have put the figure as high as half a million; others, probably nearer the truth, speak of 150–200,000. Its wall is fourteen miles long, an impressive length considering that Aurelian's wall, built round a Rome of a million inhabitants, was only twelve miles long. The Epipolae however, a ridge ten times more extensive than the whole of the rest of the city, must have had a very small population, to judge from the few ruins to be found there. At present it is even less populated, while the modern town more or less covers the three other mainland districts of the ancient city between Epipolae and Ortygia island: Neapolis, Tyche and Akhradina. I was struck, the last time I was there, by the number of new buildings I saw.

Ortygia was where the first Greek colonists settled, and the population withdrew

86. *Columns of Olympieion.*
87. *Columns of Temple of Apollo.*
88. *Entrance to Tomb of Archimedes.*
89. *The Roman Amphitheatre.*
90. *Euryeles Castle.*
91. *Latomia of Paradise. The Ropemakers' Cave.*
92. *Latomia of Paradise. The Ear of Dionysius.*
93. *The Greek Theatre.*
94. *Latomia of the Capuchins.*
95. *The Fountain of Arethusa.*
96. *Beneventano Palace.*
97. *The Cathedral.*
98. *The Syracuse Aphrodite (National Archaeological Museum).*
99. *Columns of Temple of Athene in Cathedral.*

100–104. NATIONAL ARCHAEOLOGICAL MUSEUM
100. *Roman sarcophagus (detail).*
101. *The Mother with Two Children, funerary statue discovered at Megara (560 B.C.) Detail (total height: 2 feet 8 inches).*
102. *Small Apollo (height 1 foot 6 inches).*
103. *Lekytos (5th century B.C.).*
104. *Seated goddess from Grammichele (5th century B.C., height 3 feet 4 inches).*

105–107. *By the sea.*
106–107. *Fishermen repairing hooks on lines, the lines attached to a long thin cord visible on ground.*
108. *Syracuse. The Harbour.*

86

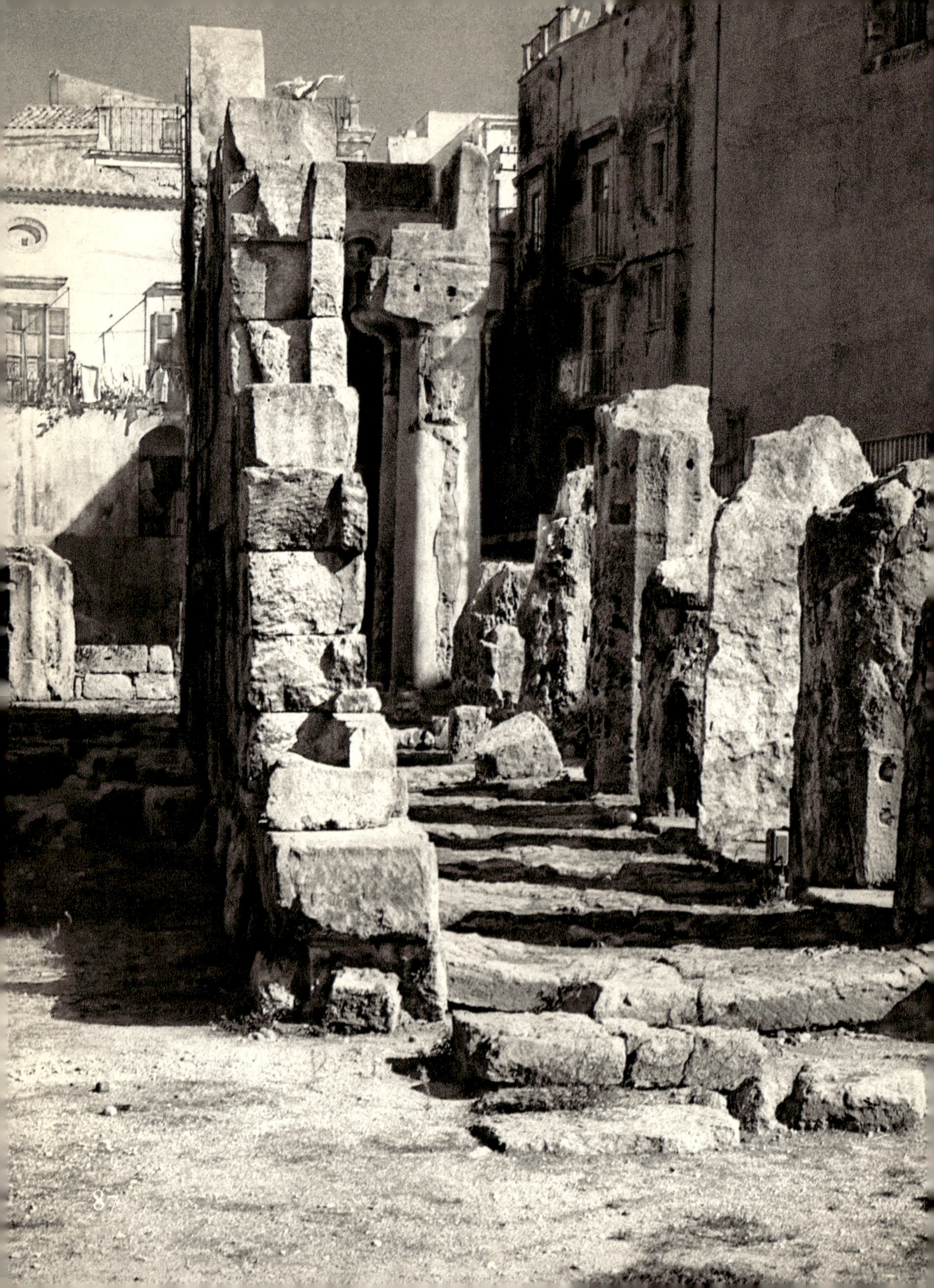

87

88

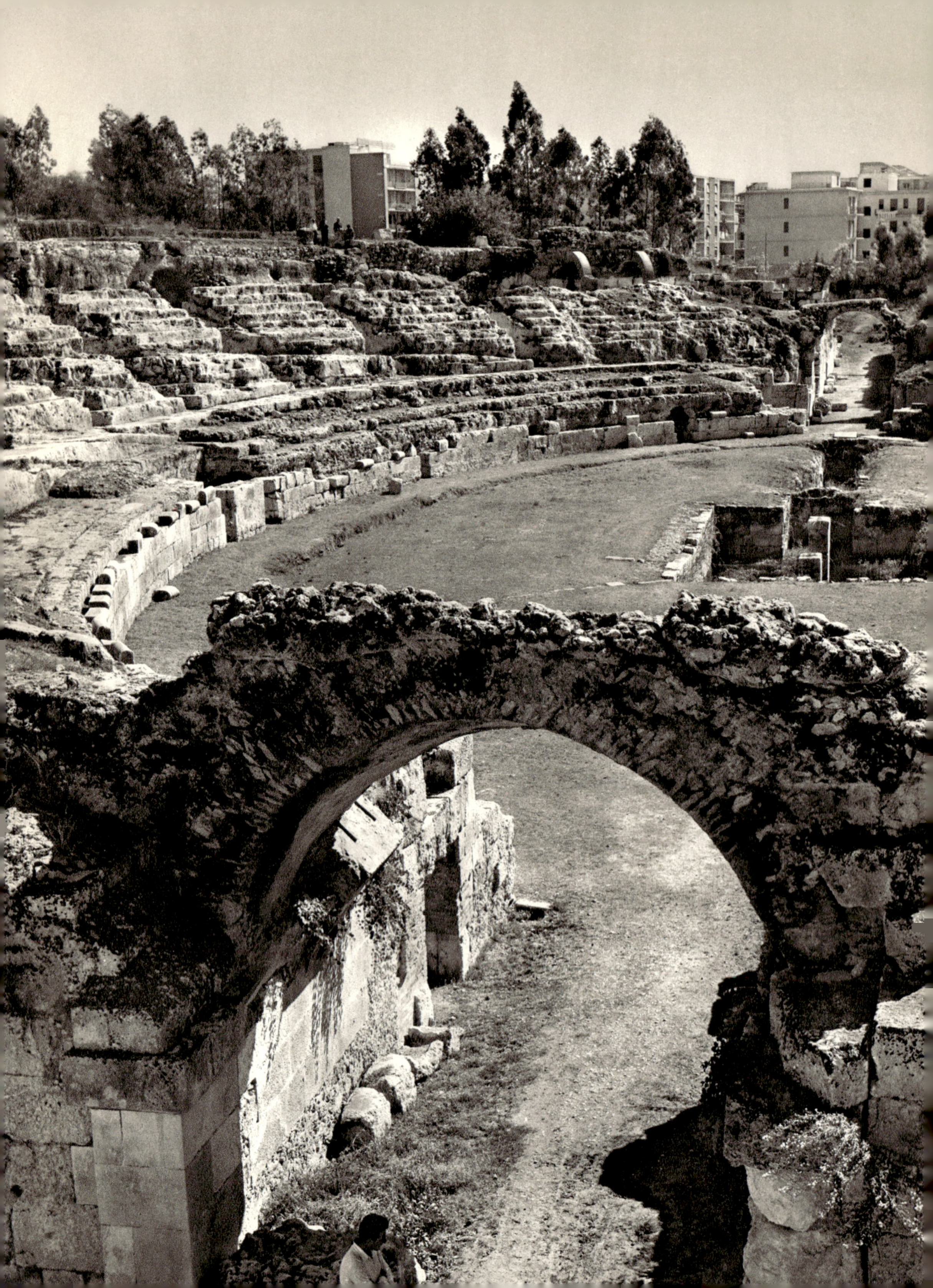

89

90

91

92

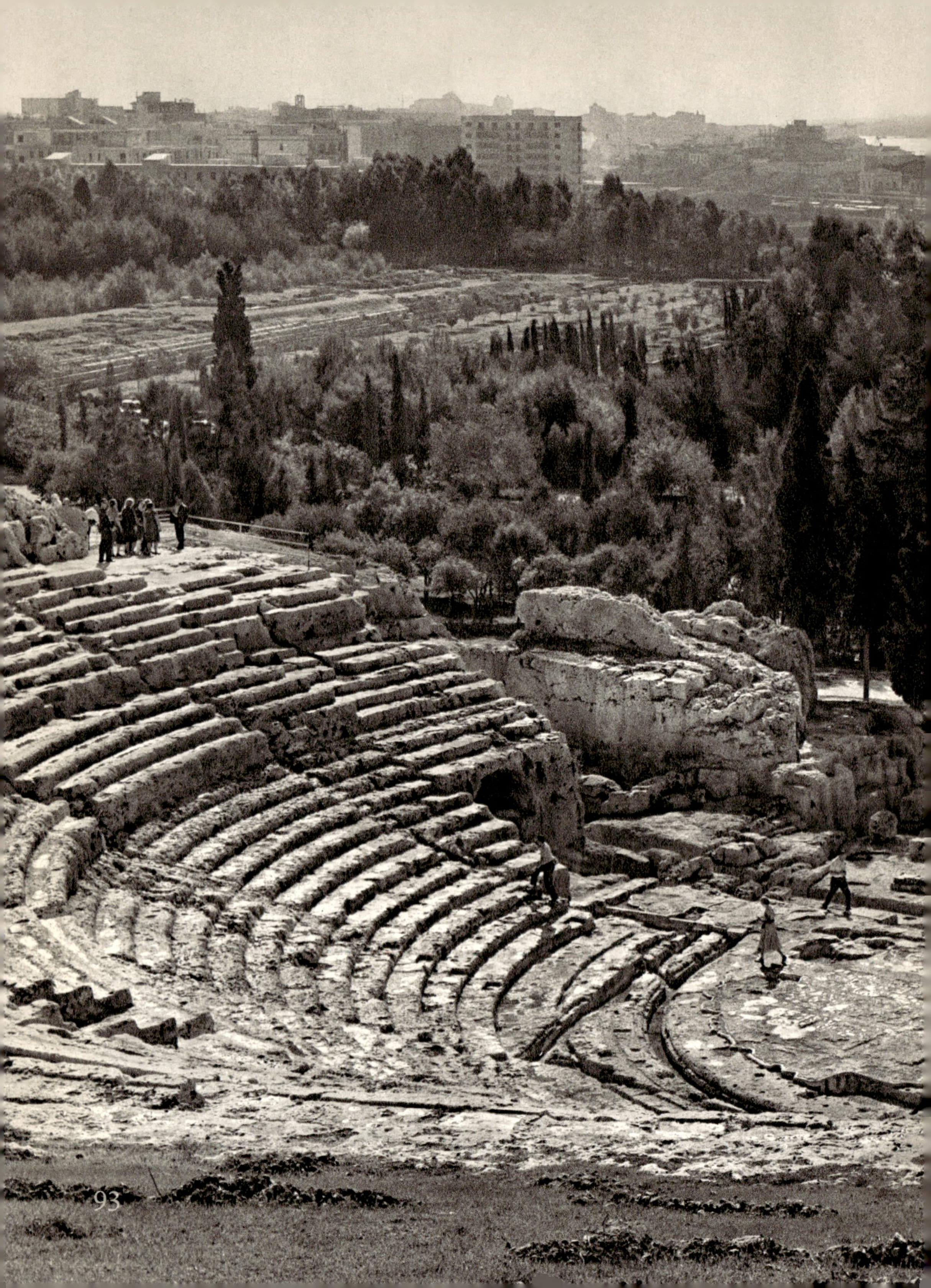

93

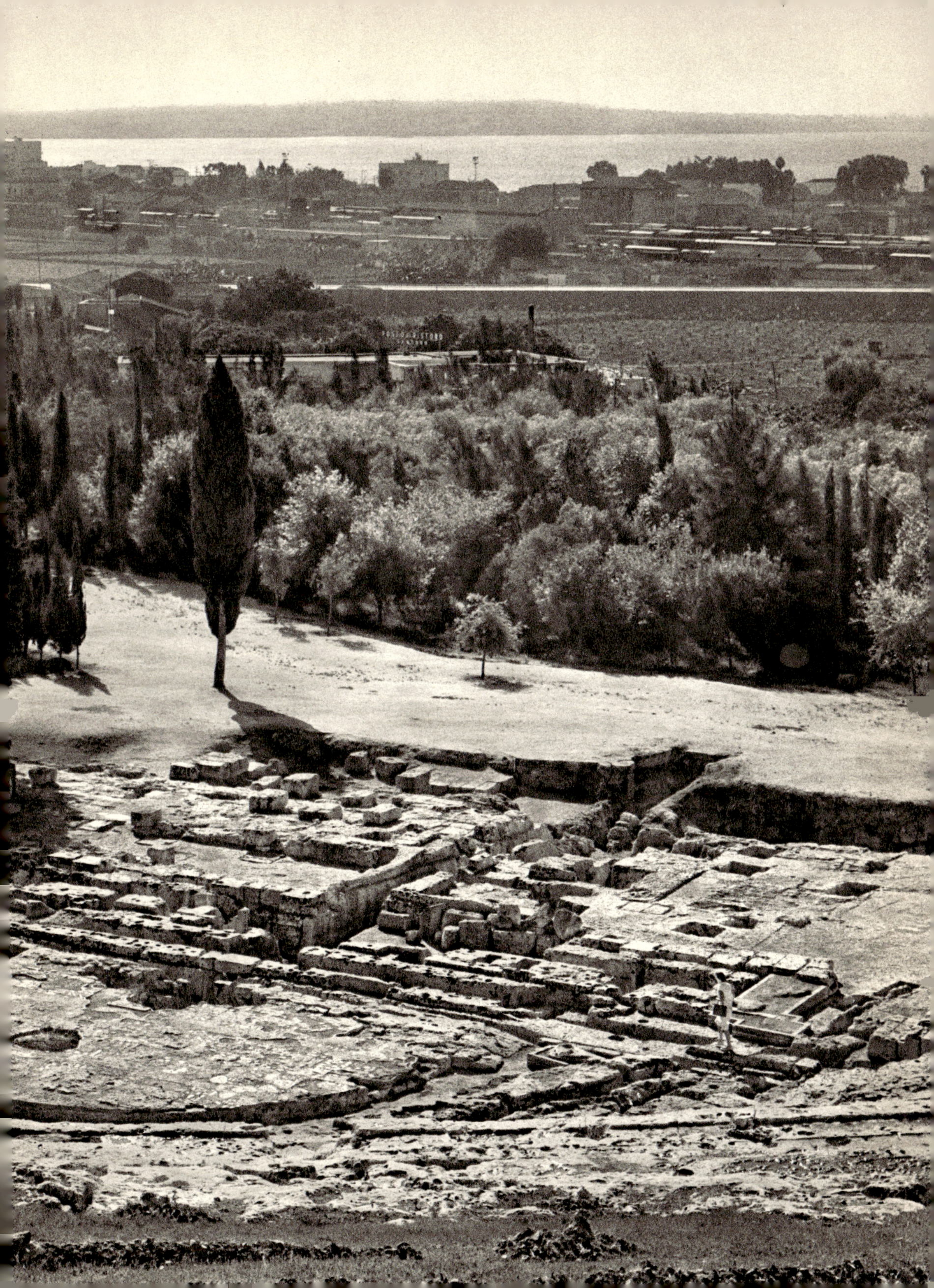

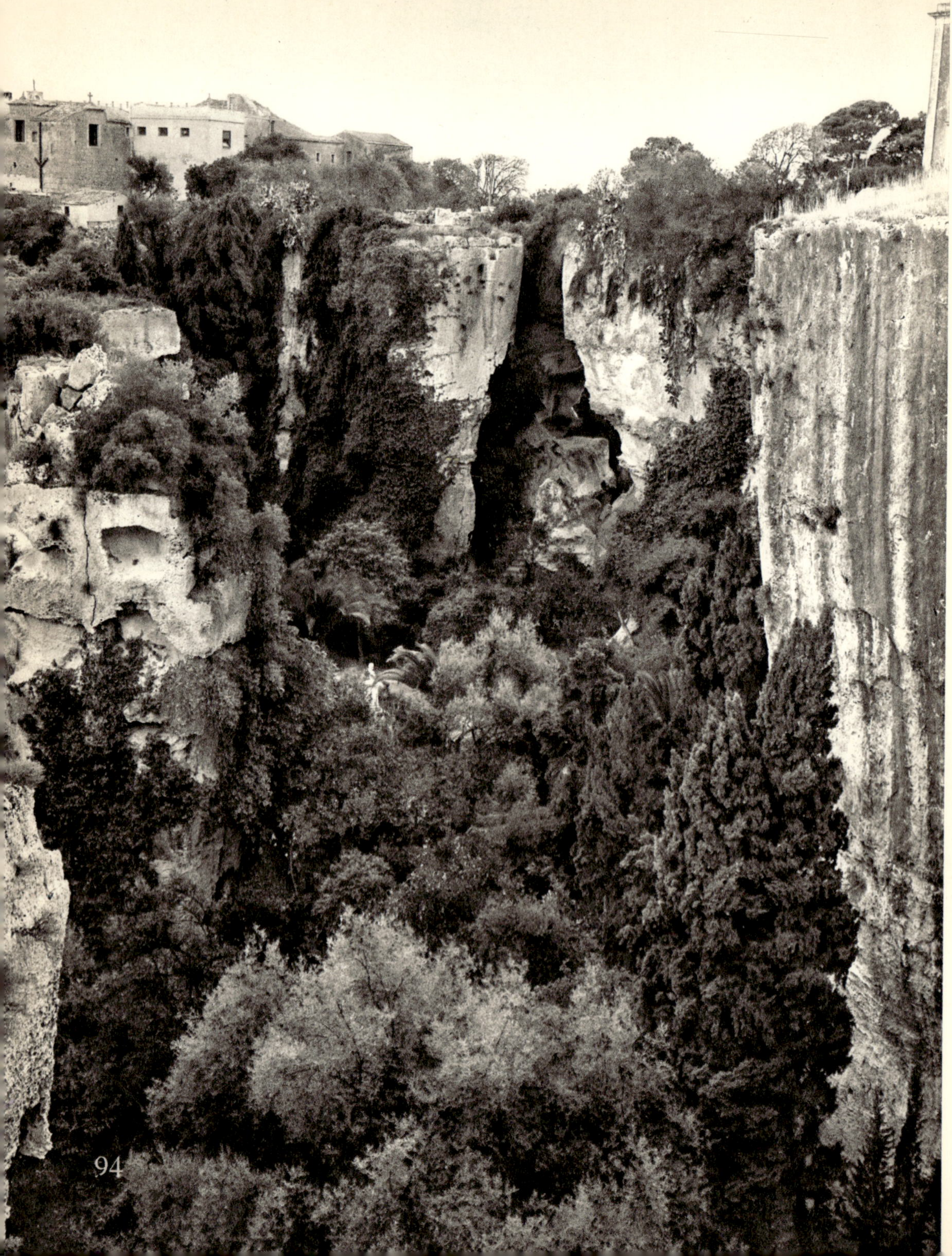

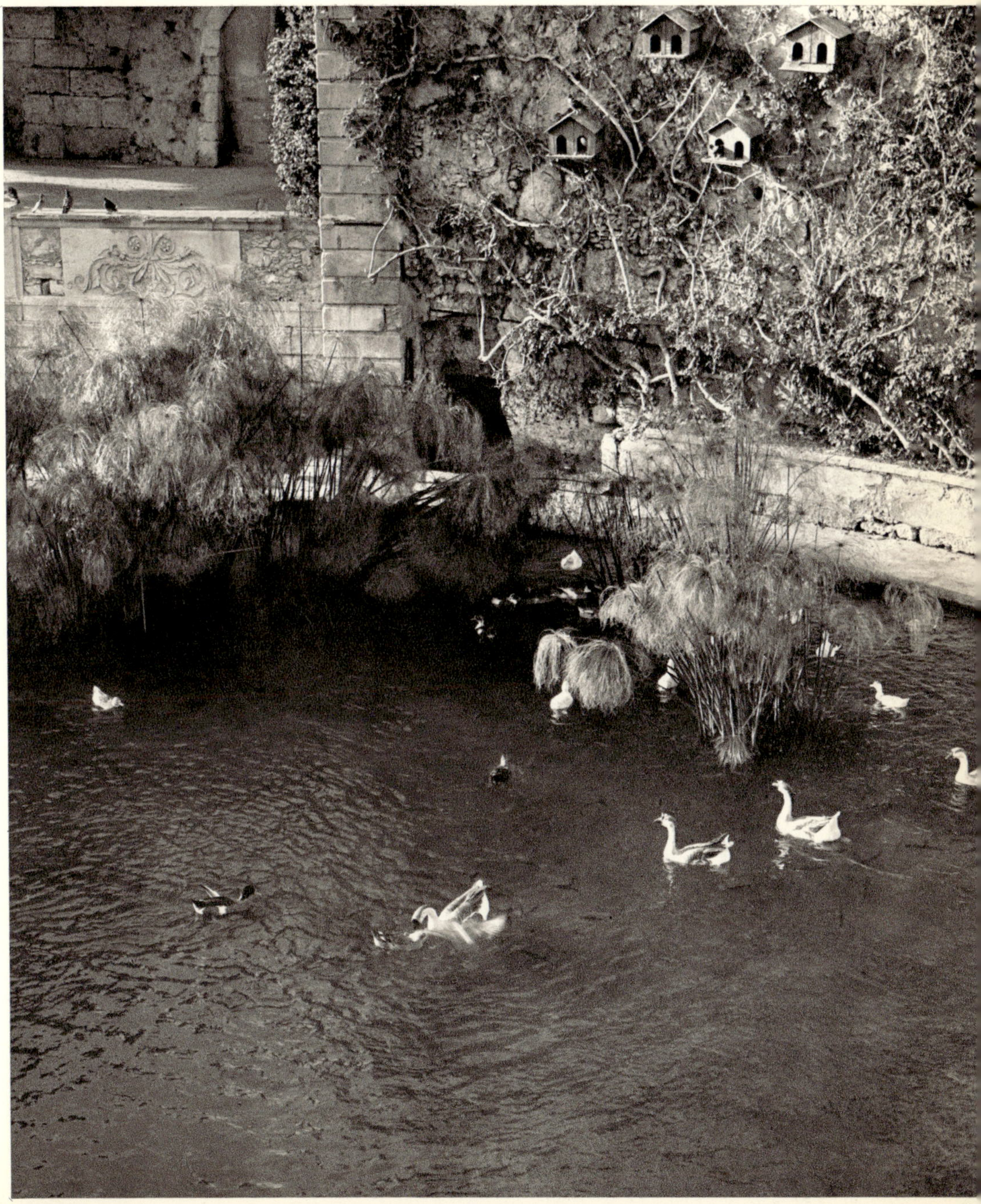

96

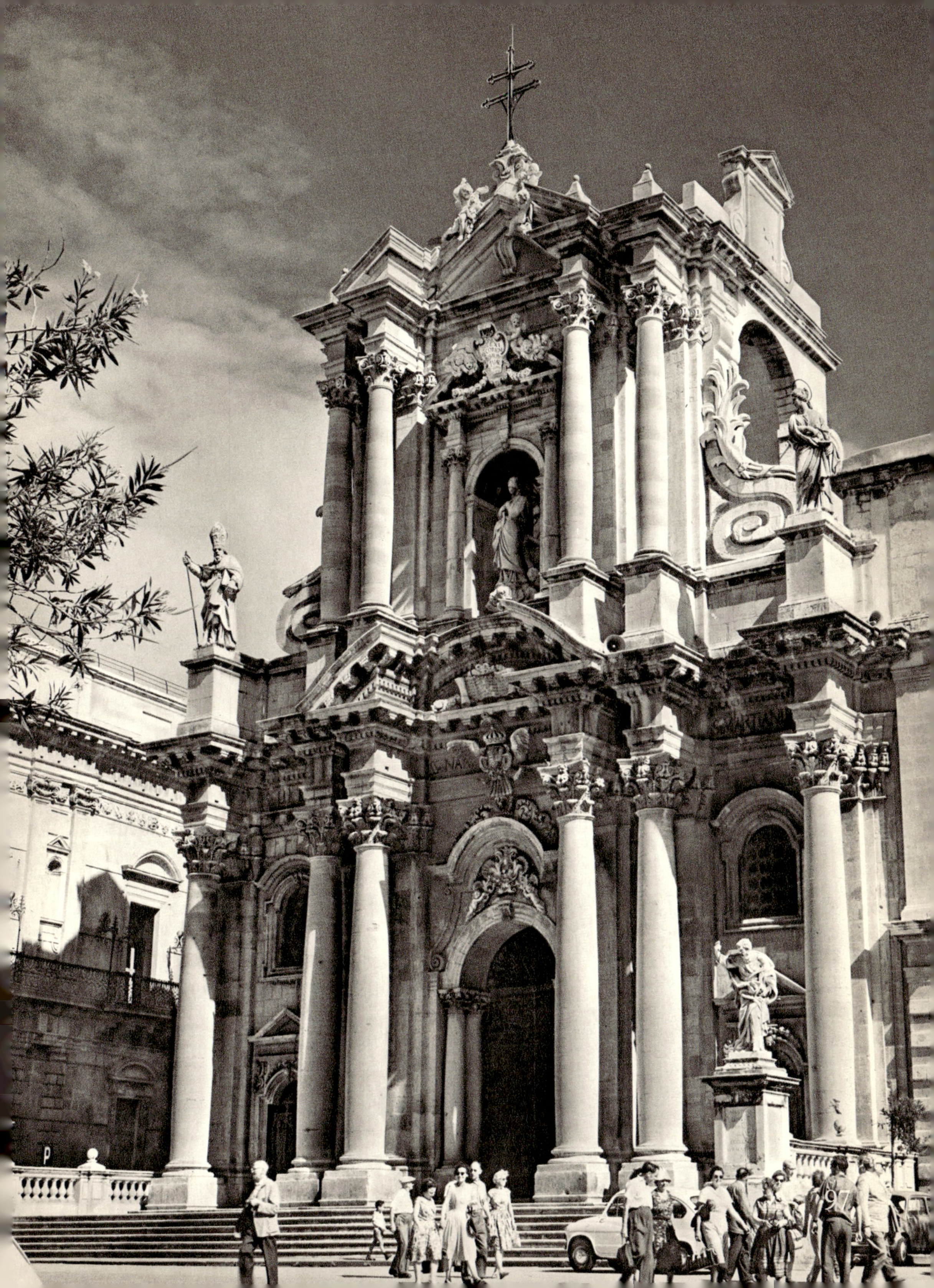

98 99

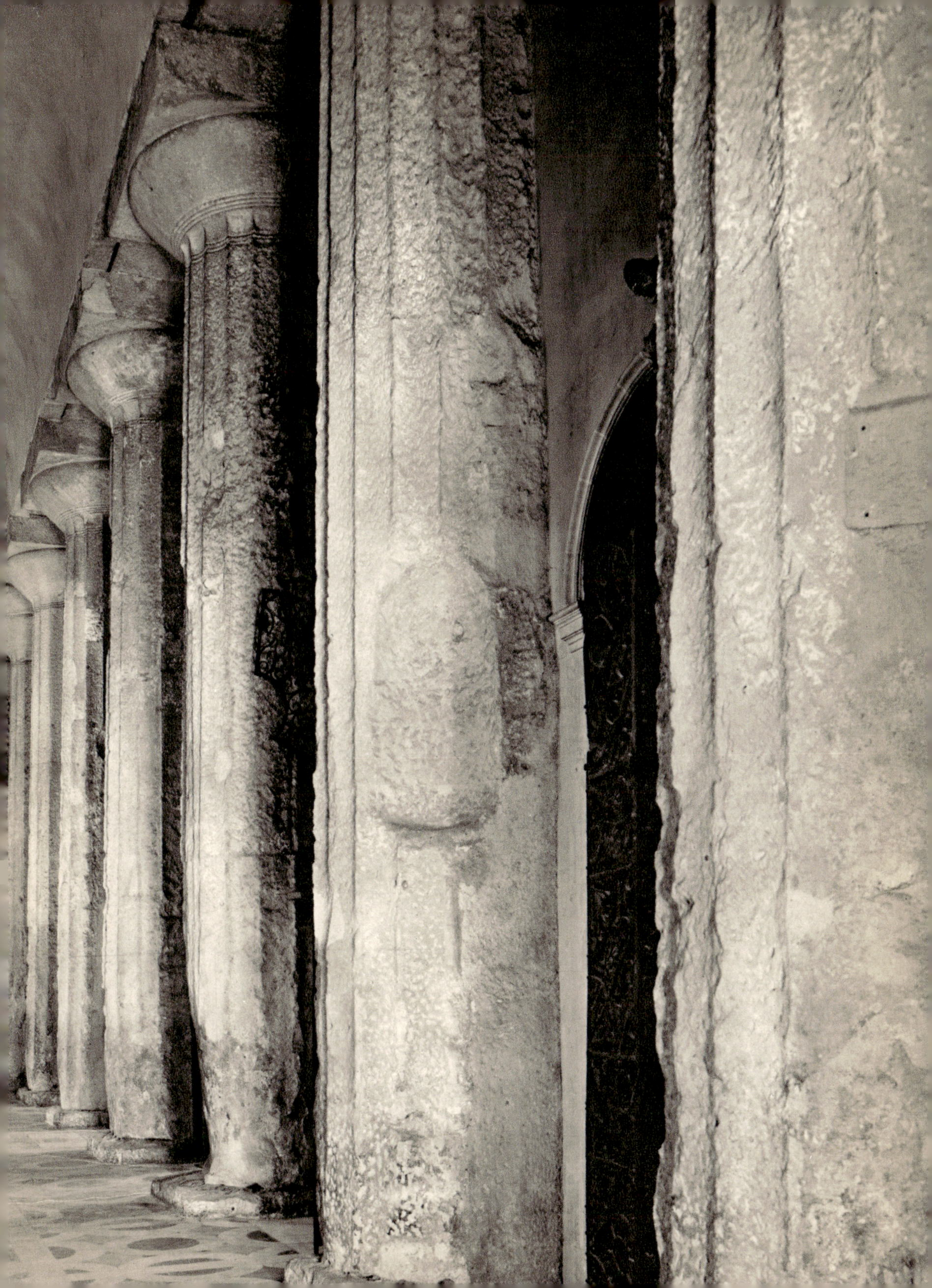

100

101

102

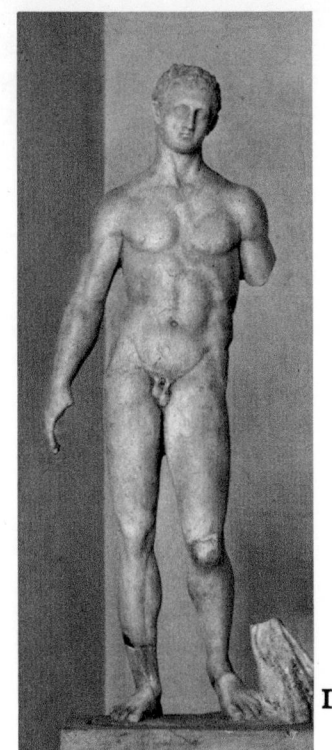

103

104

105

106

107

108

there during the centuries when Syracuse was reduced to little more than a big village. It is unchanging and will always remain so, despite the demolitions and reconstructions it has experienced during the Fascist era and since. The demolitions, however, did bring up a temple of either Apollo or Artemis, although unfortunately not much is left of it; it seems to go back to the beginning of the 6th century and is doubtless the oldest Doric temple in the Greek world.

Whether or not you put up at Ortygia, you should anyhow go there every evening, to see the sunset from the Foro Italico promenade, watch the fisherman busy with their nets, and drink Campari and soda on the terrace of a café in Pancali Square. You will find restaurants near the harbour where you are asked to choose your fish before it is grilled; you eat outside in the warm night, arguing happily with a loquacious manager and polite beggars, while your mind recalls the marvels you have seen during the day.

I would not venture, though, to recommend the method I once adopted with some archaeologist friends, which was to dine in four distinct stages round the central square (dedicated, fittingly, to Archimedes). The first was to eat in a *rosticceria* a solid Sicilian *calzone*, a sort of turn-over stuffed with mince; second stage, in the bar opposite, a glass of thick *vino nero*; third stage, grilled fish in a small restaurant; fourth stage, an ice and coffee outside a café, watching the people pass.

When describing the lay-out of the ancient and modern city, I indicated a plan which, although not the usual one nor according to historical chronology, I suggest you should follow as the best way of seeing Syracuse. First you drive up a road lined by huge barbary fig-trees, to the highest and furthest point of Epipolae, Euryalus Castle (five miles from the town centre). When you go down it will be by way of Neapolis, Tyche and Achradina; and after that you can enjoy at your leisure the delights of Ortygia.

The main reason for starting at Euryalus, a fortress built by Dionysius I as key to his defence of Syracuse, is because it will offer you a splendid panorama, which will also show you the lay-out of the town. Before you is the sea, which brought the Greeks to Syracuse, and made its trade and arms flourish. Behind you is the mountain, where the Syracusans carved themselves a kingdom extending over almost the whole of Sicily—although their enemies and conquerors, too, often emerged from the other side of that mountain.

To your right is the Porto Grande, infinitely too big for the shipping it carries today. In the centre you see the Epipolae ridge, immense and barren, with patches of limestone showing through; at the end of it you can just make out the modern town, on the tiny coastal plain into which Ortygia extends. To the left is the Gulf of Augusta, once enlivened only by an occasional destroyer from the small naval base. Today it is cluttered with big tankers, barred by new dams, smoky and fiery with the oil refineries which stand right behind ancient Megara Hyblaea, disinherited twin sister of wealthy Syracuse. You can almost see Syracusan history here in a nutshell: its greatness, decline, and now its hope of economic revival.

When you look at Euryelus Castle, you will understand why Dionysius felt he must fortify this position. First, it commands all Syracuse and surrounding country. Secondly, it was a narrow ridge connecting the plateau to the mountains, from which invaders might come. Everywhere else the plateau was defended by cliffs, so this was the only weak point. He decided to block the ridge with a series of transverse obstacles: two ditches, a bastion, another ditch, and finally the wall of the fortress proper, still well preserved with its three towers.

Notice the plan's simplicity and the quality of the masonry. These massive limestone blocks are very different from the roughly baked bricks in the upper part of the Gela wall. Starting from the bastion, you go down a stairway to the third ditch, which must have served as the bastion's inner court, for it has store-chambers all round. There are passages going off from this, and a second stairway leading to the inner court of the main keep. The whole complex, ditches, stairways, store-chambers and passages, are dug right into the rock, and one cannot but admire such an example of the Greek genius: even in functional buildings, they would make sacrifices for art, and could set off against the sky this façade and these towers, yellow, ochre or pink according to the time of day.

When Dionysius had completed his fortress he could not leave it in isolation. He had to connect it to the town, and did so by surrounding Epipolae with walls, which you can follow on foot, if you are not afraid of thistles and a long walk. But this extension of the defence system round an area with very few inhabitants was a cause of weakness. In 212, after the Syracussans had been besieged for two years, they sought consolation for not having enough to eat by drinking too much on a single 'night off'; and that night was enough for Marcellus to find an ill-guarded point in the Epipolae wall and succeed in forcing it.

There is a so-called panoramic route, which enables the tourist-in-a-hurry to 'do' the town's most famous sights without getting out of the car. Instead of taking this, I suggest you should reach Neapolis by way of its small square, where there is a Norman chapel.

On your left is the amphitheatre, which I don't much care for. It is too low and too funnel-shaped, and unlike the Coliseum, for instance, doesn't make you admire the grandeur of a stone cliff raised by the hand of man. Still on the left you will see the colossal altar of Hieron II, 220 yards in length, which must have made an awe-inspiring sight when the flesh of several dozen bulls were being burnt there in sacrifice to Zeus Eleutheros.

After this you should perhaps visit the very commercialised Latomia del Paradiso, a quarry containing an artificial cave with unusual acoustic properties which is called the Ear of Dionysius. According to a legend (supposedly originated by the painter Caravaggio) Dionysius used it to stand at the opening of the cave on the hillside and 'eavesdrop' on his prisoners shut up in the quarry; whereas it may have been only a device to produce 'sound effects' like thunder for the nearby theatre and make the wrath of the gods more terrifying. The quarry also contains the traditional 'cave of the rope-makers', who are supposed to plait rope in the cave, but really obtain pieces of rope ready-made from merchants in the harbour; still, they are a friendly 'guild', and you will no doubt have to follow the custom of so many travellers and buy their goods.

Note the wall of the cave, the vault and strong pillar supporting it; it will help you to understand how the quarries were worked. At the period when the Athenians were sent to these quarries, they were not open to the sky as later subsidence has made them. They had galleries which expanded as the blocks of stones were extracted, forming 'halls' which were sometimes quite large. By classical custom, penal sentences were served in these quarries; and the terrible condition to which the Syracusans reduced the Athenian prisoners was probably no worse than what the law prescribed for convicts in that age.

Finally you reach the most famous of Syracusan 'sights', the Greek theatre. It is far from being the same as when Aeschylus perhaps sat in the auditorium directing the production of his *Persians*; for its present tiers of seats were enlarged in the Hellenistic age and altered by the Romans. Admittedly, too, the theatre is not the equal of the one at Epidaurus, and the view it offers of the Porto Grande is marred by factory chimneys and gasometers. During the summer it is covered over with preparations for the dramatic festival, and I have even seen it used for posters in an election period. But despite all this I still carry the memory of a winter evening when I went there and sat right in the centre of the auditorium, almost hypnotised by the architectural perfection of the curves displayed before me.

Go next to Tyche, which must have been a rich residential district, and therefore liable to be looted by invaders. Hardly any traces of it have been found. But after passing the elegant romanesque porch of San Giovanni, the only vestige of Norman influence left at Syracuse, you will reach the other famous quarry, that of the Capuchins. Here the Athenians suffered their appalling captivity, but the quarry has been transformed into beautiful wild gardens, sunk about sixty-five feet below the ground, full of bushes, shrubs and trees—holm oaks, olive trees, cacti—some clinging boldly to the vertical walls; and with a strange little rock-cut stage. These gardens are pleasantly cool, which you appreciate especially on a summer day, and their only weakness is a rather paltry bust of Archimedes, unworthy of the setting and the man.

There is practically nothing left of Achradina either, the fourth district of mainland Syracuse. If you are very conscientious, you will seek out, among the streets of the modern town intersecting at right angles, some vestiges of the Greek market-place and the Roman 'gymnasium' (really a small Roman theatre); but don't fail to go and see the *Burial of Santa Lucia*, painted by Caravaggio, in the composite church which Syracuse dedicated to its patroness.

Now you can at last visit Ortygia, which is still the heart of Syracuse. Really the best way of getting to know it is to wander at random through its small streets, although they never take you very far—in fact they always bring you back soon enough to the sea. To the east the sea is dark and rough, with the mass of Etna towering in the distance. To the west it is calm and clear, in the shelter of the Porto Grande.

On your walks you will notice the essential characteristic of Syracuse after the Greek age, that it is a town of palaces: mediaeval, with Gothic porches surmounted by armorial bearings and courtyards which have staircases open to the sky; baroque, with rounded iron balconies resting on clawed consoles.

If you wish to visit Ortygia more methodically, I suggest the following itinerary, more or less adapted to historical order and geographical convenience. Start at the far point of the island, Maniace Castle: although this bears the name of the last, ephemeral Byzantine conqueror, it was built at the beginning of the 13th century by the Emperor Frederick II. It shows his liking for Arab ideas, in the contrast he tried to establish between a severe exterior, like a typical feudal castle, and a sumptuous, refined interior. Unfortunately, only the exterior of this survives, notably a noble Gothic portal flanked by two niches; they are empty today, but Frederick placed in them two Hellenistic bronze rams, one of which is now in the National Museum in Palermo.

The Bellomo Palace, from the middle of the 13th century, still belongs structurally to the Swabian period, but a century later the Catalans gave its courtyard an outdoor stairway. It contains a little museum, the pearl of which is an *Annunciation* by Antonello da Messina. The Montalto Palace, at the end of the 13th century, belongs to the variant of Gothic, already in decline, called Chiaramontain, which flourished in Sicily in the early days of the Spanish occupation. In Piazza Archimede the 14th-century Lanza Palace has late Arab touches in the decoration of its windows: and the Banca d'Italia also has a fine outdoor stairway.

We go on to the baroque palaces. At the end of Archimedes Square take the Via Maestranza, and you will be plunging into the 'Marsh', which like the one at Paris was part ghetto, part aristocratic quarter. Here you have many fine baroque buildings with rounded balconies.

Then return to Archimedes Square, cross it, and go on to the Cathedral Square, a superb baroque complex. The square is more or less in the shape of an ellipse, and you come out on it at the north end between two masterpieces: on the left the Town Hall (17th century), on the right the Beneventano del Bosco Palace (18th century) with a façade equalled in elegance only by its courtyard. At the other end of the ellipse, there is the Church of Santa Lucia della Badia, which has an extravangantly long balcony. Going down the left-hand side of the square, you come to the noble Louis XIV façade of the Archbishop's Palace, and finally, queen of the square, that of the Cathedral. This was rebuilt after the earthquake on the lines you know from Ragusa and Modica: a central tower with storeys and superimposed columns, flattened volutes and lively statues.

The Cathedral's interior has some surprises in store. Your eyes still filled with baroque light and splendour, you enter the porch and see a romanesque-looking nave with bare stone walls broken by rounded arches, as austere and sombre as anyone could wish. There is such a great contrast that at first sight you almost regret the zeal with which the building was stripped, fifty years ago, of its 18th-century embellishments, statues, paintings and stucco frills. But you will soon feel impressed by the severity and silence, by the inscription in bronze capitals which goes all the way round the Cathedral, reminding you that this was the first church in western Christianity.

Now turn, and you may well gasp in amazement. At the far end of the nave, the obverse, that is, of the tumultuous baroque façade, four Doric columns gleam quietly in the dim light, intact from base to capital, utterly pagan. In the aisles you will find others, laid out in complete rows, fourteen each on the right and the left, half built into the outer walls. Syracuse Cathedral is totally embedded in what was a Temple of Athene.

When you come out of the Cathedral, you are quite near a well-known feature, which is by the side of the Porto Grande; the Arethusa Fountain. Arethusa in the myth was a nymph, one of the Nereids, whom Artemis changed into a fountain so that she could escape the advances of Alpheus, god of a Peloponnesian river. He pursued her underground and under the sea, and finally came up on the other side of the bay at Syracuse. The nymph is celebrated by Virgil, Ovid and Shelley, and this small pool with its bubbling water and feathery tufts of papyrus must have been very attractive when it flowed freely out into the harbour. But today it is rather a sad sight, enclosed between balustrades and a gloomy wall from the Spanish period, the haunt of grey mullet, ducks and swans, but also a tip for tin cans and wrapping paper.

Equally well-known but a good deal further off is the source of the little Ciane river. Ciane was also a nymph, a friend of Persephone's, and when the god of the underworld carried off her friend whom she had tried to rescue, Ciane dissolved into tears and became the little stream which flows only two miles before being lost in the sea. To reach the spring, you have to hire a boat and cross the harbour, then go up the stream; the trip is well worth making. It is a delightful pool, with luxuriant papyrus growing wild and crystal clear water, which has been praised by Theocritus, Renan, d'Annunzio, Gide and many others.

To round off your tour, you should visit the National Museum of Syracuse (on the Cathedral Square). It is one of the finest and best organised collections in the world for Greek art of all ages. Besides such things as its pottery, and coins it has the Aphrodite of Syracuse who inspired Maupassant's comment: 'This is Woman as she is, as one loves her and desires her and wants to embrace her'—a sentiment, I dare say, of which no honest man need feel ashamed.

There are, however, other female figures in the Museum who stir me even more. They are the terracotta *kourai* (girls) with that mysterious, ironical, voluptuous smile hovering on their lips which you see on so many faces in early Greek sculpture. The last time I left Syracuse by train, a girl dashed into my compartment at the last moment, out of breath, dishevelled and not very clean. But I still remember how beautiful I found her, for she had on her lips the smile of Syracuse.

IN SICILY'S INTERIOR

PIAZZOLO ACREIDE—CALTAGIRONE—PIAZZA ARMERINA
—CALTANISETTA—ENNA—NICOSIA

109, 111, 112. *Piazza Armerina. Mosaics in the Villa Casale.*
110. *Near Piazza Armerina.*
113. *Work in the fields.*
114. *Lake of Pergusa.*
115. *Enna.*
116. *Between Gangi and Nicosia.*
117. *Near Nicosia.*
118–120. *Nicosia (119 The Cathedral).*

109

110

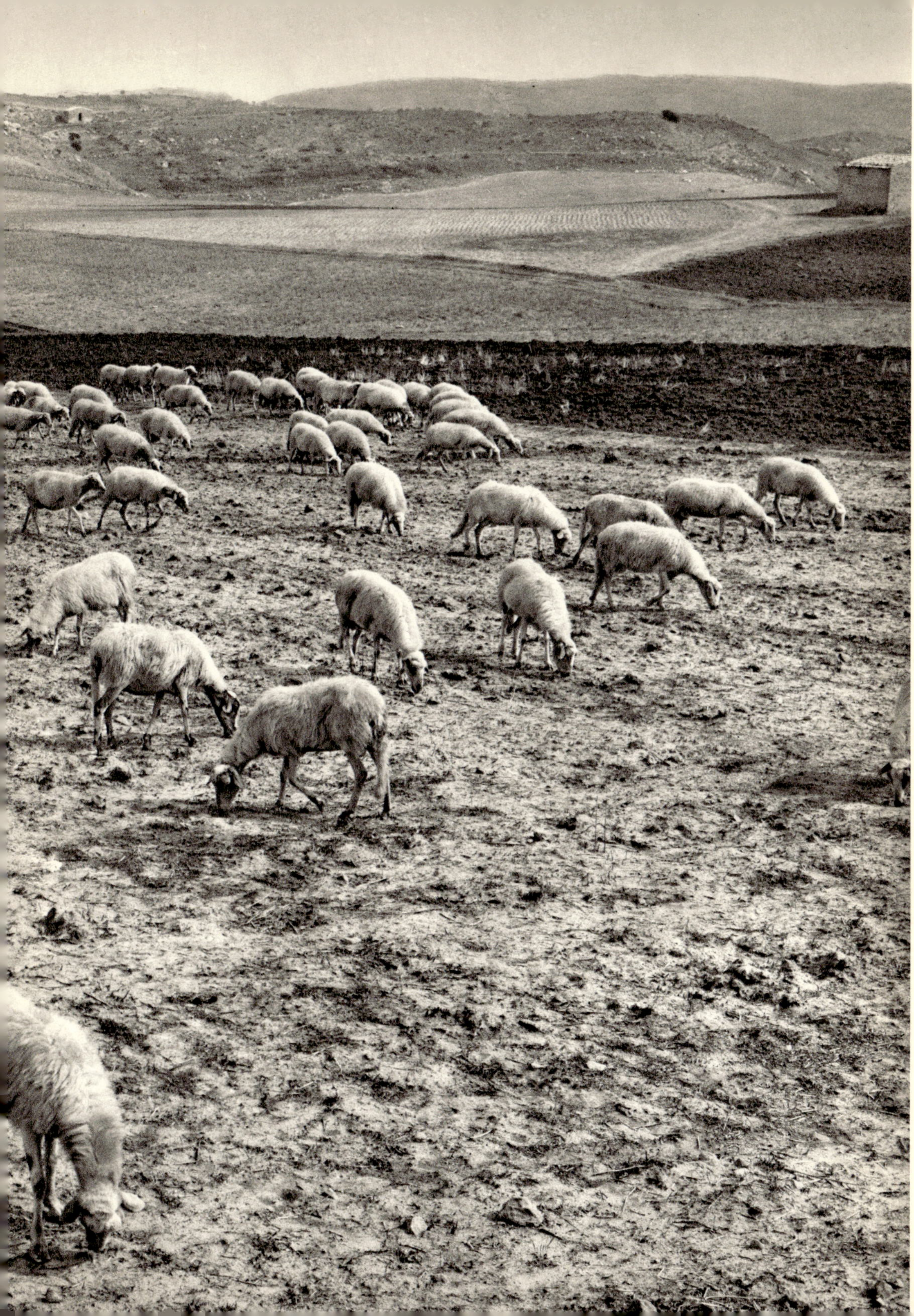

III

12

113

114

115

116

117

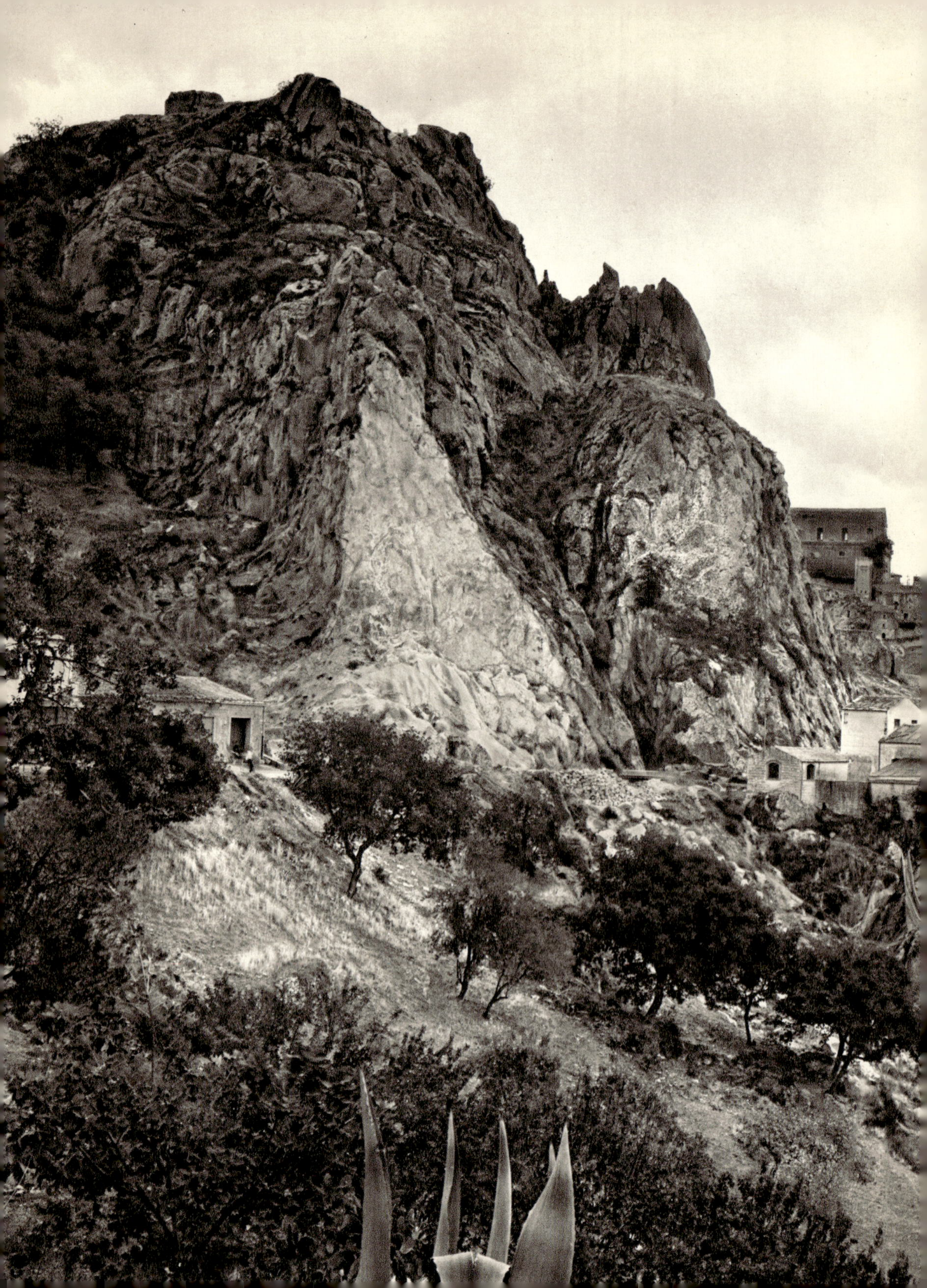

118

119

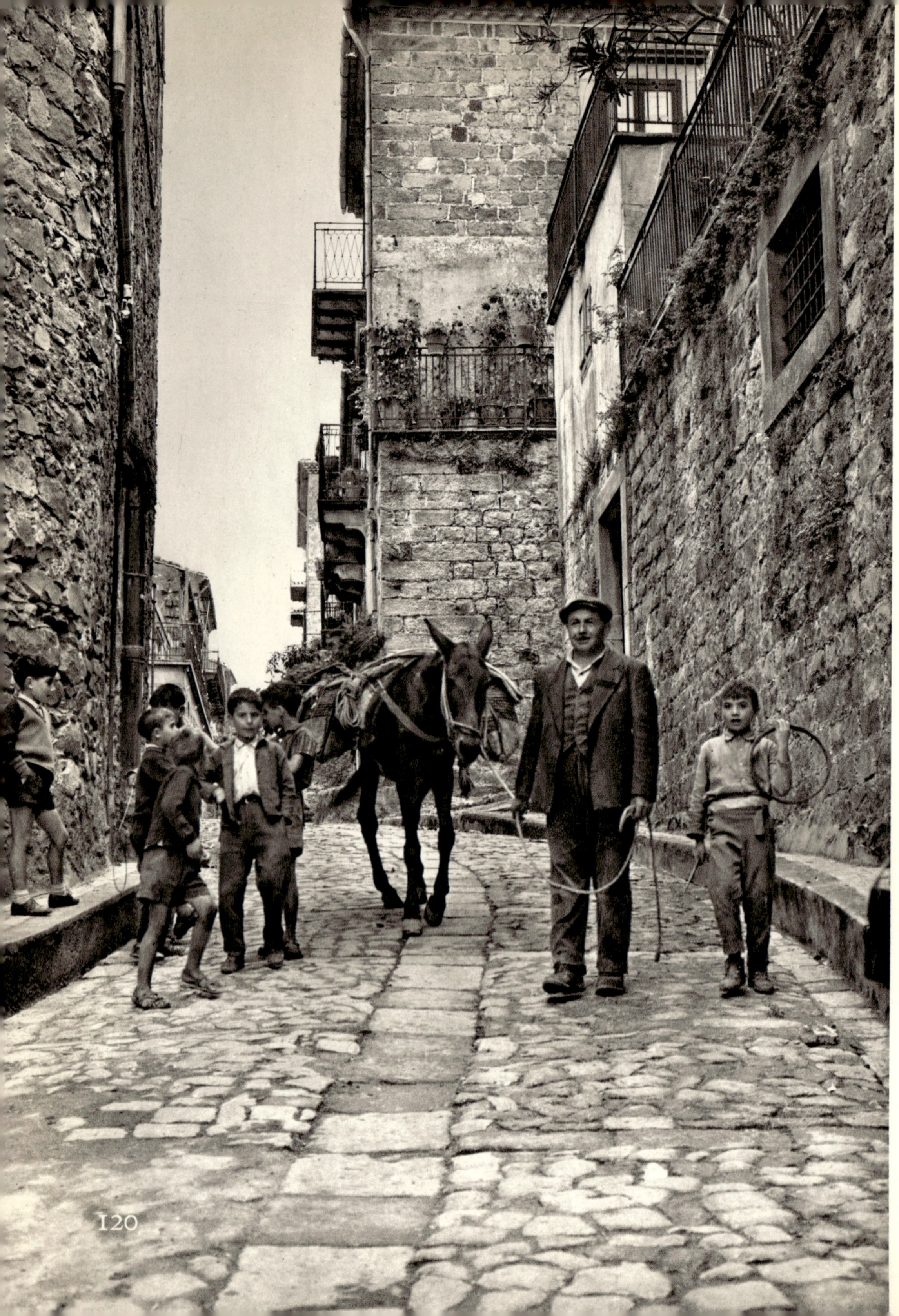

You may be wondering why I take you all the way along the coast as far as Syracuse and then bring you back westwards into Sicily's interior after 250 miles of winding roads. Besides, you have perhaps already been into the interior, either by leaving out Erice and Trapani and going direct to Segesta and Castelvetrano via Salemi, or by exploring the road connecting Palermo and Agrigento via Piana degli Albanesi and Corleone. If so, you will have seen one part of the interior, impressive certainly, but often bare and desolate, burnt by the sun which Visconti has shown so brilliantly in the sequences of his film devoted to the 'Leopard's' summer journey.

I would like to show you a different interior, which has its desolate zones too but also has forests and vast expanses of corn-fields, as becomes the chosen country of the earth goddesses Demeter and Persephone (the Roman Ceres and Proserpine).

The myth goes like this. Persephone disappeared one day when she was gathering flowers on the banks of the Lake of Pergusa. She had been carried off by one of her uncles, Hades, who took her to his grim abode and married her without informing Zeus, her brother (and head of the family!) or even his sister and mother-in-law, Demeter. Demeter was desperate and began to scour the land (which had just emerged and was in her care) looking for her child, in a chariot drawn by winged serpents. Finding nothing on earth, she felt she must search in the sea or down in the underworld, in the realms, that is, of her brothers Poseidon and Hades; but didn't know how to enter either. The only other direction being upwards, she went up to heaven and flung herself in tears on the knees of Zeus.

The king of the gods knew all about it. He was tempted, in fact, to deal severely with Hades, who had behaved like a brute, contracting marriage without asking his august permission, causing a family quarrel and even the ordeal Zeus hated most, a woman making a scene. However, being sensible and realistic, he did not care to

13

exploit his authority over his brothers, who were often insubordinate and quite capable of rejecting it. He preferred negotiation to war and succeeded in getting a compromise accepted: Persephone would spend one half of the year in the underworld with her husband and the other half on the surface, in the woody domains her mother possessed in the interior of Sicily.

Such is the legend by which the Greeks explained the rhythm of the seasons, the annual death and resurrection of nature. It must have pleased them too because it illustrated the cunning and wisdom of their god, who, when obliged to arbitrate in history's first conflict between mother-in-law and son-in-law, managed to find a compromise which many families might feel inspired to adopt. The legend was dear to the Greeks of Sicily above all, because Demeter and Persephone had adopted their fertile country. Hence their cult of these heroines of family affection, 'kindly goddesses' *par excellence*, sovereigns of the earth who were propitious for good harvests. Hence the sanctuaries of the 'chthonic divinities' you have seen, notably at Agrigento, hence the terracotta votive statues to be seen in such numbers on the shelves of the National Museum at Palermo; the archaic, Hellenistic and Roman marbles representing the mother and daughter sowing abundance or playing with one of their winged serpents.

They will not be the ones to welcome you, however, when you leave the rich area round Syracuse and begin to enter the interior, climbing the slopes of the Hyblaean Hills. You are more in the realms of Hades, and the country indeed has many 'cities of the dead'. A brief detour to the right would bring you out to a deep gorge, on the other side of which is the cliff of Pantalica, pitted all over by rock-cut Sikelian tombs.

You will be glad to reach Palazzolo Acreide and find there a pretty baroque town, rebuilt, after the earthquake, in the same style as Noto. The façade of San Paolo, convex and with a central tower, is unusual in having a portico in front, outside the church. The Corso Vittorio Emmanuele is a fine main street lined with fine buildings, including a church which contains a Madonna by Laurana; it leads to the ruins of ancient Akrae, the first colony of Syracuse. Nothing is left of this except some Hellenistic remains: a well-preserved small theatre, modest shrines in the form of grottos, and the *santoni*, rock-cut sculptures of rough workmanship, generally representing Demeter, framed in square dormer windows like funeral portraits at Palmyra.

The road to Caltagirone goes further into the realms of Hades. Following the crest of the Hyblaean Hills, it overlooks a very rugged landscape of mountains and ravines, which the gigantic, serene cone of Etna reduces to their modest proportions. It crosses Vizzini, dear to the novelist Giovanni Verga; Grammichele, with its strictly hexagonal plan; and other villages grey as the stone and always perched on some hill-top. The word 'perched' is not very satisfactory, for it evokes a bird standing on the end of a branch, whereas the villages in question are on the contrary crouched on their hill-tops like a bird brooding over its nest. The Italian past participle *appollaiato* gives the right image: it means perched like a hen, feet bent beneath the mass of feathers.

Caltagirone is a big town of 50,000 inhabitants, the first you have met with the prefix *calta* or *calata*, frequent in Sicily, derived from the Arab kal'at, a fortress. Ravaged by the earthquake (and also by the air-raids of 1943), it is naturally baroque, but more remarkable for its palaces than for its churches. It makes an impression of liveliness which is due to its ceramics industry. This gave the Arabs their blue-tiled patios, and in the baroque period ceramics were used as a main item in architecture. The result is charming in details like the balcony of the Ventimiglia house; it is less acceptable in a whole façade such as that of San Pietro, which is covered in cold-coloured tiles.

The town has perhaps another claim to glory. It was the cradle of the Christian Democrats, the political party which has been a main part of the government of Italy since the end of the war. The party's founder, Father Luigi Sturzo, was born here, and so was his disciple, Mario Scelba, one of de Gasperi's successors as prime minister. I only once saw the great Sturzo, when he had retired, old and sick, to a monastery in Rome. He was already thin and ascetic, I gather, in the period when he opposed the brawny Mussolini. Now his body seemed lost in the worn cassock, but the most striking thing about him was an aggressive nose, which would have left me with an impression of vigour even if he hadn't given me his ideas on politics. I listened admiringly, feeling that the old statesman must be a little sad that his party had come to power when he was too old to lead its government.

After Caltagirone the soil becomes richer, and there are more olive trees. You drive through wooded country, almost forests; and when, on entering Piazza Armerina, you turn sharp left for the Roman villa at Casale about four miles south west, you are soon in a shady, mossy ravine full of water.

Excavations of the villa were only started at the end of the last century, and it has won a good deal of renown for its 'Bikini girls', ten Roman athelete maidens wearing something very like modern bikinis. You may well have seen these in reproduction, but perhaps without knowing that the mosaic paving on which they disport themselves occupies only a few dozen square yards out of the 3,500 which have been excavated, and that it is not even considered one of the best mosaics.

You will realize this when you see the two major compositions; the Great Hunt, to which I shall return later, and the Labours of Hercules. Having become a god, and at last at rest, Hercules contemplates his life's work, the result of his 'labours': monstrous corpses and corpse-like monsters; in the skies are the Titans whom he has pierced with his poisoned arrows, their formidable muscles writhing in convulsions worthy of Michelangelo's brush.

There are twenty other compositions less important than these, yet finer and better preserved than the Bikini girls: above all, the delightful Small Hunt; the family scenes at the baths; the games of children and Cupids, fishing, hunting, gathering grapes and racing in chariots drawn by bustards and partridges; the quarrel of Eros and Pan; not forgetting, in one of the bedrooms, the only 'risqué' picture discovered in the villa.

In some of the passages and under the porches of peristyles you will also see nonrepresentational mosaics, based on geometrical patterns, traceries, volutes and crowns, sometimes framing small subjects or portraits of animals; the whole thing as harmonious in pattern and colour as a Persian carpet.

You may wonder who on earth the man was, so cultured, wealthy and yet secretive that he kept these marvels in a ravine in Sicily's interior. No doubt the work's merit goes back to the architect, but you also get the sense of a master's mind and eye; all the villa's characteristics seem somehow to have a personal significance.

First the situation: it is certainly out-of-the-way, but it has a great deal of game (therefore good for hunting) and it is near a big Roman road. Then there is the plan. At first sight this seems confused, but in fact it is remarkably well composed so as to use the slope of the ground and to present on three levels the three main parts of the whole: on the left the baths, on the right the representational rooms, in the centre the large peristyle with colonnades leading off to the basilica, the bedrooms and the open sitting-rooms. Finally the decoration: this must have included frescoes on the walls, levelled out today, and statues of which fragments have been found—of good Greek quality. Only the mosaics survive and, although one may criticise their construction, already slightly decadent, and their tendency to fussiness of detail, they still form the most remarkable collection the Ancients have left us in this art-form; while their colours, especially the reds and the greens with a bluish tinge, are a joy to the eye.

There is no sure evidence on which we can identify for sure this 'squire' of genius. Mr Gino Gentile, who has done so much to excavate, restore and protect the villa, thinks with most other archaeologists that it was a high personage who lived at the end of the 3rd or beginning of the 4th century A.D., perhaps even one of the emperors— Maximianus Herculius, whom Diocletian made his first co-emperor. I have always been fascinated by Diocletian, and by his decision, when he had more or less restored the Empire, to give it up and share it, under conditions which inevitably led to anarchy and civil war. So I should like to have followed Mr Gentile and taken the old man who directs the Great Hunt, and seems to represent the villa's owner, for the august Maximianus; the sacrificer in the Small Hunt for the Emperor Constantius Chlorus, with his son Constantine at his side.

I have always heard it said that Maximianus was a barbarian from Pannonia, a vain upstart and boorish soldier, used by Diocletian, who was more politician than general, to bludgeon his enemies. He was also a restless spirit, as he proved by trying to return to the throne several years after having abdicated together with Diocletian. Even if we assume that he was a great hunter, would such a man have confined himself in such a remote spot and been content with a relatively modest residence compared to the gigantic palace at Salona to which Diocletian had retired? Would he have been cultured enough to conceive this masterpiece? And wouldn't he, in the mosaic pavements, have insisted on subjects more in keeping with his vanity?

T'Serstevens is against the majority opinion. Struck by the importance given in the mosaics to wild beasts and the hunt, notably the piece of the Great Hunt illustrating the capture of live animals and their embarkment on two big ships, he has had the idea that the owner of the villa was one of the Romanised Berbers who trafficked in wild beasts for the circus games. Here, then, was a sort of Hagenbeck who after making his fortune had retired into a remote part of the country with plenty of game, where he hoped to have some chance of being forgotten by the Treasury and of getting some good shooting.

If he *is* the old gentleman of the Great Hunt, the villa-owner is certainly the Berber type, while his acolytes seem to be mostly Africans, more or less dark-skinned, and the driver of the ox-cart even looks a bit like Haile Selassi. For my part, when I saw the mosaics here, I was reminded at once of those in North Africa. Having visited the houses, or what is left of them, of the Romanised Berbers at Leptis Magna, Sabrata and Zliten, I knew what luxury they were capable of. Moreover, in the heart of the Tripolitanian Desert, in the extraordinary site of Ghirza, I had seen rising from the *hamada* the remains left by these traffickers in gold, slaves and wild beasts: their fortified foreign trading stations, and their tombs, beside which most of those lining the Appian way would cut a poor figure.

Yet I could not help feeling that the Casale Villa must be on a higher rung of the ladder of civilization. Surely historians should be able to unearth some 3rd-century Pliny the Younger, Roman citizen, of course, but one who had lived in Africa, infinitely rich and cultured, a great huntsman as well; who, to escape the troubles caused by Diocletian's inexplicable resignation, had retired from the world to this elegant retreat.

Piazza Armerina itself is quite a lively and attractive place, set on the customary hill-top and dominated by its domed cathedral, which you reach after passing several fine baroque buildings. One thing in the town you should certainly see is the monument to a certain General Cascino, which t'Serstevens describes thus: 'On a lofty rock stands a general who must have been father of a large family; for all his sons, of the same height, dressed as soldiers and cast in bronze in the same mould, are crawling up the slope of a dummy trench.'

Twelve miles past Piazza Armerina you reach a cross-roads. If you keep straight on, you can go to Caltanisetta, capital of its province. I remember little of it except a fine palace (Moncada) and a baroque cathedral. But the town has a nice situation, and it is known for its Maundy Thursday procession, during which the inhabitants of the different districts carry sculptures, representing the mysteries of the Passion, in Spanish fashion.

So let us return to that cross-roads and turn north. This is still the country of Demeter, but the red patches from the sulphur mines show that Hades is not far away. He (or it) is even more in evidence at the Lake of Pergusa, round, opaque, reddish, noxious, with once wooded banks which have now been cleared to build a motor racing track. A little depressing, so drive on in the direction of the isolated tabular mass which towers so high above the region that you see it six miles away, very intriguing in the jagged, scalloped outline of its ridge.

Is it a town perched up there? Yes, this is Enna, formerly Castrogiovanni. Its position on such an extravagant acropolis did not stop it being taken—after endless sieges, admittedly—by the Romans, the Arabs and the Normans. Frederick II liked its dry, pure air. It was ravaged once more, let us hope for the last time, in 1943.

It contains some good buildings, palaces and churches: the Cathedral, the Tower of Frederick II, the so-called Lombard Castle, also built by Frederick. This last is set on a spur, the far point of which is still today called the Rock of Ceres. In the Roman age it carried a colossal statue of the kindly earth-goddess. Frederick's Tower again shows his liking for octagonal forms after he had seen the Mosque of Omar at Jerusalem. Of the churches some are baroque, some are mediaeval campaniles; the Cathedral is early 14th-century, badly damaged by fire in the 15th, and restored largely in the 16th.

But Enna's essential virtue is to offer the widest panorama in Sicily, some twenty-five miles all round—the whole centre of the island. Fairly near, on the other side of a precipitous gorge, is the twin town of Calascibetta, grey at the top of its red cliff. Further on there are the three mountain ranges diverging from this common starting-point like the three legs of the Sicilian coat of arms; northwards the Nebrodi, north-westwards the Madonie, southwards the Ereian Hills; and right in the back, due east, is tutelary Etna. Callimachus called Enna the navel of Sicily, and looking at the map you can see what he meant.

At the foot of Enna you find the main road from Palermo to Catania, which soon leads you by way of wild gorges to Leonforte. Here you will see a baroque fountain which is considered the finest in Sicily and which to my mind is one of the finest in the world. From Leonforte you drive down towards Agira, home of the greatest historian Sicily has produced, Diodorus. By a brief detour you can obtain from the ridge-town of Centuripe an immense and unusual view on to Etna, the plain of Simeto and the Ionian Sea. Finally, at Adrano, you reach the 'round-Etna' road which descends towards Catania.

If you have time, I would advise you to spend the night at Piazza Armerina or Enna, and then turn left coming out of Leonforte, on to an impressive road along the edge of precipices. Before tackling the hill leading to Nicosia, turn left again, on to a detour of two and a half miles, to a village called Sperlinga. If you feel up to climbing the colossal slab of stone on the top of its small ruined fortress, you will read the inscription

'Quod Sicullis placuit sola Sperlinga negavit.'

When the rest of the island decided on the 'Sicilian Vespers', only Sperlinga refused to be associated in the rising and gave asylum to the French.

Possibly this is why some traces of French survive in the local dialect; although a more likely reason is that the capital of the region, Nicosia, was repopulated in the Middle Ages by immigrants from North Italy and Piedmont. In the era of Greek domination the town was called Herbita, though nobody really knows how it came by its Greek, in fact Cypriot name. It was much favoured by Frederick II, who may have christened it because of something about its situation that reminded him of Thessaly. When you go up towards it from the east, amidst a wood of umbrella pines, you suddenly see two great sugar-lumps of limestone, which are similar to the Meteorai in Thessaly.

One of these cliffs has a castle on it, the other a church; but they nearly proved fatal to the town in 1757, when they collapsed on to it in a landslide. The result is that Nicosia was largely rebuilt in the 18th century, and it has pleasing, if slightly over-elaborate, baroque buildings. The landslide spared the Cathedral, however, with its Gothic campanile and lateral portico. So here is a small Sicilian town with a Greek name, with a splendid situation, where you hear bits of French in the dialect, and where a small Gothic complex is surrounded by buildings in the rococo style. Altogether an unusual place, and I don't think you will regret your detour to Nicosia.

121. *Arrival at Catania.*
122. *Catania. Former Benedictine Monastery, now a school.*
123. *Catania. Biscari Palace.*
124. *Taormina. Public Gardens.*
125, 126. *Taormina. Greek Theatre.*
127. *Taormina. Marionette and painted panels from an antiquary's front.*

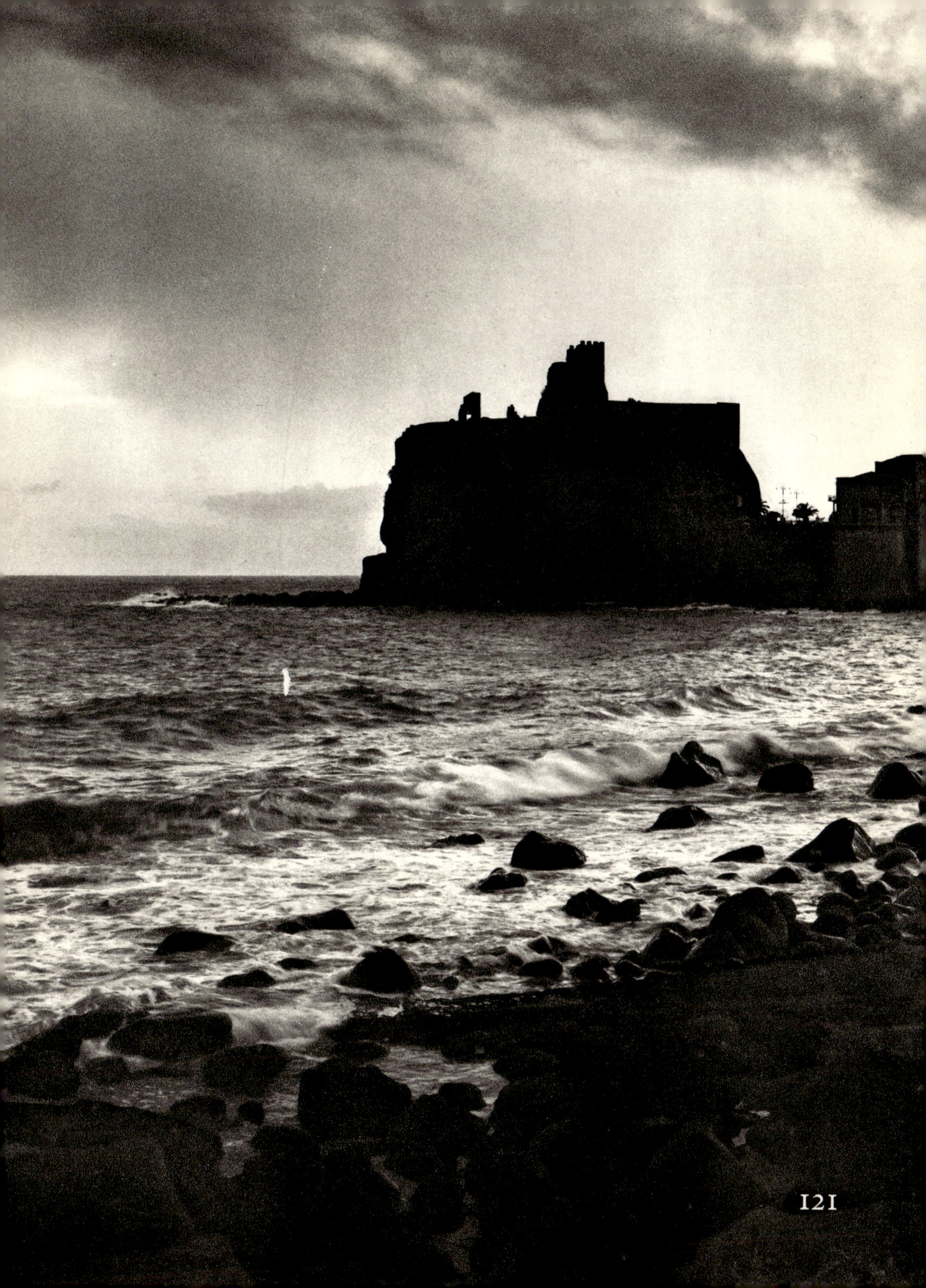

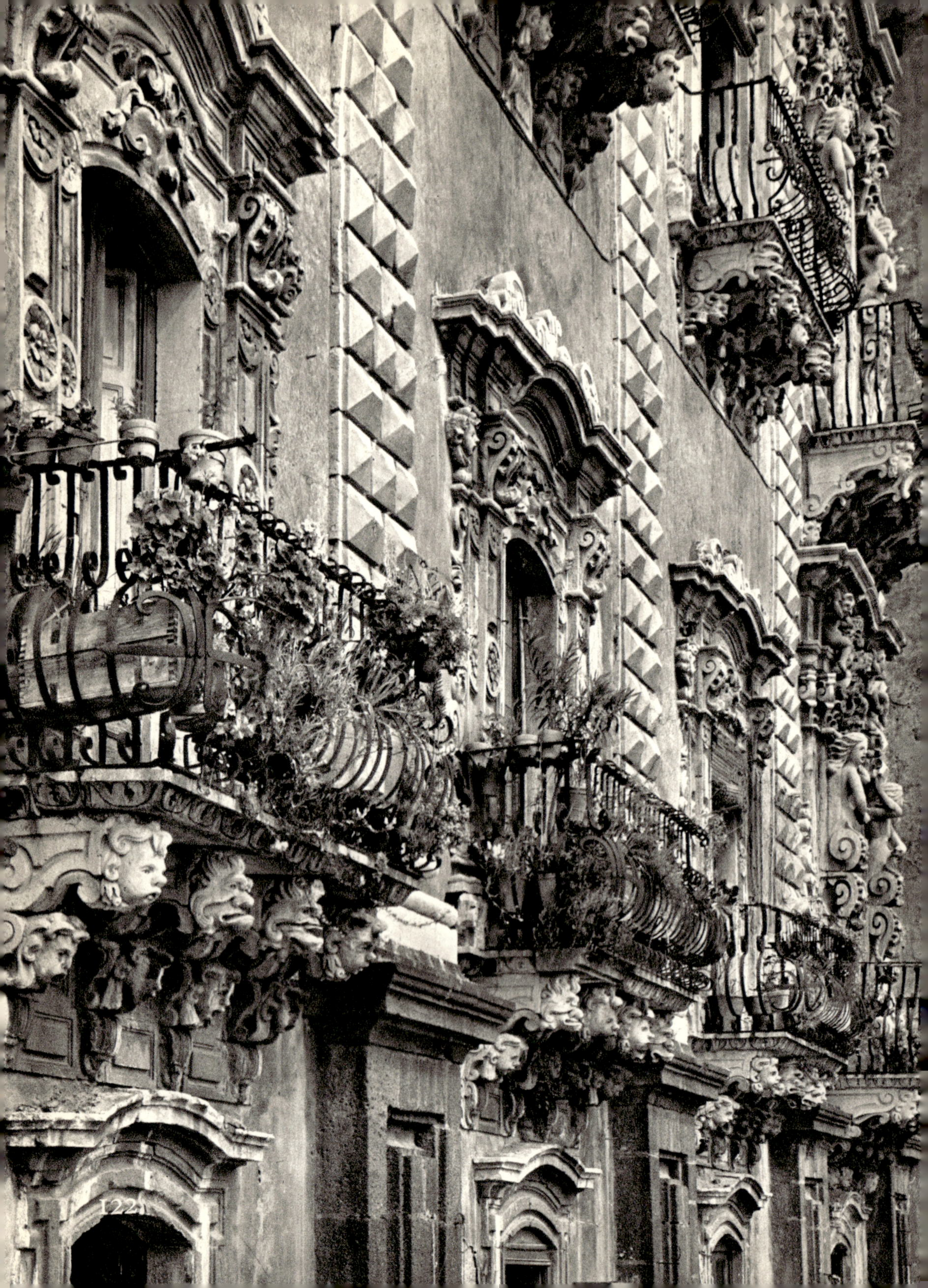

122

123

124

125

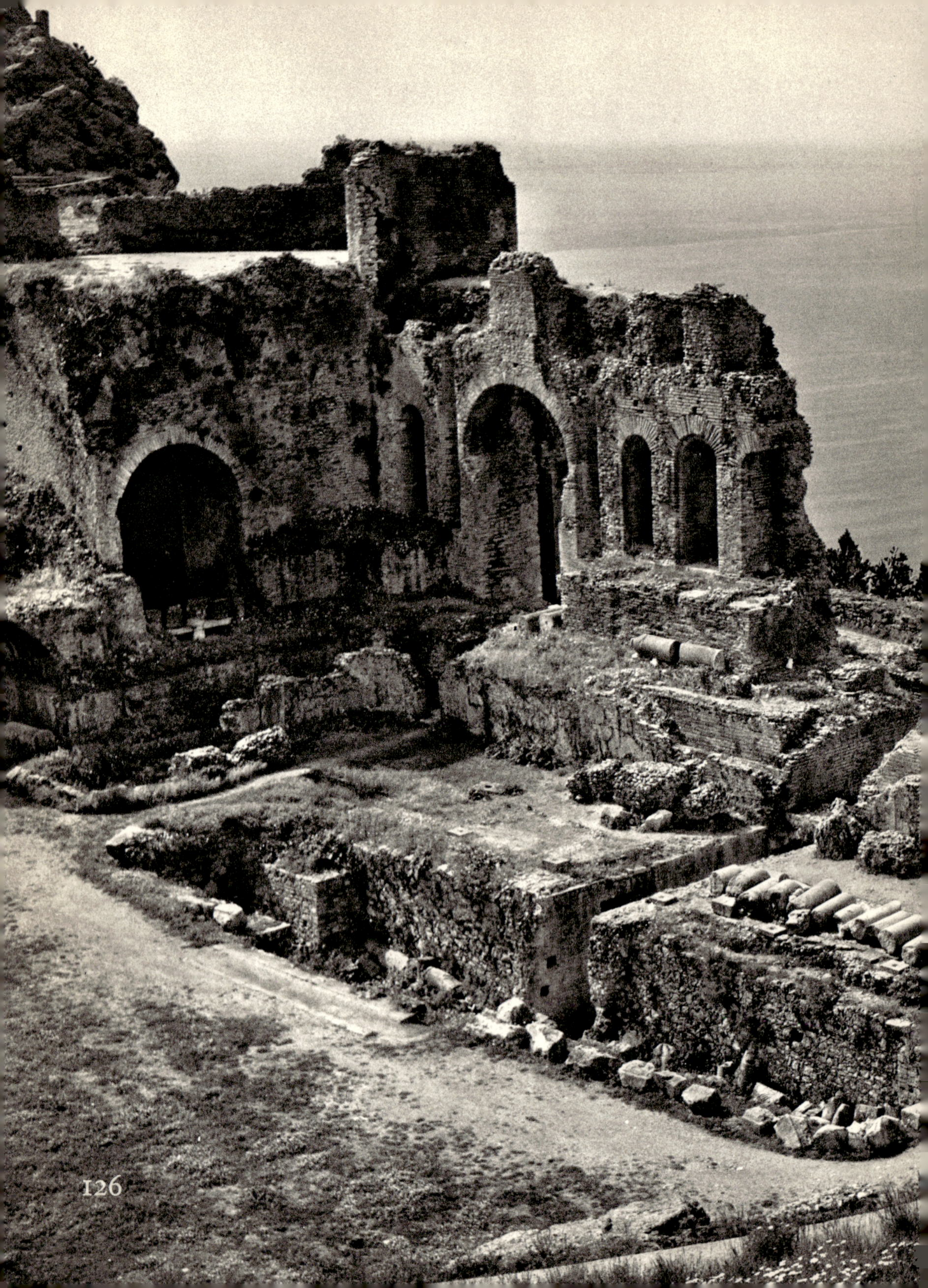

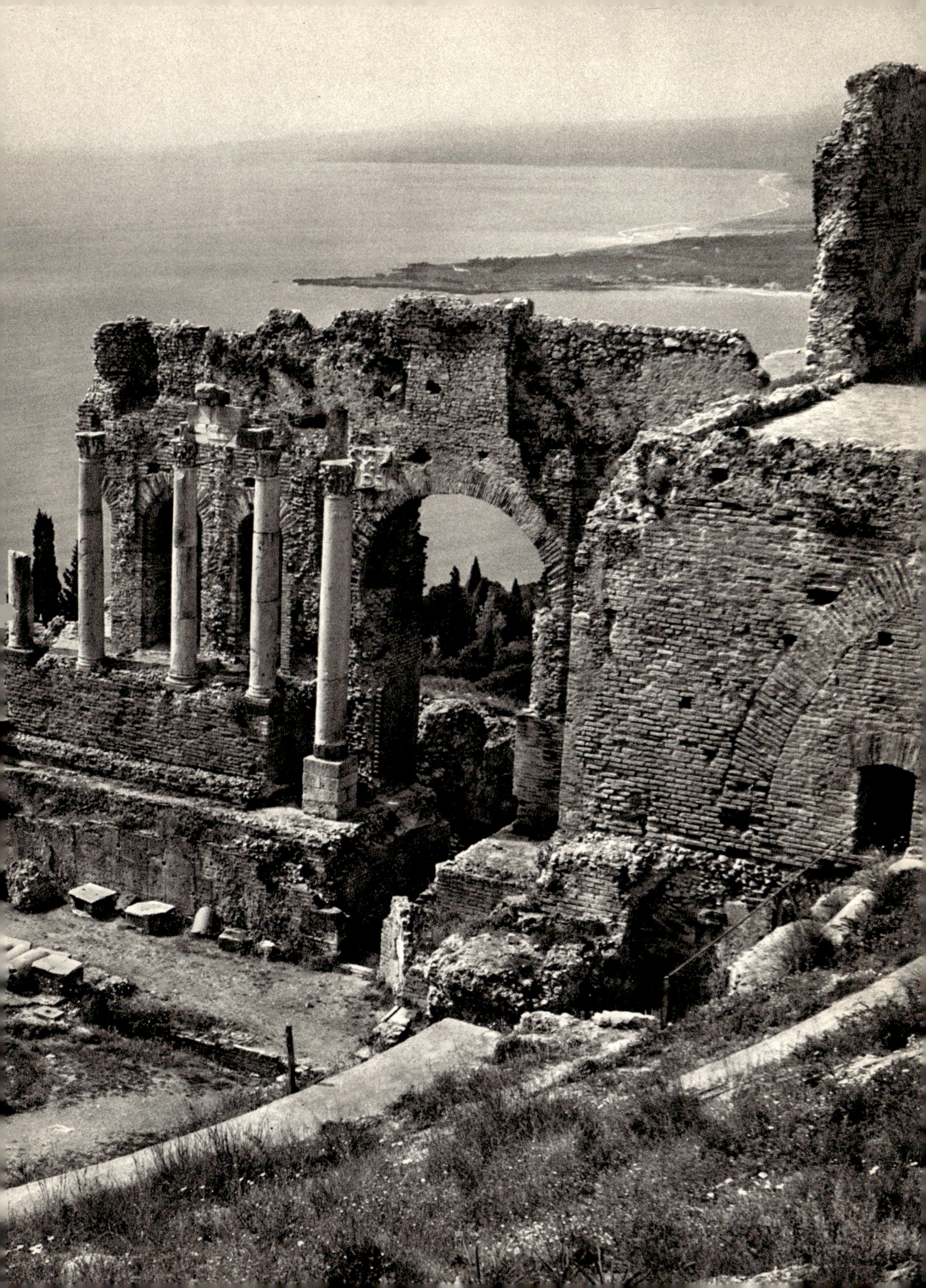

127

CATANIA AND ETNA — TAORMINA

CATANIA has nearly as large a population as Palermo, and makes an equally strong impression of being a town in full development, to judge merely by the building works in progress there. It is developing fast in other economic sectors as well, especially the engineering, canning and chemical industries. It was lucky to become the main town in a region which from Sicily's earliest days has always been the most active and the richest agriculturally. But nowadays it has another trump card, for oil and natural gas have been discovered there; so Catania has become its economic and financial centre.

You can feel that it is growing richer at all levels of society. There are more cars than at Palermo; and the last time I passed through it, I was struck by the new districts I saw, above all by the bold and large-scale replanning works to open up and modernise the old districts between the station and the centre.

Catania was founded in 729 B.C. by Sicily's first Greek colonists, from Chalcis, who settled a few years before at Naxos near Taormina; since then, till the air-raids in 1943, its history has been a succession of reconstructions following political or volcanic catastrophes. It was destroyed by Hieron and by Dionysius of Syracuse, then by the Vandals and by the Saracens. It was even more badly damaged by the eruptions of Etna in 121 B.C. and 1669, and by the earthquakes of 1169 and 1693. Yet although it has led revolts against various occupying powers and has in its cathedral the proud inscription—'Do not offend the city of St Agatha, for she is capable of avenging injuries'—Catania seems naturally pacific.

In classical times the poet Stesichorus and the philosopher Xenophanes decided it was a peaceful place to settle; and it has indeed been a leading city intellectually as well as economically. In the Middle Ages the Aragonese sovereigns endowed a university there, which has remained lively and prosperous ever since. The composer Bellini was born in Catania (in 1801) and several well-known novelists were born or have lived there. One is Giovanni Verga, who promoted realism in Italy at the period when Zola was doing so in France. Another is De Roberto, author of *The Viceroys*, which foreshadows *The Leopard*; and in recent times there is Vitaliano Brancati.

The first thing you will want to see is the most highly considered personality in Catania—its symbol, which adorns its coat of arms. This is the elephant of the Elephant Fountain, in the town's traditional centre, the Cathedral Square. Constructed by Vaccarini (in 1736) out of an antique elephant in black lava, he perches on a fountain and carries on his back a small Egyptian obelisk. He is not, admittedly, as graceful as Bernini's elephant in Rome's Minerva Square. Produced in the late Roman period, he is rather crude and heavy; and the white marble saddle-cloth makes him look like a negro in a shirt. Still, with his mocking eye and poised trunk, he clearly finds it amusing to look down on the town's life.

Next you must pay your homage to another equally important personality, St Agatha, patroness of Catania, in the Cathedral. Of the former romanesque building the earthquake of 1693 has only left three apses. The rest has been reconstructed, and the façade, Vaccarini's work, of course, is a baroque which shows the influence of Borromini. I do not myself like it so much as the style Gagliardi favoured in Noto and its surroundings, which I find much more elegant and personal.

There are things to see in all directions from the Cathedral Square. First go east on the Via Vittorio Emanuele, passing the concave façade of St Agatha's Convent, to the fine circular courtyard of the Cutelli College (also Vaccarini's work); then south, through the Porta Uzeda, which leads to the port and has handsome baroque buildings in the Archbishop's Palace and the Palazzo Biscari. Here in the 18th century Ignazio Paterno Castello, Prince of Biscari, amassed a famous collection of antiques which delighted Goethe. You can see them if you turn west from the square and visit the Ursino Castle, a typical fortress of Frederick II, which houses the museum. From here take a look at the theatre, more Roman than Greek, and its annex, the Odeon, used for 'intimate performances'—it has only 1200 seats!

Returning to the Square, you can now set out on to Catania's Oxford Street, the Via Etnea, which runs dead straight towards the cone of Etna. It is a lively street, with many pretty girls, Milanese business men, Sicilian priests, sitting outside at café tables; rich stores; handsome baroque façades, the Town Hall, the University, the San Giuliano Palace, the Collegiate Church.

Soon you turn left into the Via Antonio di San Giuliano, and on your left again you can admire a unique baroque complex: the Via dei Crociferi, well-framed by the Arch of San Benedetto which spans it, and lined by the façades and railings of the Churches of San Giuliano, the Jesuits and San Benedetto. Then you come to the semicircular Piazza Dante, and are confronted by the strange sight of the Church of San Nicolo.

It is apparently the largest church in Sicily, and its façade is unfinished, showing the enormous stumps of eight gigantic columns. There are many other stumps of columns in Sicily, starting with those of the Doric temples—which are ruins, however;

whereas these are simply unfinished, like primitive works of art or sketches by artists who lacked the inspiration to complete them. That is why I find them disconcerting and rather ugly.

Happily, you will find beauty right beside them in the Benedictine Monastery, which has become a school. Its courtyards are luxuriant gardens with porticos across them. Its façade, to my mind at least, is a masterpiece of Spanish-Jesuit baroque. Under a strong cornice, supported by pilasters worked in nail-heads, there are tiers of windows with elaborate frames and portly balconies, mostly with flowers in them. Overloaded perhaps, but what style and gaiety!

Returning to the Via Etnea, you will perhaps end your visit by relaxing in the Gardens of the Bellini Villa (the composer's birthplace). Catania is very proud of these gardens, and they are delightful. Bellini is in evidence here through his operas, the titles of which are given on the borders, in capitals made from geraniums and begonias. You may find this a little excessive for a composer who, although of great talent, did not produce a great volume of work before he died prematurely. But think what he might have produced had he lived—considering that Chopin admired him so much he wished to be buried near him.

Amidst the flowers of these gardens in the Catania streets enlivened by pretty faces and baroque buildings, among new blocks of flats and the most modern factories, you will not think for a moment that all this prosperity might be swept away. It is hard to imagine that less than three centuries ago torrents of lava filled the moats of the Ursino Castle.

Yet the giant Etna is very close and still smoking, 'heaven's column, father of eternal snows, whose chasm vomits forth the purest sources of inaccessible fire' (Pindar). It is at the end of the Via Etnea, in fact. If you keep straight ahead along it, you are on a reasonable road for climbing its flank to a point over 8,000 feet up, where there are hotels, restaurants and guides. From here you can apparently reach the crater in four hours' climb.

I say 'apparently', for I have never been up to the top, although I have been all the way round, a drive which I recommend. You will be able to admire the mountain's lines from all points of the compass—never identical but always perfect. For ninety miles you will be driving along the successive or superimposed layers of lava which it has spewed up. There is an extraordinary contrast between those time has weathered to make its soil the most fertile in the world, bursting with human and vegetable life, and the more recent layers, thinly covered with some sparse broom, still raw, sinister, black like rivers of coal. Your road suddenly plunges into a dark cutting with a board saying '1923 lava' or '1929 lava'; in 1950 the crater disgorged a million cubic yards of it; and there on your left, behind that orange grove glittering with brilliant fruit, that friendly house with a garden of enormous yews cut in human form, above that nice, flower-decked service station, in a week or a month a black wall with incandescent gleams might rise and advance inexorably.

Leaving Catania on the Taormina road, you start your round tour of Etna keeping by the coast, in a region celebrated in the Odyssey. Aci Castello was perhaps the peaceful cove where boats 'did not need to tie up to each other nor cast anchor nor secure their stern to the shore'. The rocks in the dark blue sea off Aci Trezza are those with which the blinded Cyclops, Polyphemus, vainly bombarded Odysseus's fleeing ship. The name of Acireale, which is set on a high lava cliff and has fine baroque churches, recalls the shepherd Acis: the same Polyphemus, when he was still sighted with his one eye, bombarded him too, but this time successfully, after catching him in the arms of Galatea.

Giarre, the next village along the road, gives the impression of being in the middle of exceptionally fertile country. But the village after that, Mascali, looks very new, and that is because it replaces an earlier village, a few hundred yeards further on, which was swallowed up by the eruption of 1929.

After Fiumefreddo you plunge inland. The road rises, passing Linguaglossa, and the country becomes rugged amidst the lava outflow of 1923. Randazzo appears next, finely situated, forming an interesting Gothic complex; the Cathedral, the Campanile of San Martino, palaces, small streets with Gothic arches. But all this is built in black lava, and when the rain is washing the town, the very mud becomes decomposing black lava!

After Randazzo the scenery grows even grimmer. The road reaches about three thousand feet, and it is very cold. Instead of the meadows there are beech and chestnut woods. The sky and the view open out; you have 'rounded the cape'. First you have wide vistas on the side opposite Etna, over the Caronie range and the rich valley of Simeto.

Then you see the big town of Bronte, presented by Ferdinand III to Nelson, whose descendants have held on to it firmly and are evidently in no hurry to hand it over for agrarian reform. Consequently, although the peasants are very ready to grumble, you need not be too surprised to watch a Rolls Royce incongruously emerging round a corner.

Finally, you view Etna itself from a new angle. On its flanks there are a proliferation of monstrous pimples, cones and adventitious craters, yellow, red and black. In the eruption of 1669 one such cleft in the volcano was opened from the summit down to Nicolosi, sending down a vast flow of lava to overwhelm a large part of Catania.

Adrano was celebrated in classical times for its sacred dogs. A thousand of these were set to guard a temple against robbers, whom they tore to pieces, and to protect drunkards, whom they gently led back to their homes. The present town contains plenty of descendants of these intelligent animals, but nothing is left of their temple. You will, however, see some remains of a Greek wall; a handsome and well-planted avenue dominated by the square tower of a feudal castle; and the baroque but sober façade of the Santa Lucia Monastery. As you come nearer to the sea, the land grows more and more fertile again, and the gardens of orange trees multiply between the lava outflows. As a result Paterno, like Adrano, is a large agricultural town; it is set on a basalt cliff, and has a fine Gothic castle and church.

Your drive is coming to an end. You return to Catania by the Garibaldi Gate, an astonishing baroque construction, of alternating layers of black lava and white limestone. But before you reach it, stop once more to look at Etna. It is more beautiful seen from here than anywhere else. Its lines are as pure and satisfying as those of Fusi-Yama in Japanese paintings. Yet beneath its mass Enceladus the Titan of the legend suffers his torment still; and in the hope of reducing it he might at any moment writhe once more and make the volcano erupt.

I rather like Taormina. It may not be as wonderful a place as you have heard, but nor is it merely an over-praised, sophisticated resort favoured only by stupid tourists, dyspeptic old people and snobs. It is a small town of limited artistic interest, with no history or industry, which people either love or hate, generally depending on their mood and who they are with. I like it without being in raptures over it, and I hope you will like it too.

At any rate, and whatever its detractors may say, it is one of the most scenically beautiful spots in the world. You have admired Erice's wonderful view; Taormina has two such views, at least as sublime and entirely different from each other. The first, almost vertical, embraces a jagged collection of headlands, small islands and creeks, in a setting which might be that of a Japanese painting. The second extends over a vast distance, the Ionian Sea, an apparently endless coastline, and a whole province dominated by the mighty mass of Etna. The first is the view you get from the western district of Taormina, especially from the well-known palace built in the former Dominican Monastery, the second is the view you get from the Greek theatre.

This is, indeed, the theatre's main interest. It was no doubt Greek in origin, though from the Hellenistic era; but the Romans completely altered it, much more than they did with the one at Syracuse, to adapt it for the cruel games of gladiators and men pitted against wild beasts. It is imposing, all the same, and vast enough for you to go to the top of its tiers—which are incomplete—and contemplate in peace the view framed in a large gap right in the centre of the 'scena' back wall.

Suppose, however, there had not been this gap? The same question naturally comes to mind when you visit the theatres of Segesta and Syracuse? Why did the Greeks build their theatres on sites with magnificent views if these were going to be blocked by a back wall? If such a wall really existed, how could Thucydides have written that the Syracusans watched from the theatre their sailors fighting the Athenians in the harbour? If the wall was so necessary acoustically, as is claimed, how is it that at Epidaurus, where the wall has completely disappeared, from the topmost row of the colossal auditorium one can still hear an attendant tearing up a piece of paper right down in the middle of the orchestra? In fact, it was the Romans who erected these walls up to the level of the highest row. The Greeks, more artistic, tried to preserve for their audiences' benefit the view which had made them choose their theatre sites; so they confined themselves to smaller back walls. The one at Taormina, therefore, seems to me to be largely a Roman addition.

Because this theatre is the biggest in Sicily after the one at Syracuse, it does not mean that Taormina was an important place in classical times; although it was certainly very ancient, for traces have been discovered of a Sikelian village. If you reverse the syllables of its name, you can reach 'Minotaur', which has made some scholars suggest that it was founded by the Cretans in the Minoan age. At any rate, it is established to have been an extension, and a place of refuge, for the first Greek colonists who settled in Sicily—at Naxos. You can see the site of this when you look towards Etna, on a flat peninsula which extends for some miles. But Taormina's history was afterwards that of so many other Greek towns and large villages, tossed between the great powers of Syracuse, Cathage and Rome. It began to feature a little more prominently with the Saracens and the Normans.

Its most interesting buildings are consequently in the mixture, now so familiar to you, of Arab, Byzantine and Norman styles: for instance, the Badia Vecchia (which has only its splendid tower left) and the small palaces of Corvaia and spectres of Santo Stefano. The façades of these are feudal, but they have beautiful Gothic double windows, frames, cornices and blind arches, made of that patchwork of white, black and grey stone—limestone, lava and pumice—which you saw on the apse of Monreale. The Cathedral, too, despite additions and restorations, is still in the style of a battlemented Norman church.

These buildings, interesting though they are, would not, of course, justify Taomina's reputation, and make very little impression compared to its views, which I have already described, and its gardens. Public gardens, hotel gardens, private gardens of villas hanging on the mountain side, above the town and below—they are the real commemorative monuments of the age when Taormina came into its own, when German, French and above all English tourists of the 19th century discovered its exceptional situation, decorating it according to their romantic and rural taste. In the 20th century it almost lost its glories as a result of pointless American bombing.

The tourists are thus an integral part of Taormina. Better accept them with indulgence and humour, remembering that after all you are a tourist yourself! Sit outside a café in the main square with its little Church of St Augustine and its 'Queen's Oak', and watch them pass in their strange accoutrements, pouncing on *carrozzelle* (small taxis), claiming their satisfaction in many languages. Mingle in their incessant flow, along streets and alleys which are too neat and clean, lined with shops in which astute shopkeepers display so-called antiques and local or pseudo-local souvenirs. Follow these tireless tourists to Castel Mola, a village which manages to be perched still higher than Taormina, and in a still more venturesome position with regard to the laws of gravity. Watch them proudly signing their names beneath those of many illustrious predecessors in the famous autograph book of the Caffè San Giorgio.

Perhaps you will feel irritated by the tourists with their little foibles and vanities, by the shopkeepers with their almost Oriental persistence, craftiness and haggling. But they are only one side of Taormina; the other side will amply make up for it, such moments as you attain in the view from the Greek theatre of the sun setting over Etna's snows.

128. *Outside the 'mussel park'.*
129, 130. *Messina at night (129 The Harbour; 130 Outside the station).*
131. *Cathedral façade. Left, detail from central door.*
132. *The Fountain of Orion, outside the Cathedral.*
133. *The astronomical Clock and the Cathedral.*
134. *Chevet of the Annunziata dei Catalani.*
135–140. MESSINA NATIONAL MUSEUM.
135, 136. *Altar-piece of the* Annunciation *by Antonello da Messina.*
137. *Christ on the cross (15th century).*
138. *Marble statue (Hellenistic type) representing Igea (3rd century B.C.; height 5 feet 8 inches).*
139. *Madonna and Child. Marble statue carved by Baboccio da Piperno (1st half of 5th century; height 6 feet).*
140. *Scylla by Montorsoli.*
141. *Ceiling of Cathedral.*

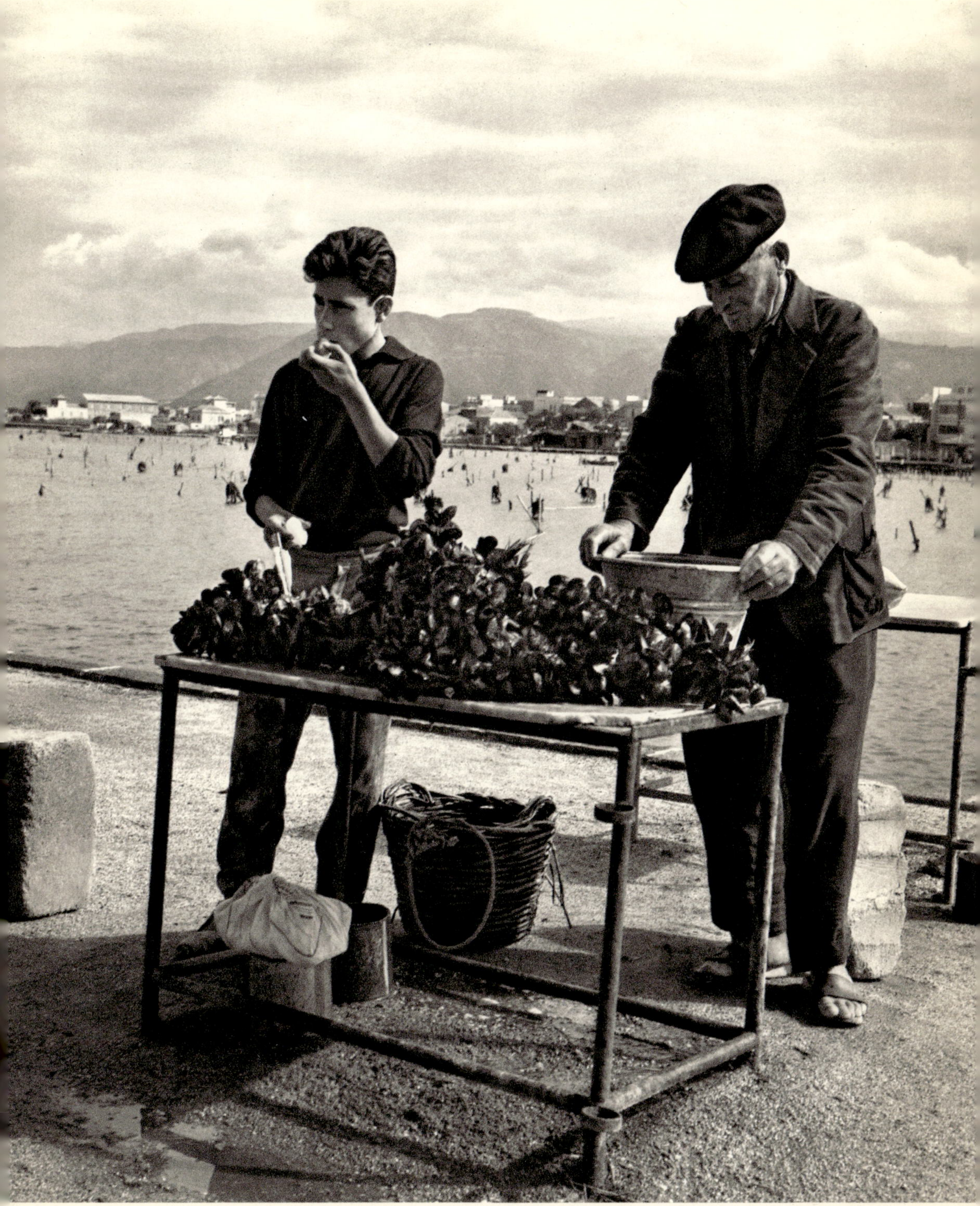

129

130

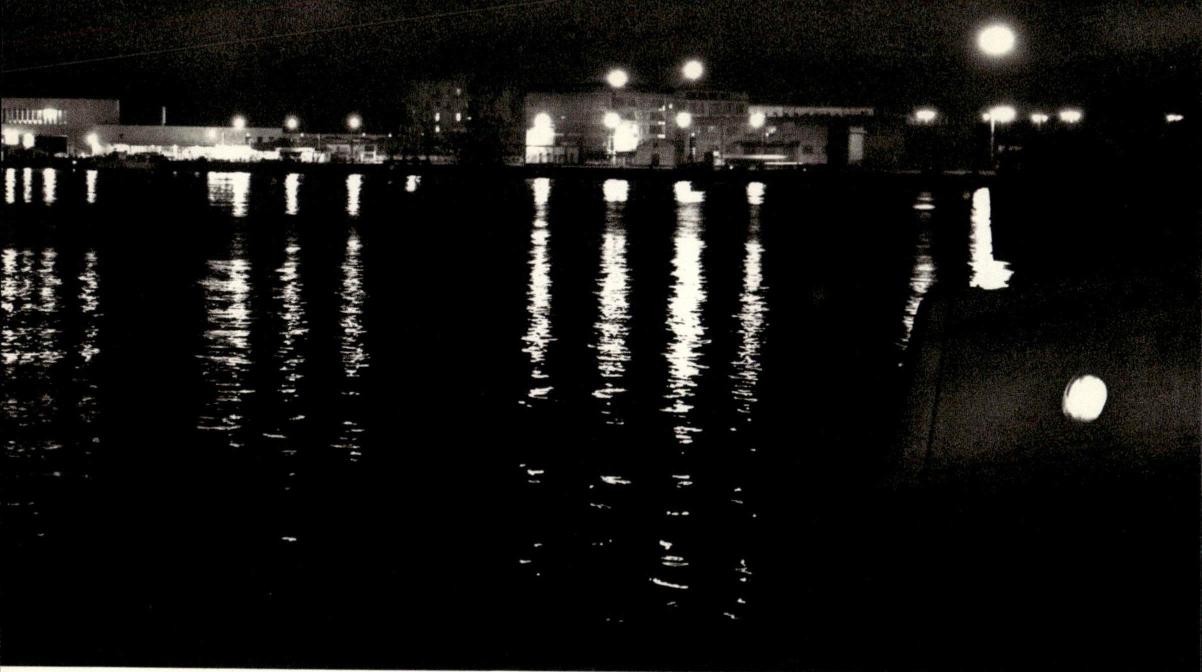
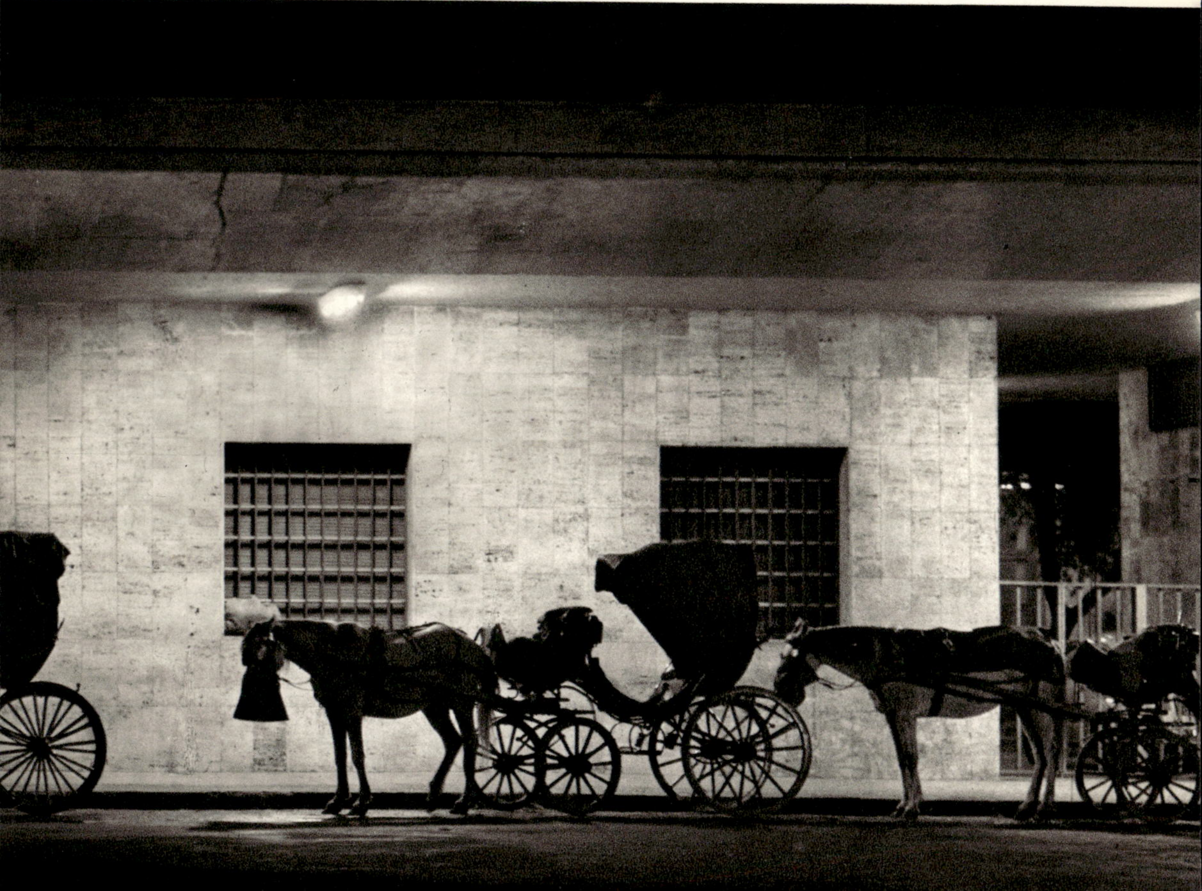

131

132

133

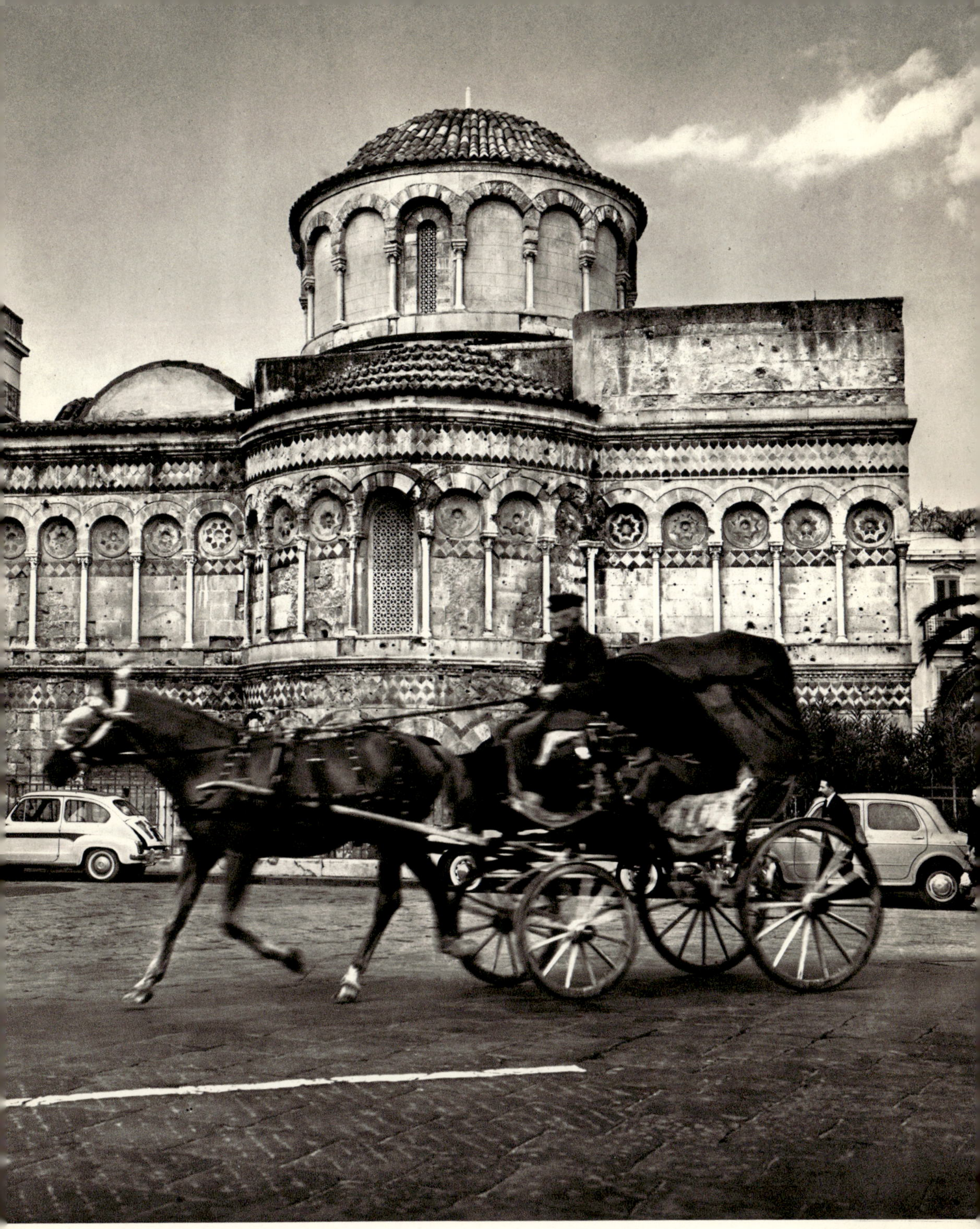

135

136

137   138   139

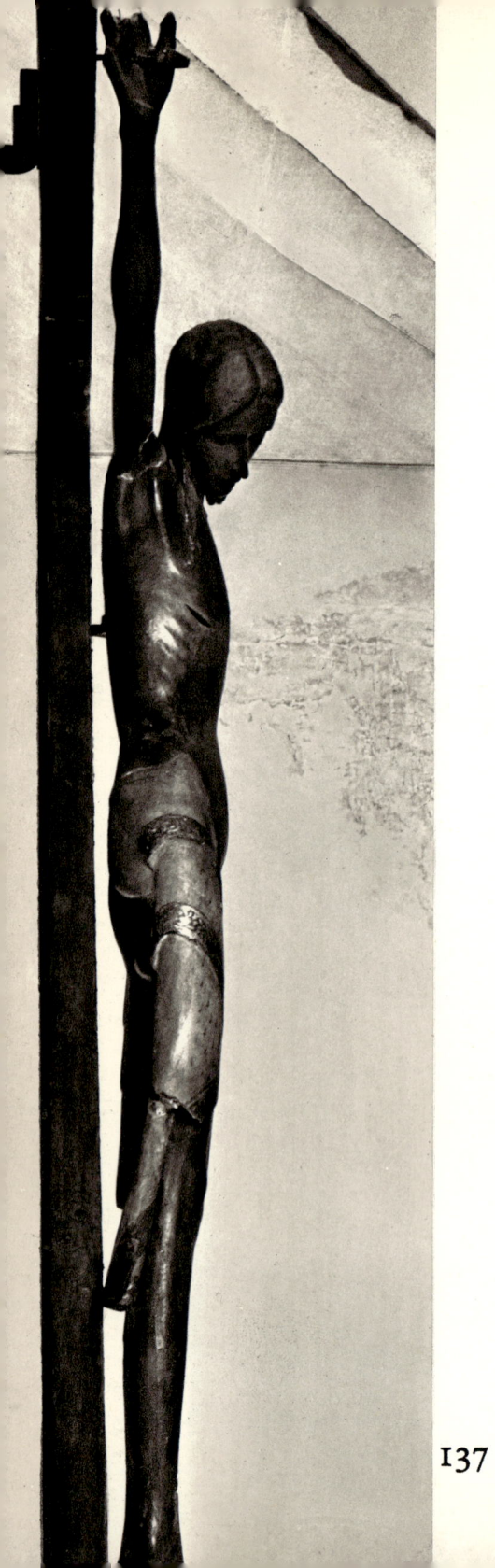

140

141

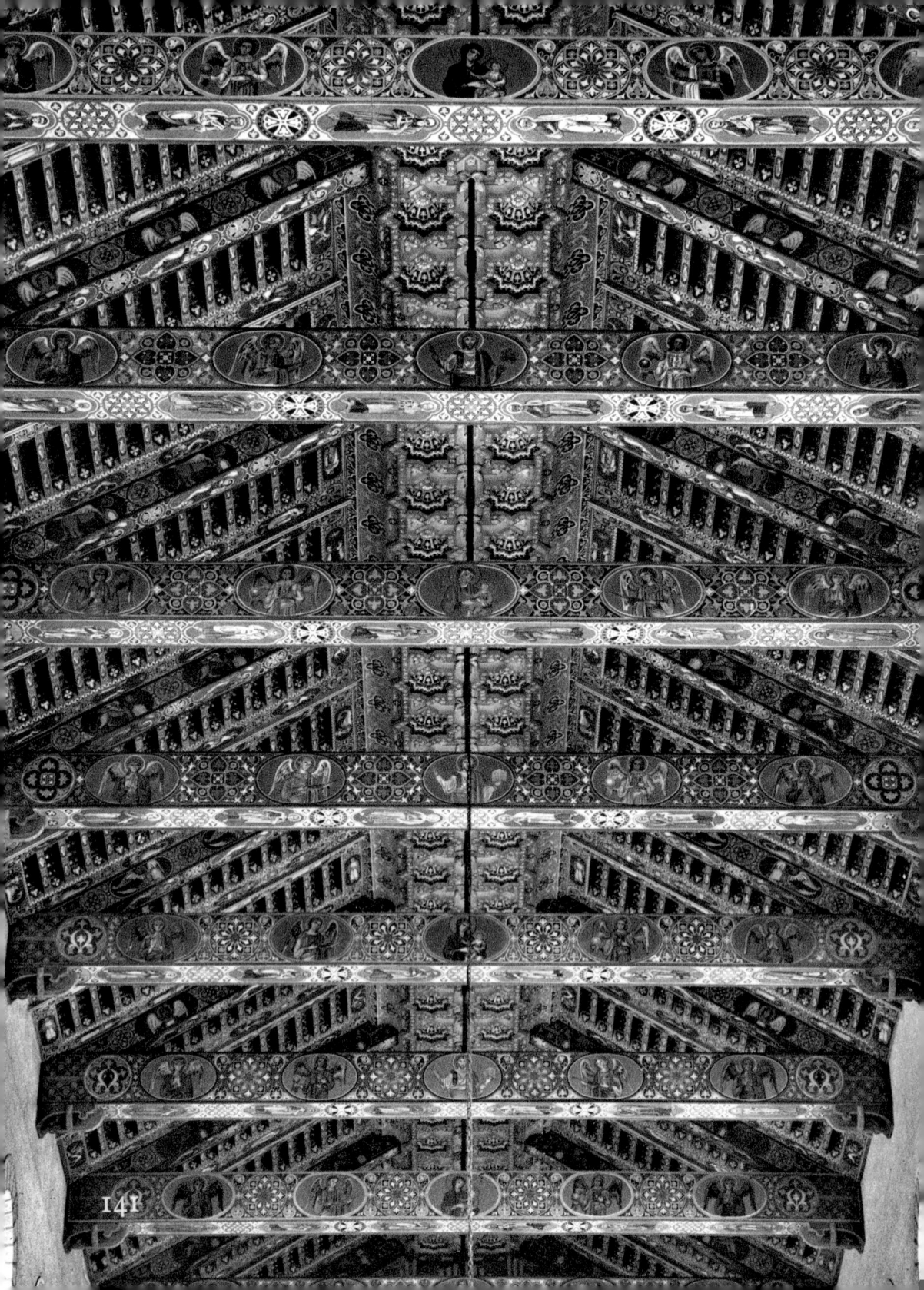

MESSINA

A ROAD that is really the main street of a continuous series of villages will take you to Messina, a town which has quite recently played an important part in European history. The decision was reached here which led to the establishment of the European Common Market. It was an inspired choice of meeting-place for the original conference, because few towns can have shown so much courage, tenacity, ingenuity and will to live. No other town in Europe, not even those periodically ravaged in war or Catania, victim of Etna, has been as often destroyed as Messina from top to bottom, by man or nature, and been obliged to rebuild from the ruins.

Its harbour is remarkably sheltered, behind a semi-circular spit of land which made its founders, the Greek colonists of Naxos, call it Zancle (sickle). It commands the straits between mainland Italy and Sicily and also, therefore, the passage from the Tyrrhenian to the Ionian Sea. Owing to the harbour and its situation, men have been constantly fighting for three thousand years to gain control of it. It was first destroyed by the Carthaginians in 396 B.C. Both Roman and Norman invaders of Sicily used it as a beachhead. In 1678 it revolted against the Spaniards, appealing for help to the fleet of Duquesne and the army of the Duke of Vivonne; but they finally had to leave it to its fate, and the Spaniards crushed the rebels. It revolted again in 1848, against the Bourbons, and was battered by naval guns.

Nature, however, proved more destructive still: fire in 1559, plague in 1743, cholera in 1854, earthquakes in 1783 and 1894; and the disaster of 1908, the most terrible in recorded history before those at Hiroshima and Nagasaki.

On 28 December 1908 it was a town of 136,000 inhabitants, more remarkable for its commercial activities and wealth than for its buildings, many of which had been destroyed over the centuries. Yet palaces, churches and monasteries survived, and it had a unique sea-front, the Palazzata, a line of sumptuous neo-classical palaces running for nearly a mile along the waterfront.

At 5.21 a.m., after thirty five seconds of the most violent earthquake shock ever recorded, Messina was rased to the ground. The survivors, injured, dazed, panic-stricken, rushed instinctively to the docks, where they thought they would be safer on the other side of the still crumbling walls. But they were swept away, along with the boats and even ships, by the tidal wave which came a few minutes after the earthquake. Fires were blazing all over the place, and in their light, with day dawning, the extent of the disaster could be seen.

The number of dead was later estimated at 60,000 for the town alone, and between 100,000 and 160,000 for the district (the exact numbers were never known). 91 per cent of the buildings were totally destroyed, and not a single one was completely intact. On the front, as the sea calmed down, the façade of the *Palazzata*, sturdily built and no doubt facing the direction of the earthquake, was still standing, apart from a few gaps. There was nothing left behind it; and as it was dangerous to lean ladders against it, as there was a great deal to do looking after the living, the naked body of a dead girl remained hanging by the feet to one of the balconies for several days.

Even that was not to be Messina's last ordeal. In 1943 the air-raids cost the town a thousand dead and also 94 per cent of its houses rebuilt since 1908 (a third completely rased, a third seriously damaged, a third only slightly affected).

Once more a new Messina rose, like a phoenix, having taken the precaution of enlarging its streets and limiting the height of its houses. Today it is swarming with life and activity, in shipping, commerce and industry. It offers a wonderful view over the straits and the Calabrian mountains, and it retains its charm as a Mediterranean town, with its cafés in the shade of fig-trees, its cabs drawn up outside the station, some handsome buildings and an excellent museum.

Its main building, the Cathedral, is obviously only a pastiche. Each time it has been destroyed, notably in 1943, the people of Messina have piously rebuilt it using all that survived and restoring what was missing. The surviving parts grew fewer and fewer with each calamity, so there had to be ever bigger restorations. Nevertheless, it still looks very like the Norman church built by King Roger II. You will appreciate the painted beams of its ceiling, completely redone after 1943, and its central porch, more or less authentic. Despite its Gothic shape, this is still romanesque in its decorative sculptures, respectable saints next to naked small children playing amidst vines.

You may wonder why Messina had the strange idea of flanking its cathedral with a campanile (built in 1933) in the form of a Flanders belfry, which has a huge astronomical clock (of pure Strasburg inspiration) with figures which perform daily. Whatever the reason, you will be amused to watch this curio of gilded bronze start up its jerky ballet on the stroke of noon, the Jack-of-the-clocks hitting their bells, the lion rearing, the cock beating its wings, the biblical characters gesticulating, and the Madonna handing ambassadors from Messina the signed letter which in A.D. 42 she deigned to write to the town. Unfortunately for our curiosity, the letter has disappeared in some disaster.

You will find more aesthetic satisfaction looking at the Orion Fountain outside the Cathedral and the Fountain of Neptune on the water-front. Both are the works—or copies of works, naturally—by a Tuscan called Montorsoli, who must have been a great admirer of his compatriot Michelangelo. There are also two 12th-century churches. One of them, the Annunziata dei Catalani, has mostly been miraculously preserved; it is a type of romanesque reminiscent of Pisa or even more of Greece. The other, the St Francis of Assisi, has been almost entirely rebuilt in austere Gothic and even Germanic form.

The museum contains four remarkably contrasting items of the first quality, two sculptures and two paintings. Of the former, one is a *Christ on the Cross*, in dark wood, like a skeleton and rather terrifying. The other, the *Scylla* by Montorsoli, is an original, or what is left of it, disfigured by the calamities but still powerful, tormented and dramatic. Of the paintings there is a splendid *Resurrection of Lazarus* by Caravaggio and a still finer *polyptich* by Antonello da Messina. This is the only work Messina's most illustrious citizen left in the town of his birth. In its central panel a ravishing Madonna offers cherries to the Child, who holds an apple, and two angels hold a crown of roses over her head; of the flanking panels the two above show the Annunciation, the two below show St Gregory and St Benedict.

Finally, there is Messina's greatest attraction, the view of the Straits and the mountains of Calabria reflecting the successive phases of the setting sun. Drive up on the mountain road; or else along by two salt lakes where mussels are reared, harvested and sold on the road, until you come to the lighthouse, which is Sicily's most easterly point.

The sun is still high. You look out on the whirlpool of Charybdis and the silky currents of the Straits. Opposite you, on the Calabrian shore, stands the rock of Scylla, and in the background the whole of Mount Aspromonte is still bathed in gold. The sun dives behind the barrier of the Peloritan Mountains: the Strait grows pale, then darker and darker till it is an inky blue; while Aspromonte, with the light fast escaping towards its summit, turns from orange to pink and then purple.

Now night has fallen. The lights go on at the end of lighthouses and beacons, in the portholes of ships, in the thousands of buildings on the coast. A fishing boat passes, near enough for you to make out a man leaning against the mast, in the position of Odysseus, bound so that he could listen to the Sirens' song without succumbing. Make the most of this glorious spectacle, for in a few years' time it will be broken up by a gigantic bridge, vital, unfortunately, for trade and tourism.

FROM MESSINA TO PALERMO
THE NORTH COAST AND CEFALU

THE road from Messina to Palermo keeps very close to, and sometimes high above, the Tyrrhenian Sea. In the narrow coastal plains, it passes over beaches and the mouths of wide brooks with more pebbles in them than water. There is a long line of mountains from east to west running roughly parallel to the coast. When the foothills meet the coast directly, forming steep and often high headlands, the road clings to the sides, climbing right to the top, so that you can see the cliff faces dropping sheer into the sea—a sea colder in colour than anywhere else in Sicily. The road crosses the barrier of the Peloritan Mountains and goes through many north-coast villages. In this part of it a skilful rural administration has turned it into a real 'park drive', lined with geraniums, china-asters and oleanders.

About twenty five miles from Messina a side-road to the right leads to Milazzo, a small town on the neck of a peninsula facing north. Because of its situation and the waters round it, Milazzo was one of the battlefields most fought over by Sicily's various invaders. Caius Dullius defeated the fleet of Carthage there and Agrippa defeated Sextus Pompaeus's fleet. Duquesne and Ruyter had their first engagement at Milazzo, Garibaldi won a victory there over the Bourbon army which completed his conquest of Sicily. It is a pleasant town, its wide docks planted with trees, its Frederick II castle standing out on the side of the Greek acropolis. It has a busy harbour, and is the port for the Aeolian Islands.

The nearest of these is Vulcano, a paradise for sunworshippers, underwater fishermen and students of volcanoes—it has five. Behind it, hiding the twin peaks of Salina, you can see Lipari, the main island of the archipelago. The town of Lipari is attractive and picturesque, and one of the earliest inhabited places in the western world; this is because there is a seam of obsidian in the area, that black, gleaming volcanic stone, hard and sharp, which primitive men used for making their tools and weapons. Circular neolithic huts have been found there, traces of an Aegean settlement; confirming the Homeric legend that the islands were occupied by invaders from Italy, ruled over by the famous Aeolus, master of winds and friend of Odysseus, who gave the archipelago its name. In the west you can just make out the islets of Alicudi and Filicudi on the horizon. In the east Panarea stands out, and further back, Stromboli, which erupts punctually every twenty minutes and has a perfect conical shape.

Perhaps a word is due here about Sicily's other two archipelagos, the Egadi Islands in the west (off Trapani and Marsala) and the Pelagian Islands in the far south west. I have several times flown over solitary Pantelleria, on the west of the Pelagians, a wooded fertile island with many vineyards and the crater of an old volcano in its centre, and rugged Lampedusa with its tremendous cliffs, a sort of Heligoland in the Mediterranean, or a piece of Sahara strayed into the open sea. I have never been to any of these, however, and have never even flown over the Aeolian Islands, so I can describe them even less—or I would have put you on a boat for them from Milazzo.

On the right of the road Tyndaris appears, on a cliff about a thousand feet up, dropping sheer to the sea. Although it was a Greek colony, it has a large Sanctuary of the Madonna, a famous Sicilian place of pilgrimage. There is also a village on the cliff, and a small field of ruins. These include a basilica (sometimes wrongly called a gymnasium) rather unusual in design (the main arch of its long gallery rested on nine stone arches, which are still standing); a Byzantine fort; and above all, the Greek theatre. The theatre is not very well preserved, and of course was turned into an amphitheatre by the Romans. But like the theatres at Segesta and Taormina, it has a wonderful view—over the Tyrrhenian Sea, the Gulf of Patti and the Aeolian Islands.

Cefalù lies at the foot of a white limestone crag, in which the Greeks saw the shape of a head (hence the name, *Kephalos* meaning a head). This is imposing because of its massiveness, because it is dominant in views from every angle, and because it forms a worthy backdrop to the noblest church in Sicily.

Cefalù Cathedral was founded in 1131 by King Roger II, who was caught in a violent storm at sea and vowed he would build a church in the first harbour where his ship found shelter. Despite the warmth of colour given it by Sicily's sun, it is full of the fervour and relief of a man who remained a Norman and a Christian in moments of truth, although he set out to protect the Arabs and liked dressing up as a Byzantine King. Of all Sicilian buildings this Cathedral is nearest the romanesque style as seen at Caen, showing Arab and Byzantine influence only in its decoration; the general design and structure is clearly that of its architects, no doubt Benedictine Cluniac monks. The Aragonese Kings remained faithful to Norman ideas when they asked a North Italian, Ambrosio da Como, to build the porch which in 1471 completed the façade.

The simple, elegant porch, three arches resting on slender columns, serves to emphasise two striking features of the façade: the wide distance between the two square battlemented towers with their small spires; and its bare decoration, only two galleries, with blind arches. The people of Cefalù were not to be offered a spectacular piece of

142. *Tyndaris. The Theatre.*
143. *Tyndaris and the Aeolian Islands.*
144. *Cefalù. Cloister capital.*
145. *Cefalù. Cathedral façade.*
146. *Cefalù Cathedral. Mosaics on apse.*
147. *Cefalù. General view.*
148. *Solunto. Roman House.*

142

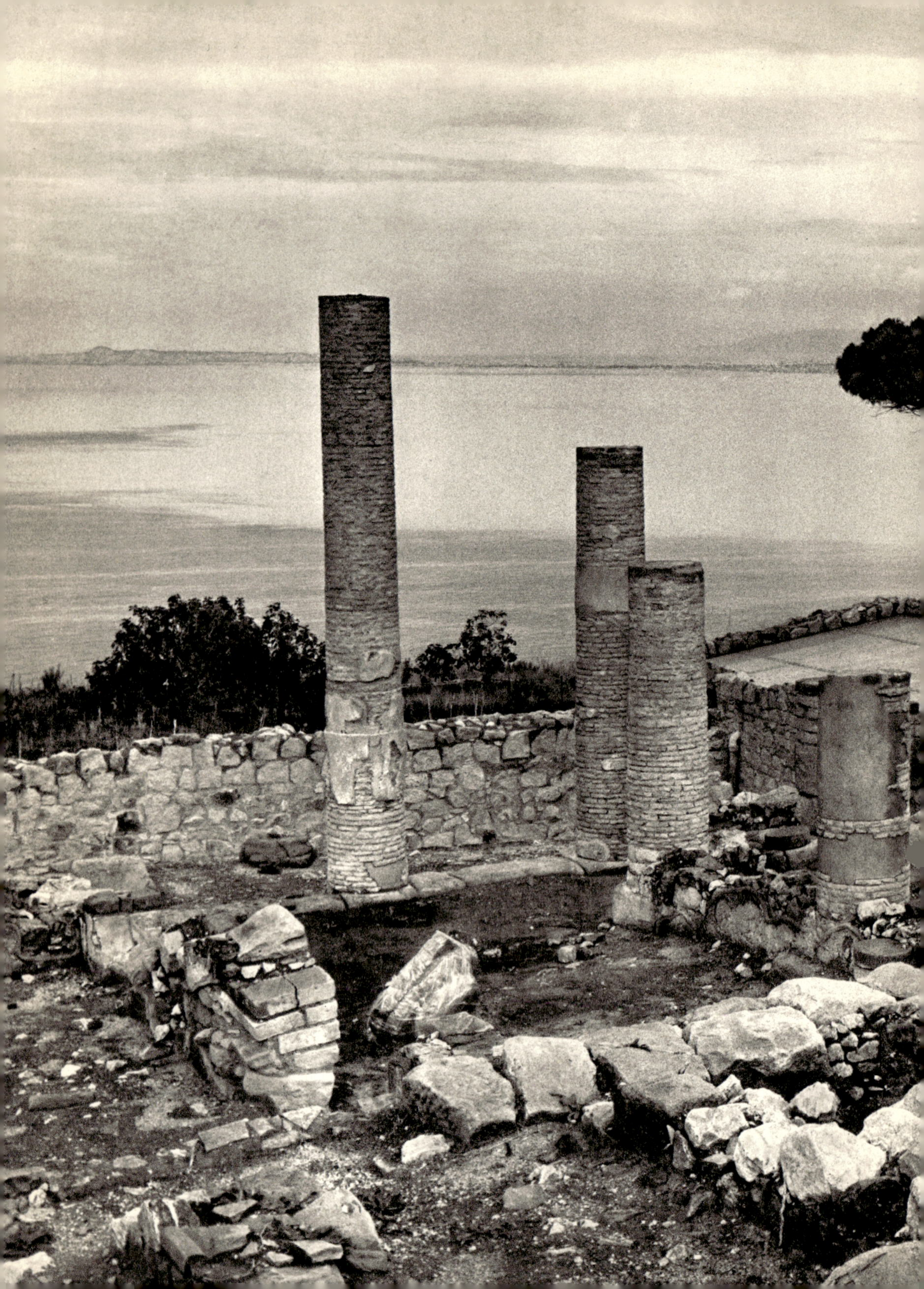

143

144

145

146

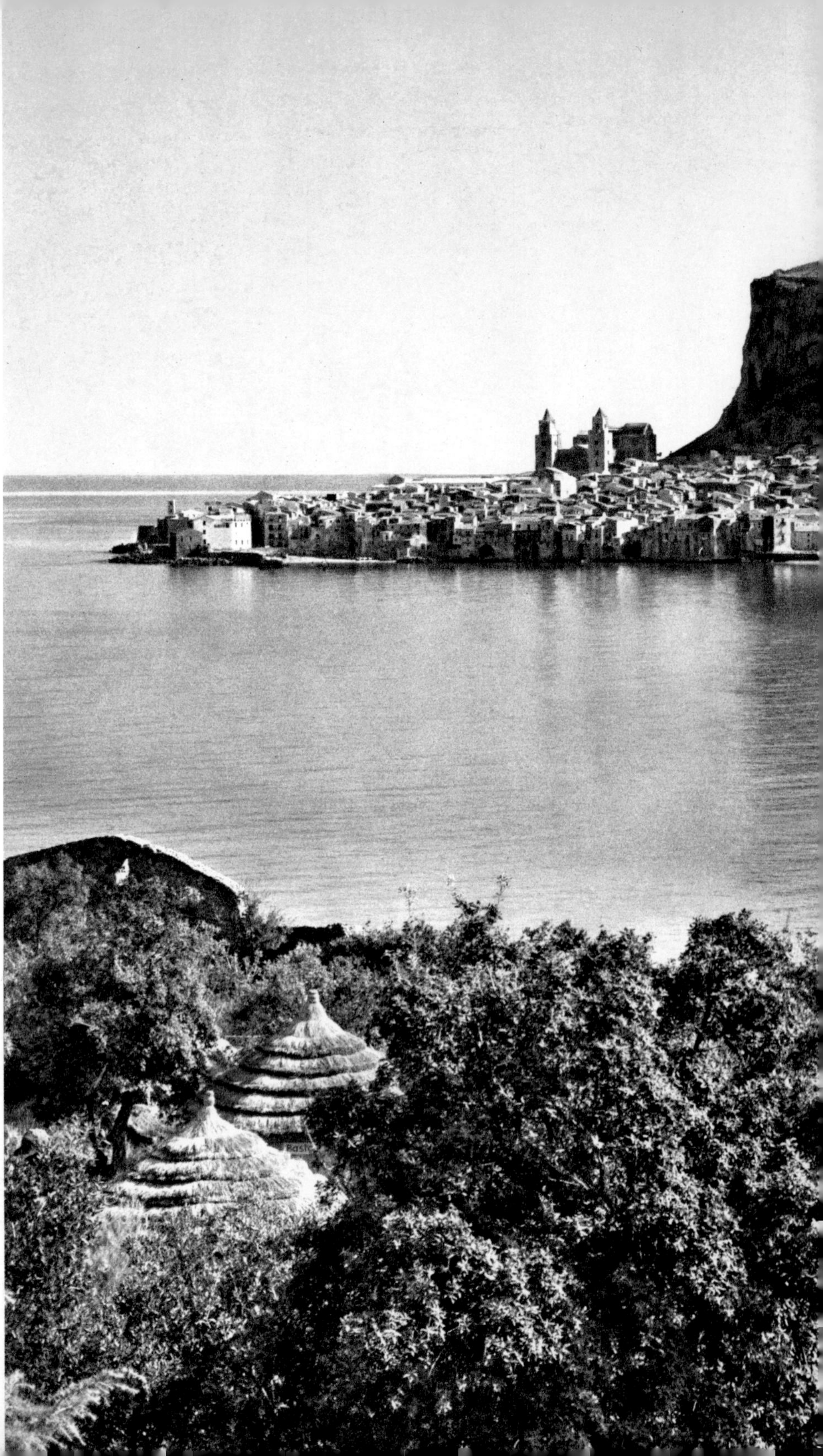

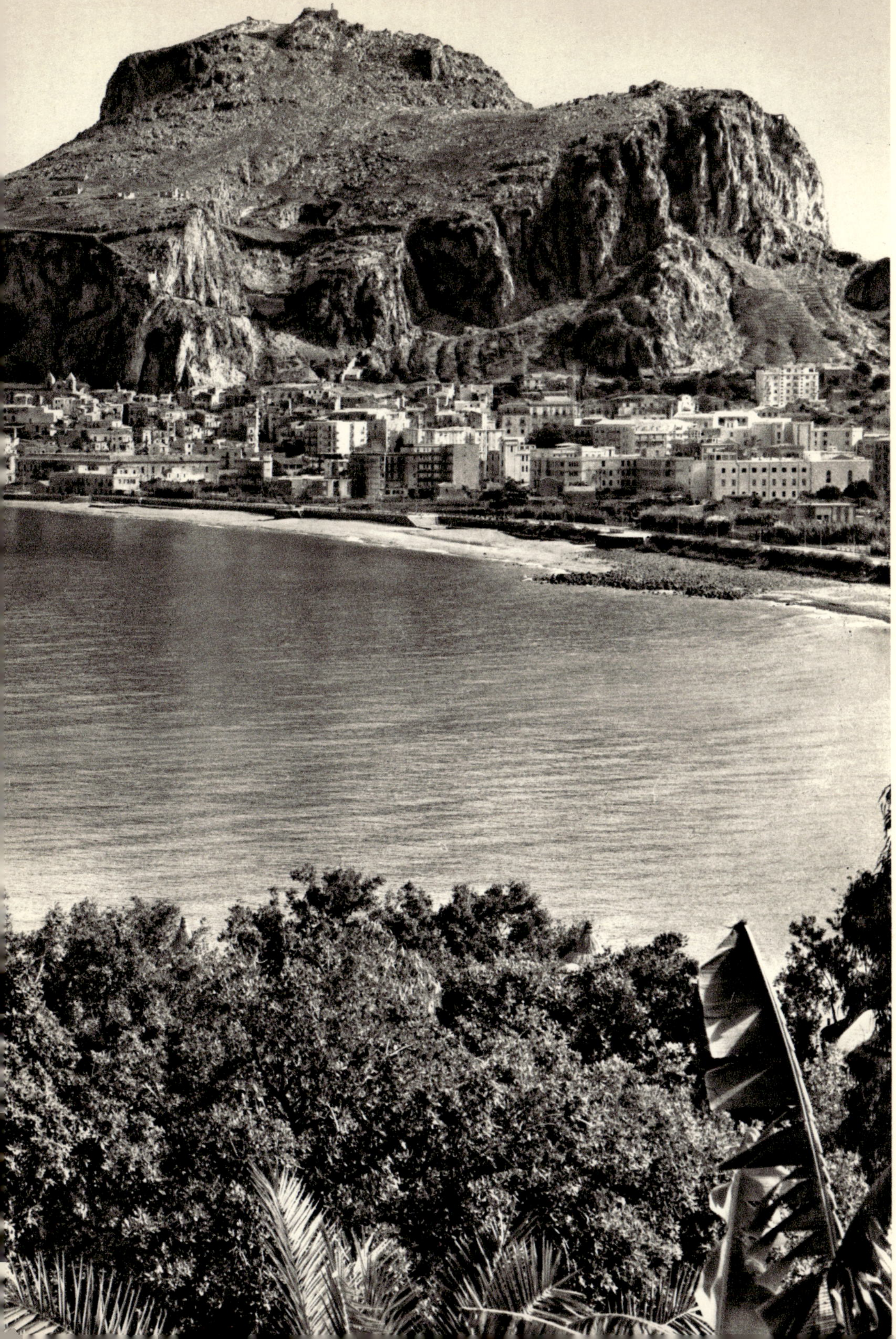

148

baroque, but a church to stir their souls and make them pray to the Christian God. The façade is certainly a masterpiece of architecture, and also a Norman crusader—against the lurking shades of Olympus and Islam—fully armed yet proclaiming forgiveness and peace.

The design of the interior derives from the same concern to lift man's mind towards God. The nave is vast, with classical columns, blind arcades between them somewhat arabesque in style, and an open-timbered roof which still shows traces of 13th-century painting. The transept is even vaster and higher, borne aloft by huge columns, and leads to a raised choir, looking down on the apse. This is entirely covered in mosaics, and is dominated by the tremendous figure of Christ.

He is completely Byzantine, however, a Christ who gives stern judgment as well as benediction; there is no trace of tenderness on that ascetic face. Below him, as with most Byzantine churches, there are other portraits at three levels: on the top one the Virgin, with archangels on each side of her; below, the twelve apostles in four groups of three, on each side of the apse window. The vault contains Cherubim and Seraphim with six crossing wings. The whole work is a recognised masterpiece of Byzantine mosaic, and at first sight it may be surprising in a church of purely Norman conception, testimony to a Norman king's prayer and vow. We should remember, no doubt, that Roger had the bold idea of bringing about the synthesis of East and West in his kingdom of Sicily; and even when fulfilling his vow, he still had this idea in mind. But we can see in the Cathedral that although he accepted the Eastern origins of his religion, and was ready to allow the East all manner of decorative frills and flourishes, he still meant the West to be responsible for building and architecture, for government and the secular arm.

From the north aisle a door leads into a pleasant cloister, between the bulk of the cathedral and the towering rock. And before you leave Cefalù, you should go to the local museum to see Antonello da Messina's marvellous portrait of an Unknown Man. He is middle-aged and not very handsome, but you will be struck by his ironical, slightly mocking smile—rather like the smile on the faces of those *Kourai* at Syracuse. Finally, at the end of the Bay of Cefalù, there is a special holiday village belonging to the Club Méditerranée (run by a French organization); and on a grassy esplanade near it you get a wonderful view of the small town, the cathedral and the rock.

The village is on the coast road to Palermo, which will take you past what remains of the ruined Doric temple of Himera, built by the Greeks to celebrate their victory in 480 and pulled down by the Carthaginians during their 'counter-offensive' of 409.

If you are not in a hurry, however, to get back to Palermo, I don't think you will regret a last plunge into the interior, in one of Sicily's most imposing regions. Either go back the other side of Cefalù for six miles and turn off to Castelbuono, or carry on towards Palermo for nine miles, then wind round via Collesano and Isnello, also reaching Castelbuono eventually. This village is the start for a drive round the Madonie Mountains—used for motor-racing, a favourite sport of Sicilians. The Madonie are a limestone range, one of the four parts of the great line of mountains parallel to the Tyrrhenian Sea, and they contain the highest peak in Sicily after Etna, the Pizzo Antenna, over 6,500 feet. In clear weather it apparently offers a superb view on to the coast, the Gulf of Castellanmare, the peninsula of Milazzo, the interior as far as Enna, Etna, and even the African Sea.

The peaks are mostly bare with sheer rock faces, the colours of which change with the hour of the day. But the open slopes and the valleys are covered with woods and copses quite large by Sicilian standards. The population, which is said to include plenty of pretty girls, has retained the traditional honesty and warm-heartedness of mountain-dwellers; indeed Frederick II granted to one big village the privilege of adding 'generous' to its name. This is Polizzi Generosa, which has a triptych of the Flemish school, locally attributed to Memling, though we may wonder how it arrived at Polizzi.

Castelbuono has a mediaeval square recalling that of Nicosia, and a delightful chapel decorated with stucco work by Serpotta; it is overloaded and double-gilded like an 18th-century drawing-room. Geraci Siculo is dominated by a sugar-lump rock, with the walls all round it of the fortress of the Ventimiglia family, lords of the Madonie. The church of Petralia Soprana looks rather fine, standing out against the sky at the far end of a spur. As to Caltavulturo, obviously of Arab origin, it has an amazing situation on a sort of shelf, on the side of a vertical cliff which is several hundreds of feet higher and extends the same distance below it.

Back on the Messina-Palermo road you pass Termini Imerese, quite a big town and port, and also a spa, which is supposed to have had Hercules as one of its first clients taking the waters. Then comes Trabia, owned by the great Lanza family; then Santa Flavia, from which you make a brief detour for a glance at the ruins of Solunto.

This was a Carthaginian and then a Roman town, never Greek; yet the least well preserved of the ruins, the so-called gymnasium, really the peristyle of a large and rich villa, is surprisingly Greek in appearance.

When the Romans built in Sicily, they were clearly at pains to adapt to local traditions. This need not only suggest a lack of creative imagination or an inferiority complex towards Greek culture. No doubt they hoped to preserve the unity of a tried and tested style which harmonised with the surroundings. Outside Sicily, on the other side of the Mediterranean, I know another example of this scruple: a proconsul in the 1st century B.C. produced a Doric porch, a masterpiece of tasteful pastiche, for the new market-place of the ancient Greek city of Cyrene.

Anyhow, before you enter the suburbs of Palermo, you should certainly see the six Doric columns at Solunto, and the view to which they form a frame. Although Roman, they will be the last image you carry away of Greek Sicily.

RETURN TO PALERMO AND CONCLUSION

149. *Quattro Canti Square.*
150. *Panorama from the Normans' Palace.*
151. *Melons for sale.*
152. *The Pretoria Fountain at night.*
153. *Evening street scene.*
154. *The art of living.*

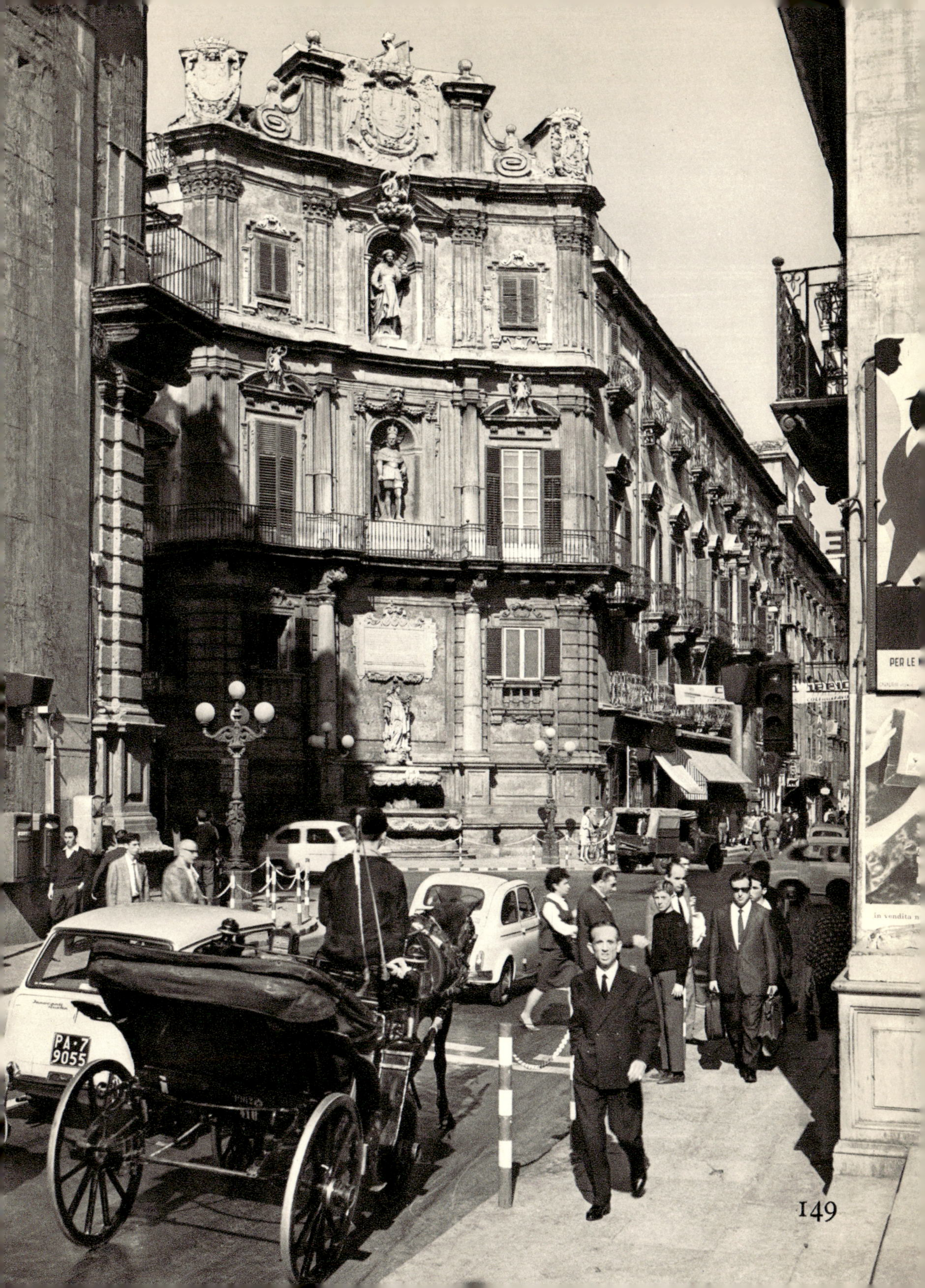
PER LE
PA·7
9055

150

151

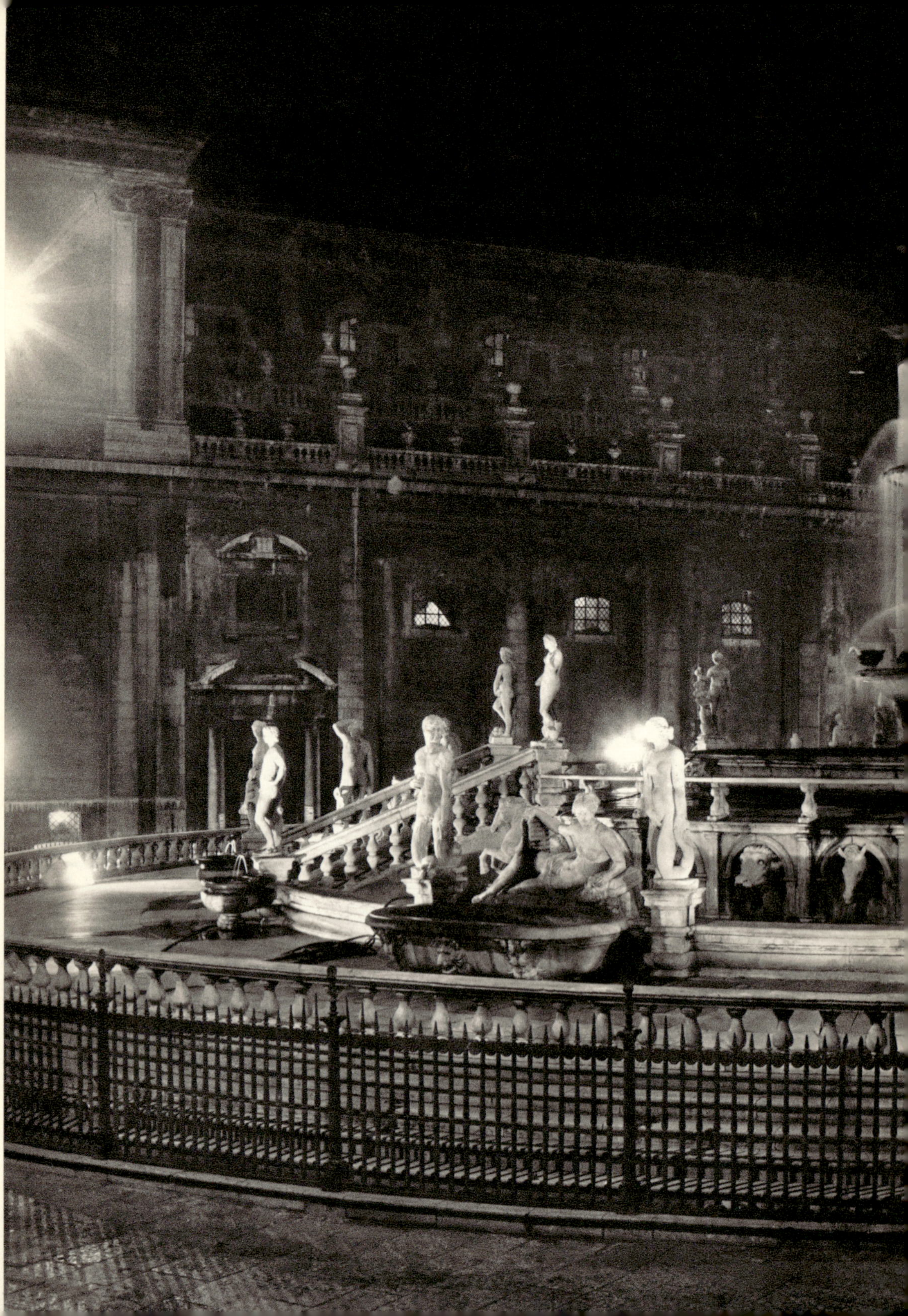

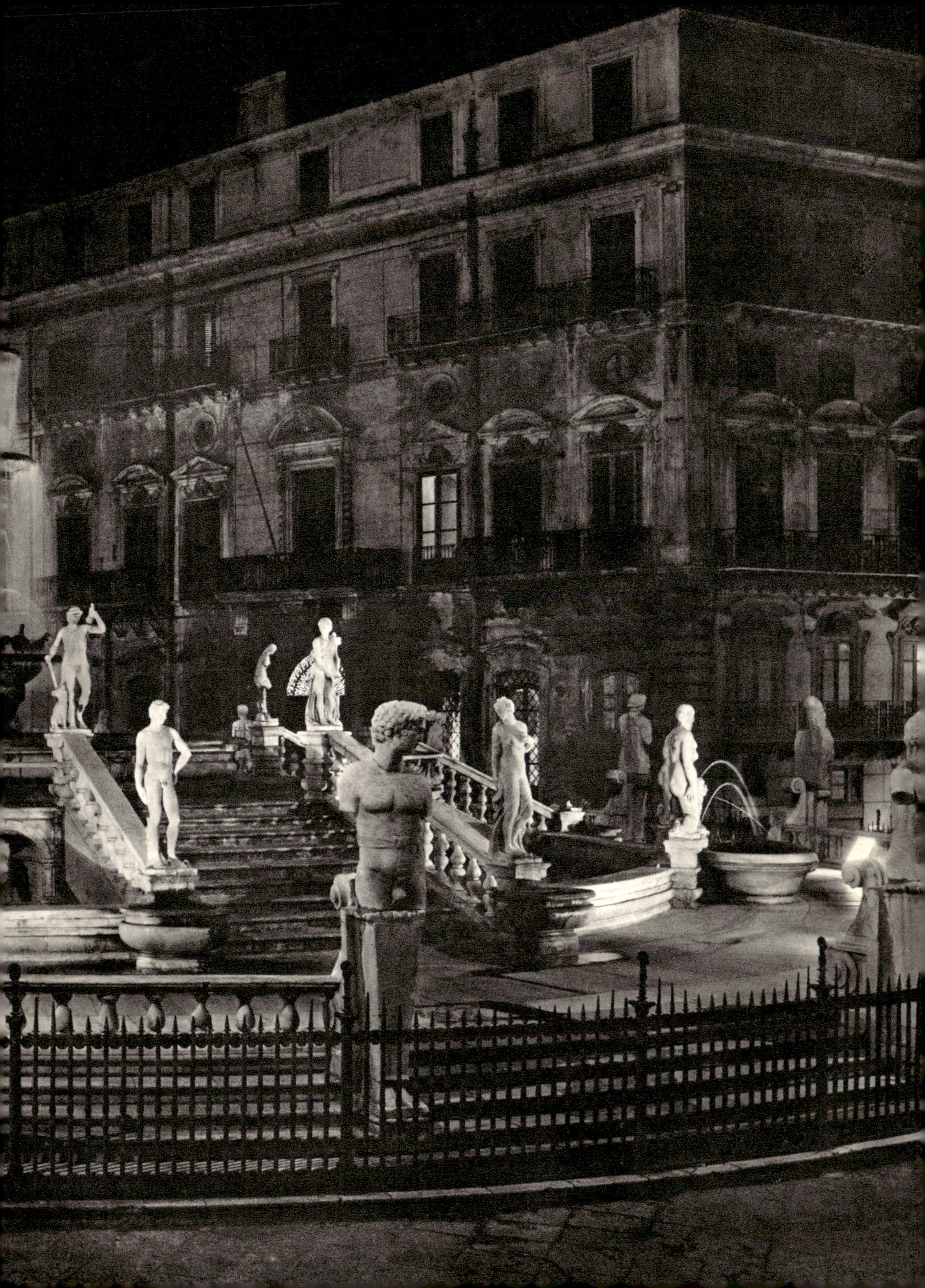

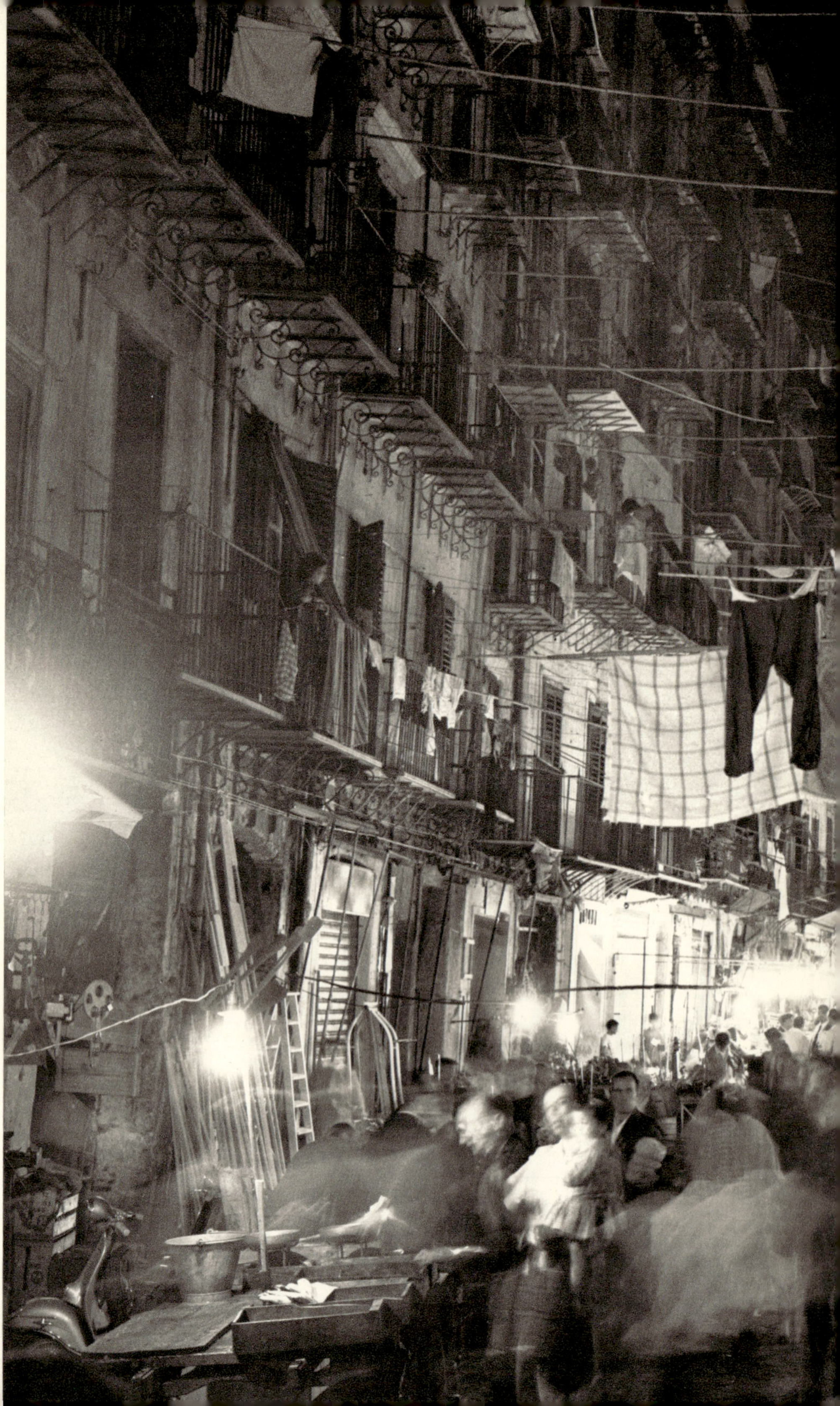

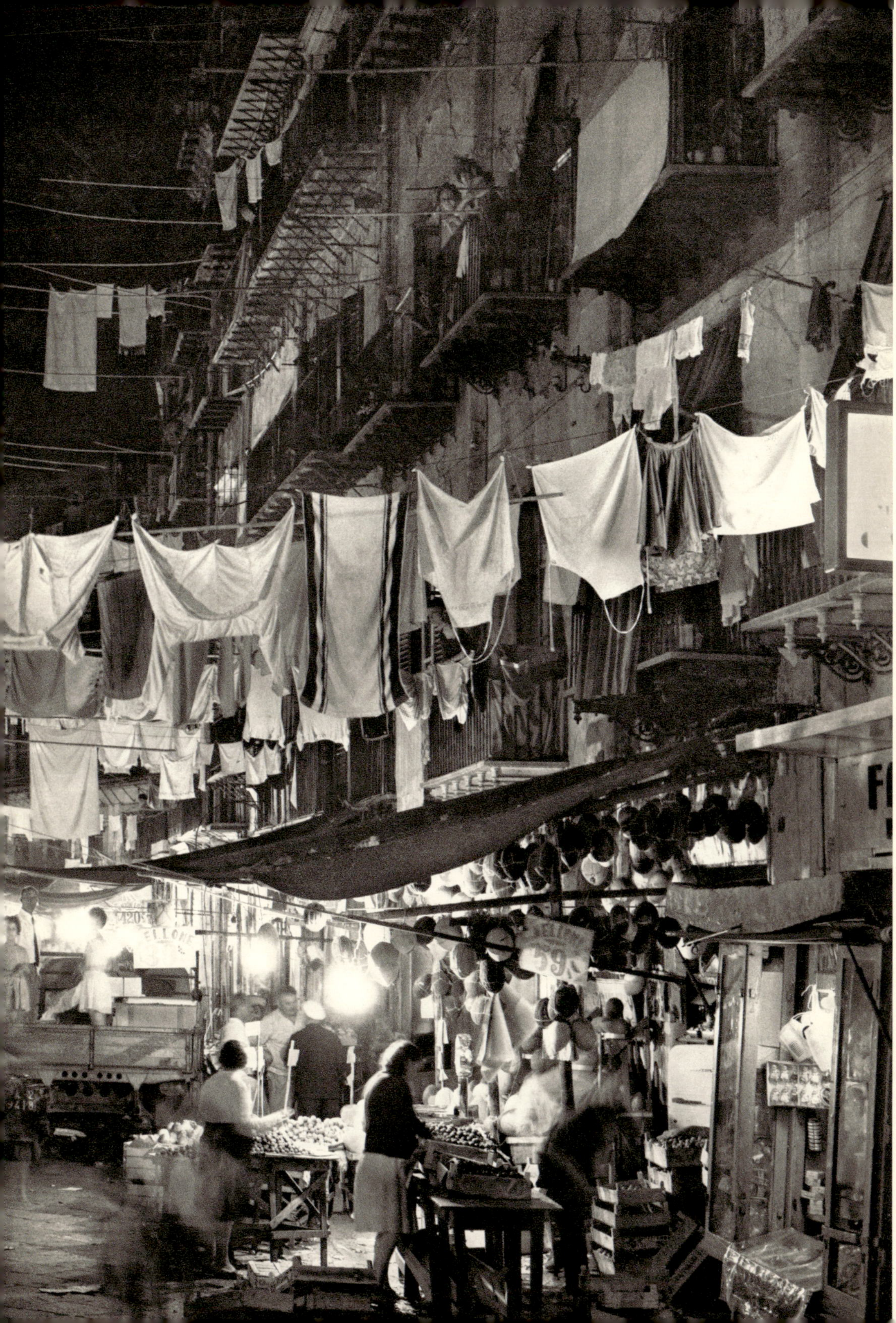

154

Passing endless suburbs, you come into Palermo. Amidst a stream of traffic you drive down the Foro Italico along by the old harbour, on the new sea-front boulevard, opposite the mass of Monte Pellegrino which stands out imposingly against the setting sun.

After your trip round Sicily, you will probably be quite pleased to get back to the capital for the few days of your holiday that are left, to enjoy the same tranquillity as you experienced beneath the pines of Mount Eryx, on the beaches of Mazaro and Cefalù, in the gardens of Syracuse and Taormina. You feel like leaving your car in the garage so as to ride in a *fiacre*; or better still, stroll round on foot; you feel like taking your ease in the cafés of Castelnuovo Square, at the foot of the absurd but endearing 1900-Ionic bandstand; bathing every morning in the Mondello lido and going to the opera in the evening or out to dinner in friendly company with plenty of good talk. Above all, I dare say, after a surfeit of sight-seeing, you feel like having a rest, lazing away most of the mornings, taking a nap in the afternoons.

Once you are rested and have become a Palermitan by adoption, you will want to get to know 'your' town; for on your last visit you saw only the main sights customary with tourists in a hurry. So the time has come for me to take you on those minor expeditions I promised you, which will allow you to discover the real Palermo and also to think at leisure over all you have seen in Sicily.

I have eight such expeditions to suggest, four in the town and four on the outskirts. You can easily do two a day without sacrificing bathe or siesta.

The first four start from the Quattro Canti, the fine baroque square you already know, which is the centre of old Palermo. So before setting out, you will be able to refresh your memories of the fountain in Pretoria Square, massive and elegant by day, and still more so at night when it is floodlit.

First expedition, south-east: mediaeval and Arab Palermo. Starting from Pretoria Square, you pass the baroque façades of St Catherine and St Anne. Piazza dei Vespri— where many Frenchmen were massacred at the 'Sicilian Vespers'—contains the Aiutamicristo Palace. This work by the architect Carnevilari belongs, like the Abbatelli Palace, to the artistic transition period between the Middle Ages and the Renaissance: the exterior, or what remains of it, is that of a Norman castle; the inner court with its porch is that of a Loire *château*. You walk past the Cistercian Church of la Magione, and come to the Piazza de la Kalsa. This name, al Khalesa, is all I can show you of Arab Palermo, unless you have enough imagination and acquaintance with the Middle East to picture it in the square's dusty irregularity, in the features of the children playing and old men dozing there.

Carrying on towards the harbour, you are back in parts you know, outside the baroque Church de la Pietà and the Abbatelli Palace next door to it, where you may want to take another look at the *Triumph of Death*, the bust of Eleanora of Aragon and Antonello's *Annunciation*. Then turn to the right, by the church of la Gancia, and you suddenly meet banian fig-trees, just as they were described to you in school botany classes, with roots growing from their branches and hanging downwards like fat snakes.

The Garibaldi Gardens are a good place to rest in the middle of your walk. They are between Santa Maria dei Miracoli, a small masterpiece of Renaissance virtuosity, and the Chiaramonte Palace, commonly called Lo Steri, a strong, stern mediaeval keep despite some pretty triforic windows; its rebellious owner was beheaded there in 1396, and it has long been used as law-courts. A little further on there is another work by Carnelivari, this time completely Renaissance, the façade of the Church of Santa Maria della Catena; the harbour used to be closed every night with a chain stretched across it at water-level, and the church, being near the join of the chain, derives its name from this (catena = chain). So here you are back at the old harbour, which you saw when you first arrived at Palermo.

Second expedition: south-east, the 'Serpotta' walk. For you will be walking along tortuous streets in search of the astonishing 18th-century sculptor of stuccoes, Giacomo Serpotta. You will recognise his signature in the lizard which he always put in some corner of his work, on the grounds that the local name for a lizard, *sirpuzza*, sounded a little like his own. You find him chiefly in the three oratories of San Lorenzo, the Rosario di San Domenico and Santa Zita. These oratories were used by religious and charitable brotherhoods for holding services and meetings.

Up to six foot above the ground they are strictly conventional: at the end the altar-piece is by Caravaggio in the San Lorenzo, by Van Dyck in the Rosario; at the sides the benches are in inlaid mother-of-pearl, suggesting a distinct taste for luxury in these brethren. How they must have laughed under their cowls whenever they looked higher than that to the walls and ceiling decorated by Serpotta. There are a great many religious pictures in stucco high-reliefs, very small compared to the framework round them: This consists of swarms of stucco *putti*, clownish little boys, naked or in comical fancy dress, whirling about, fighting, playing ball, giving each other a leg up to pinch fruit; statues representing female saints or respectable virtues in the form of pretty girls wearing classical attire.

The material is only cheap stucco, the movement is excessive, and the composition is swamped by its details; yet some have justly compared Serpotta to Boucher. And what a contrast between these oratories and the surrounding churches: the austere Gothic of St Francis of Assisi, the baroque vastness of St Dominic, the Bramante-like severity of St George, the bareness of St Zita, completely restored owing to bomb-damage; or the sad palaces on the Knights-of-Malta Square, once sumptuous, today cracking and degraded; or the alleys decked with drying clothes, where children much less chubby than Serpotta's *putti* play in the gutters, between the piles of melons and tomatoes in the picturesque market of la Bocceria.

North-west expedition: the baroque palaces, or what is left of them. The Via Maqueda offers you several. First walk a short distance in the direction of the station to see the Santa Croce and the Comitini, today the seat of the prefecture. Make your way back towards the Opera, going through carriage gateways which sometimes lead into fine inner courts. Then make a detour through a district little frequented by tourists, occupying a depression which was formerly a swampy extension of the harbour. Here you will find the palaces of Monte di Pietà and the Gothic church of Sant'Agostino, which has an excellent Gagini side-door.

This detour will bring you out into the Corso Vittorio Emmanuele by the cathedral, and the Corso is *the* street for baroque palaces, although unfortunately they were badly damaged, by air-raids. You can admire the Santa Ninfa, however, with its Louis XIV main door and its court, where the great antiquarian Daneu is installed. The Church of San Salvatore has an elliptical plan as strange as its walls, which are covered with all the different marbles Sicily produces. After passing that, stop in the Piazza Bologni to look at the façades of the Villafranca and Ugo Palaces.

South-west expedition: the great baroque churches. At Modica, Noto and Syracuse you have seen splendid examples of Sicily's 'Jesuit baroque', but your taste for this style, I should warn you, may be more severely tested here by St Joseph of the Theatines and the church abutting on the Casa Professa, parent establishment of the Jesuits in Sicily. The former is rather too extravagant, in fact, with its gigantic columns of grey marble and its mediocre paintings framed by heavy festoons of gilded stucco.

The church of the Jesuits will at first sight seem just as overdone: marbles of all colours, paintings and statues and stuccoes; all this strung together so as not to waste a square inch of wall or ceiling, and superimposed to form festoons and astragals in bright on dark marble or *vice versa*. If, however, you stop and look for a bit, you will, I hope, be gradually caught by the strange charm emanating from such exuberance of imagination and richness.

The contrast will be all the more striking when you come out of this sumptuous 'temple' straight into the Alberghiere district, where the prince of swindlers, Giuseppe Balsamo, alias Count Cagliostro, was born in 1743. This has always been one of the

155. *Baroque ornament in the Oratory of San Lorenzo.*
156, 157. *Politeama Garibaldi.*
158. *Olive trees at Zucco.*
159. *Villa Igea.*
160–164. *Bagheria. Villa Palagonia.*

155

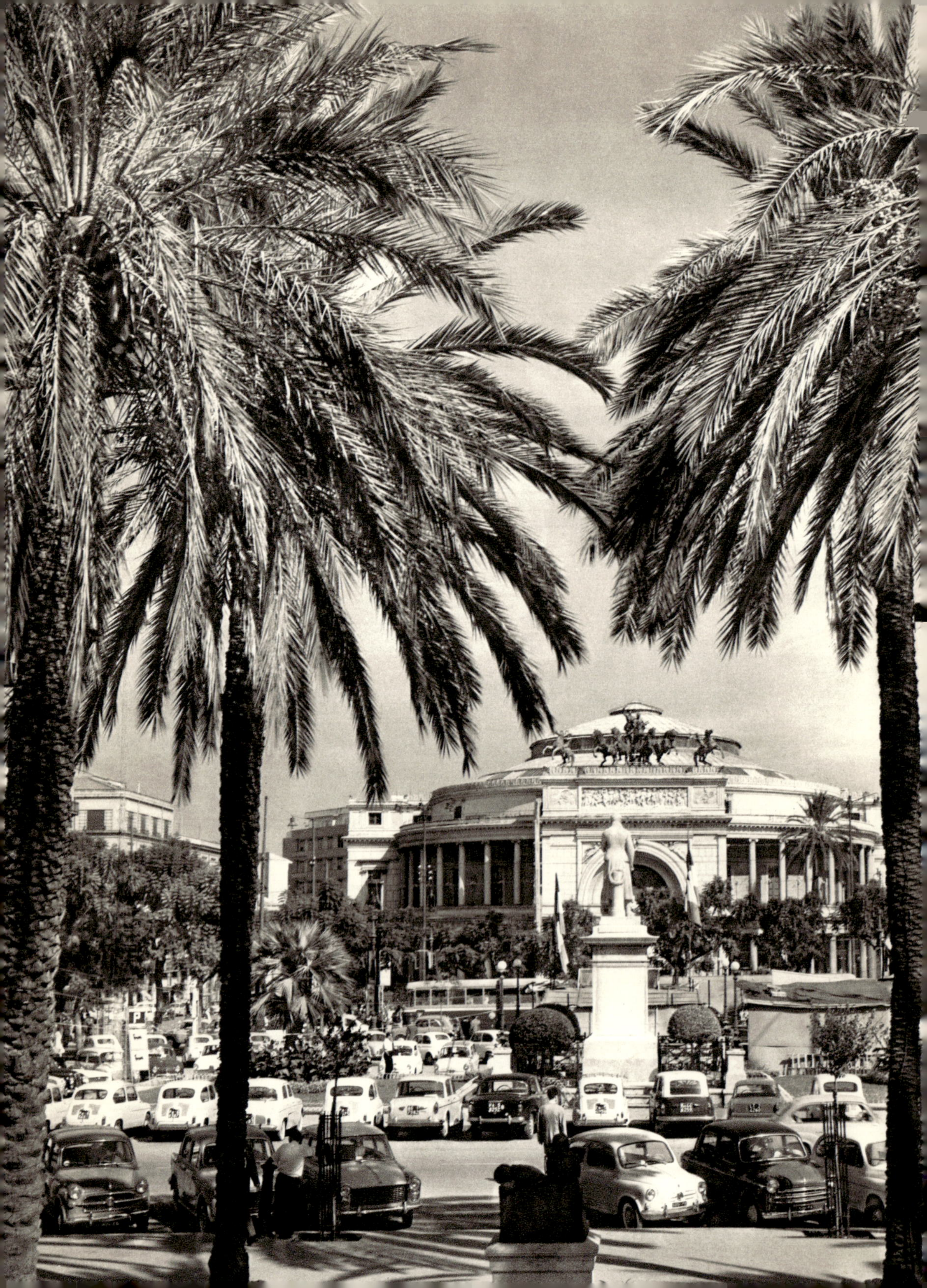

156

157

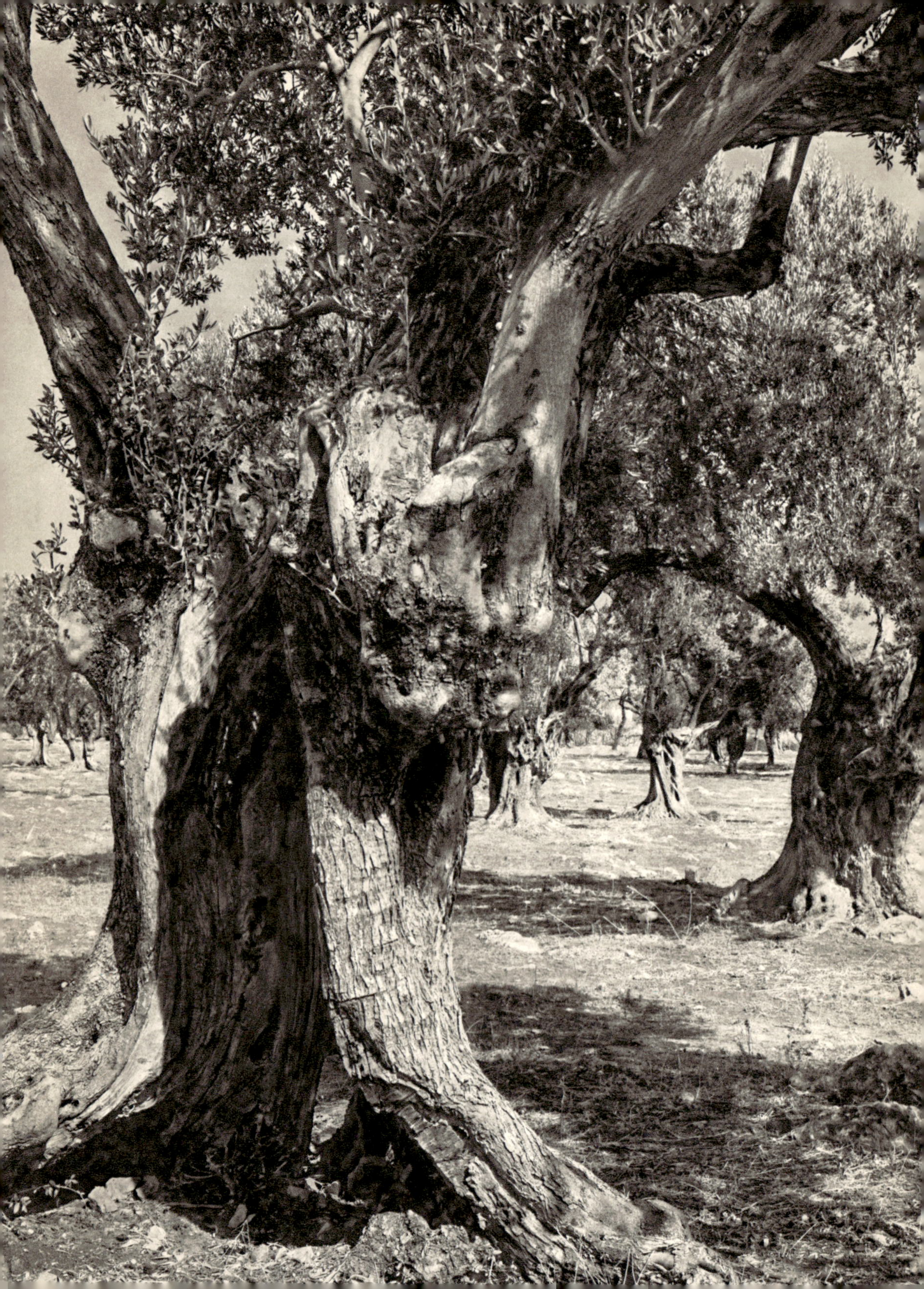

158
159

160

161

162

163

164

oldest districts in Palermo and one of the poorest; on top of that, it was ravaged in the air-raids. It makes a powerful impression, though, of the more or less cheerful poverty appropriate to the capital of Sicily. Still, when you leave it, passing the Sclafani Palace, one of the vastest in Palermo, you will probably be quite glad to have a rest beneath the shady trees near the Villa Bonanno, listening to a singer of traditional ballads, or in the cloister of San Giovanni degli Eremiti, which will bring you back to Sicily's more idyllic side.

The first of the 'suburban' expeditions will not take you far, only to the hills above Palermo in the north west, where the Norman Kings had their Arab architects lay out a park in Arabian-Nights style. There is nothing left, alas, of the gardens, fountains and pools. All you will see is a garden kiosk in the form of a marabout shrine, the Cubula; a pavilion, la Cuba (from the Arab *Kubbeh*, a dome); and a small palace, the Ziza—the name comes from the adjective *azizia* (delightful), and it deserves it.

As often with Arab buildings, the exterior of this is austere, a massive block with narrow windows and a few arches. The whole decorative effort has been reserved for the interior; there is a hall with bees-nest vaults, walls covered by mosaics like those in King Roger's Room, and from the back wall a fountain spills its water on inclined planes through a trough and pond let into the marble paving. In the silence, coolness and dim light so restful to the eyes, you can feel part of the delicate, tasteful, unobtrusive luxury and harmonious relaxation, which—to judge from the buildings they left—characterized the Palermitans of the 1st century.

But if you insist—and I am not forcing you—you can see directly afterwards, a few yards away, the morbid tastes which evidently characterised the Palermitans of the 18th and 19th centuries. The catacombs of the Convent of the Capuchins are only too well-known, and all I need say about them is that during those centuries ten million bodies were hung up along its walls, clad in their finest attire, bearing on their necks a label giving their names and degrees, more or less well preserved in a 'mummifying' atmosphere.

After this macabre underground episode you will be refreshed by the second suburban expedition, to the top of Monte Pellegrino, the hermitage and tomb of St Rosalia. The mountain itself has nothing refreshing about it—a rocky *djebel*, without a tree, disfigured half way up by a hotel which I have never seen open. At the top delights await you: the cool dry air; the immense view over the town, the gulf and the Conca d'Oro; the sanctuary itself, a dripping grotto behind a simple façade—the only pretentious thing in this is the grandiloquent inscription commemorating Goethe's visit to it.

The story of St Rosalia is rather refreshing, too. She was the daughter of a Norman prince, who shunned the pleasures of the Zisa and the pomp of the Royal Palace, and retired into this airy hermitage, where she deliberately sought the world's oblivion. Four centuries later, in 1664, when the plague broke out in Palermo, a 15-year-old girl, already married, was one of the victims. Her inconsolable widower tried to distract his grief by going hunting on the slopes of Pellegrino, but found no game

17

among these bare rocks. He was feeling sadder and sadder when he saw a woman of resplendent beauty appear at the entrance to a cave: it was St Rosalia. She told him that in pity for Palermo's troubles she had chosen him, so harshly tested, to put an end to them. 'Seek out the clergy and the authorities; dig in this corner of the grotto; you will there find bones—my bones; give them a decent burial, and the plague will cease.' This was done, and the plague did cease. Since then the people of Palermo come every year to give thanks to St Rosalia on Monte Pellegrino on the evening of 3 September.

The third suburban expedition will bring you more contrasts. There is nothing more peaceable and Franciscan than the churchyard, court and fountain of the little church of Santa Maria di Gesù, south of Palermo. However, when from the nearby belvedere you gaze at the view, one of the finest you can get of the town, the first building to attract your attention will be the sombre San Spirito Church just opposite you, outside which the Sicilian Vespers began. Moreover, the road taking you back to town is the Via Ciaculli, an ordinary road containing characterless houses and garden-walls; but for ten years it has become the battlefield of the Mafia.

The fourth and last expedition is to Bagheria, a big village nine miles out of Palermo on the Messina road, which in the 18th century was a resort of aristocratic Palermitans. Other villas there, Valguarnera, Butera and Trabia, are worthy of their founders, and so is the Villa Palagonia, but in a different way. Ferdinand François Gravina, Prince of Palagonia, who had once governed somewhere in Latin America in the name of the king of Spain, was one of the richest land-owners in Sicily, and a highly eccentric character. Goethe records having met him in full dress in the Via Maqueda, attended by liveried servants bearing silver plates to collect money for the ransom of Christian slaves held by the North African Moslems. He was very fond of practical jokes, arranging statues so that passing wigs would get caught on one of the hands, or chairs with one leg which bent when you sat down on them.

Just as the owner of the Villa Casale at Piazza Armerina left his imprint on that, the Prince certainly left his imprint on the Villa Palagonia. You come to a huge sun-baked square with a gate supported by two bizarre telamons six foot high, one wearing Egyptian dress, the other in sloppy strawberry-coloured breeches. Going through this gate, you are in a garden full of seedy-looking palm trees, cacti and rank weeds; and on the wall round this garden there is a continuous 'frieze' of statues, about three foot high, representing comic dancers and instrument players, cripples, hunchbacks and monsters: animals with human heads and humans with animal heads.

The villa itself, however, has a handsome convex façade—but no door. You walk through the only opening you can see, into a sort of tunnel, lined with further phantasmagoric statues. The tunnel winds through the house and leads you out into the façade at the back. This is concave, and also very harmonious; it has an open staircase which makes a double turn. But there is no room to step back and admire that, you are too close to a wall with more grotesque statues on it. The gate in this wall has telamons even more freakish.

The interior is just as extravagant, but depressing because it is dirty and neglected. You reach it by an oval-shaped hall with dummy colonnades which are quite stylish apart from the layer of dirt over them. By pushing open a dilapidated door, you enter the gallery along the convex façade, and this is full of heaped-up remains of delightful ornament, mirrors, stuccoes and panels inlaid with coloured glass. The main hall has a ceiling covered with Venetian mirrors, set in gold, but broken and mildewed. There is nothing left now of the Prince's joke sculptures and furniture.

So your last expedition in Palermo and in Sicily was to this unusual and somehow attractive 'folly'. I arranged that deliberately so as to dissuade you once more from reaching too definite, one-sided conclusions about Sicily as a whole.

Probably I needn't have worried. You know Sicily now, and will smile when pretentious people tell you they have discovered the truth about a country where, as Pirandello pointed out, everyone has his own 'truth'. When the unsatisfied groan 'What a beautiful place it would be if only . . .', you will shrug your shoulders, as the 'Leopard' did when his Jesuit chaplain made the same sort of remarks to him. You will be indignant if jaundiced folk say they have seen nothing but poverty in Sicily, and amazed at uncritical enthusiasts who have hardly noticed any poverty.

Indeed from now on, being used to Sicilian contrasts, you will find it natural that Sicily can have its light and its dark sides, can be both very rich and very poor, an idyllic country and one of the most under-developed in Europe. You now see it for what it is, a country quite in the image of a man, with its qualities and its defects—and a country where you have enjoyed a wonderful holiday.

You know that you love Sicily. That is, I believe, the only conclusion you *could* reach, and a very happy one too.